RELIGION &

RECONCILIATION

IN SOUTH AFRICA

RELIGION & RECONCILIATION IN SOUTH AFRICA

Voices of Religious Leaders

Audrey R. Chapman and
Bernard Spong, editors

Templeton Foundation Press
Philadelphia and London

Templeton Foundation Press
Five Radnor Corporate Center, Suite 120
100 Matsonford Road
Radnor, Pennsylvania 19087
www.templetonpress.org
Designed and Typeset by Kachergis Book Design
Printed by Versa Press, Inc.

LIBRARY OF CONGRESS CATALOGING-IN-PUBLICATION DATA
Religion and reconciliation in South Africa : voices of religious
leaders / Audrey R. Chapman and Bernard Spong, eds.
p. cm.
ISBN 1-932031-28-6 (pbk.)
1. Reconciliation—Religious aspects. 2. Religious leaders—South
Africa—Interviews. 3. South Africa. Truth and Reconciliation
Commission. I. Chapman, Audrey R. II. Spong, Bernard.

BL2470.S6 R45 2003
200'.968'09049—dc21
2002153740

Printed in The United States
03 04 05 06 07 08 10 9 8 7 6 5 4 3 2 1

Published in South Africa with Cluster Publications.

This report is a product of the American Association for the
Advancement of Science (AAAS) Science and Human Rights Program.
The interpretations and conclusions are those of the authors and do
not purport to represent the views of the AAAS Board, the AAAS
Council, the Committee on Scientific Freedom Responsibility, or
the members of the Association.

CONTENTS

PREFACE

THIS VOLUME HAD ITS ORIGINS in a project designed to understand better the interrelationships between truth-finding and reconciliation in South Africa. The American Association for the Advancement of Science (AAAS) began a multidisciplinary study with several South African collaborators shortly after the Truth and Reconciliation Commission (TRC) submitted its final report to the Mandela administration in October 1998. Both the AAAS Science and Human Rights Program and its major collaborator, the Johannesburg-based Centre for the Study of Violence and Reconciliation, had been involved with the TRC.

It is important for any study of the process of and prospects for reconciliation in South Africa to take the role of the religious communities into account. One important source is the personal perspectives of religious leaders. The AAAS therefore decided to undertake a series of in-depth interviews with a cross section of key persons in various religious communities. The objective was to elicit their views about the TRC and the prospects for reconciliation, and to find out more about the status of relevant church-sponsored programs. Audrey Chapman, the project director, asked Bernard Spong, the former Director of Communications of the South African Council of Churches and a former colleague, to conduct the interviews, and he agreed to do so.

To begin the process, we decided on a series of open-ended questions that could serve as the basis for a conversation with a range of religious leaders. We then drew up a list of potential candidates. The letter to all who were invited to participate in this project stated that the purpose was "to share the thoughts that arise and, hopefully, be a useful input into the ongoing task of reconciliation in South Africa."

Bernard Spong conducted the interviews in this volume over a period of twelve months beginning in August 1999. The same instrument was provided to each person so there is an obvious pattern throughout, but the conversations—a more appropriate characterization for the meetings than a formal interview—allowed room for the priorities of each person to receive attention. This flexibility has given an added richness to the overall content. There were times when the particular status, situation, or past experience of a person drew further direct questions, again adding another layer of viewpoints to a number of the exchanges. In reading the interviews that follow it is important to keep in mind that they are conversations and not essays, and need to be understood as such.

Moreover, it is important to keep in mind that the conversations did not take place in a vacuum. They were held within the context of an emerging democracy and against the background of a world where issues and priorities changed. The issue of blanket amnesty for apartheid perpetrators was very much in the forefront when the questions were determined. It quickly changed to the priority of reparation and compensation for victims. Farm invasions in Zimbabwe, amnesty applications by well-known figures, and a general election all took place during the course of the interviews and made their mark on these meetings as much as on any other conversations in South Africa during those times.

The selection of interviewees is wide, although no attempt was made to mathematically calculate the exact numeric representation required to cover the South African religious population as per the latest census. We tried to include activists and theorists, leaders and local representatives. Many were invited to take part; some agreed, some declined, some could never quite find time, and others made numerous promises that never materialized. We regret that this means some of the voices we would like to have heard are not included in this volume. On the other hand, we are delighted at the number of people who gave generously of their time and reflections.

We particularly regret that we missed the voice of more representatives of indigenous African churches and faith groups. The issue of reconciliation is obviously not a priority for them. We are reminded that, despite much pressure, the leader of the Zionist Christian Church remained silent when he attended the religious community hearings of the Truth and Reconciliation Commission. Perhaps there is a need to listen to that silence!

The vast majority of the interviews conducted are people from Gauteng

Province.[1] This is a change to the original plan that had greater geographic coverage. The practical difficulty of getting people in a particular area to be available within a reasonable period of time was enormous. This is not, however, the reason for the shift. Two other things happened. One was that some of the leaders who were approached asked us to be in contact with Gauteng surrogates to be interviewed on their behalf. Second, it became obvious after a short time that the geographic placement of a person was not the important issue within the conversations, and the views within a short distance of Bernard Spong's home were varied enough to cover a wide spectrum of national viewpoints.

There is a predominance of Christian participation. This is not only a matter of relative numbers. It became obvious during the conversations that the issue of reconciliation in South Africa is a matter that the Christian churches especially have to face. It is the churches that hold within them those who supported and sustained the apartheid regime. It is the churches that hold those who spoke out against, and in some cases fought hard against, that same regime.

This is not to deny the role that people of all faiths have to play in the creation of a non-racial, non-discriminatory society. It is to emphasize the baggage that the Christian church carries from its past and needs to face in its own internal struggle for reconciliation.

The interviews, which were taped, were then transcribed, slightly edited, and given to the interviewees for any changes or revisions felt necessary. The result is a wide collection of views with two commonalities: they are all from a religious perspective and all around the theme of reconciliation.

The interviews were originally intended to be a resource for the larger study of the nature and dynamics of reconciliation. But as we read them over, it became clear that they deserved to be shared with a wider audience. Once we decided to publish an edited volume based on the interviews, we prepared the introduction and commissioned several commentaries. As in the case of the interviews, only some of the commentaries materialized in time to be included in this volume.

We would like to thank all of the religious leaders who agreed to be interviewed and worked with us to edit the transcripts of their interviews. We realize that they all are busy people with many demands on their time.

We would also like to acknowledge the generous support of the John Templeton Foundation. A grant from the Templeton Foundation to the

AAAS has served as the major source of support for the research project and enabled us to prepare this volume.

Audrey R. Chapman
Bernard Spong
March 2002

NOTE

1. Gauteng Province is the region that includes Johannesburg and Pretoria and therefore has the central offices for many religious communities.

RELIGION &

RECONCILIATION

IN SOUTH AFRICA

INTRODUCTION

RELIGION AND RECONCILIATION

IN SOUTH AFRICA

AUDREY R. CHAPMAN

L IKE MANY OTHER COUNTRIES emerging from periods of repression and conflict, South Africa confronts a legacy of deep social,
economic, and political divisions, which in the case of South Africa also
have a significant racial overlay. Unlike most contemporary transitional so-
cieties, the institutionalized racism, injustice, and violence at the heart of
the apartheid regime made South Africa an international pariah. The international anti-apartheid movement, led by nongovernmental and religious
organizations, and its successful efforts to impose economic sanctions reinforced the domestic opposition forces within South Africa and helped bring
about a transition to majority rule. So too, post-apartheid South Africa's
efforts to come to terms with its past, particularly its Truth and Reconciliation Commission's emphasis on forgiveness and reconciliation, have inspired many in the world community.

South Africa's 1993 Interim Constitution recognized the importance of
reconciliation to South Africa's future. The post-amble to that document
stated that "the pursuit of national unity, the well-being of all South African
citizens and peace require reconciliation between the people of South Africa
and the reconstruction of society." It went on to note: "There is a need for

1

understanding but not vengeance, a need for reparation but not for retaliation, a need for *ubuntu* but not victimization."[1]

Taking up this theme, South Africa's widely heralded Truth and Reconciliation Commission (TRC), led by Archbishop Desmond Tutu, a Nobel
peace prize winner and South Africa's most senior Anglican cleric, sought to
balance truth-finding with reconciliation. Truth commissions are tempo-
rary bodies mandated by governments or international agencies to investigate and make findings about acts and patterns of violence and gross human rights violations that took place during a specified period of time.[2]
Their role typically is documenting and acknowledging a legacy of conflict
and vicious crimes as a step toward healing wounds and shaping a shared
future.[3] In contrast with most of the major truth commissions that preced-
ed it, the TRC was mandated to go beyond truth-finding and "to promote
national unity and reconciliation in a spirit of understanding which tran-
scends the conflict and divisions of the past."[4]

This volume is intended as a contribution toward understanding the
implications of the South African experience to promote forgiveness and
reconciliation among former adversaries. Despite its critical importance to
a wide range of countries, the process through which parties in a divided
society can achieve reconciliation is relatively unexplored. Almost all of the
research on forgiveness and reconciliation to date has focused on interpersonal or small group relationships, and the relevance of these findings to
wider societal processes is unclear.[5] The introduction to a recent publication, for example, comments that "no comprehensive research has been
conducted on the dynamics of interaction between justice, reconciliation,
and the pursuit of peaceful coexistence among parties"[6]

South Africa offers an unusual opportunity to explore the interaction
between justice, forgiveness, reconciliation, and reconciliation on a national, social, and political landscape and to evaluate the strengths and weaknesses of utilizing a truth commission body for promoting societal reconciliation. In addition, this volume has the additional benefit of being part of a
broader multidisciplinary study of the TRC.

The volume focuses on the relationship between religion and reconciliation and does so particularly by providing the perspectives of leaders of a
wide range of faith communities.[7] During 1999 and 2000 the Rev. Bernard
Spong, the former communications director of the South African Council
of Churches, conducted a series of in-depth interviews of thirty-three key
religious figures as one component of a more comprehensive assessment of

the TRC conducted by the Science and Human Rights Program of the American Association for the Advancement of Science, with the collaboration of the Johannesburg-based Centre for the Study of Violence and Reconciliation. The interviews sought the views of these actors on a series of topics with as little intervention or direction as possible.

While the relevance of the South African experience to understanding reconciliation is clear, the focus selected here needs further explanation. During much of South Africa's history, religious communities, particularly many of the Christian churches, have had significant public roles. Some of the earliest colonizers were missionaries, and the Christian faith was sometimes used as a rationale to defend colonial rule. During the apartheid period, churches and religious bodies served as both a major source of support and opposition to apartheid regimes. Many politicians on both sides of the apartheid divide, particularly members of the Afrikaner-dominated National Party, had some religious training. Some were ordained as ministers, and religious doctrines were offered as rationale to bolster and critique apartheid policies. After the democratic transition, religious leaders continued to play important roles. In contrast with other truth commissions, the TRC was led by clerics rather than lawyers and judges. And the TRC's approach to reconciliation was shaped by and imbued with religious content. Thus the role and influence of religion in South African society are central to efforts to assess the problems of and prospects for reconciliation in that nation.

The Apartheid Legacy

The apartheid system of compulsory racial separation enabled a white minority amounting to some thirteen percent of the population to monopolize economic and political power and relegate the black majority to a subordinated and politically powerless status. Apartheid ("apartness" in Afrikaans) supported white supremacy through an elaborate set of laws that reserved eighty-seven percent of the land and virtually all natural resources to the white population and skewed access to good quality education, decent medical care, and well-paying jobs to the white minority. An official population registration apparatus provided a documentary basis for birth-to-death racial classification and discrimination against the African, Asian, and mixed race population. The Group Areas Act of 1950 and its various amendments defined separate areas that legally could be owned and occupied by various racial groups. To enforce the Group Areas Act, the government forcibly relocated people, primarily Africans, by deporting them to "homelands" or native reserves and instituted a vicious system of pass laws to control the movement of the black population. The Reservation of Separate Amenities Act mandated the reservation of separate (and significantly unequal) services, buildings, and conveniences for each racial group. Other laws sought to entrench white political power by stripping many black South Africans of their citizenship and relegating them to membership in unviable homelands.

To maintain their control, the Afrikaner-dominated government used instruments of state power, including violence and gross human rights abuses, to repress legitimate demands for greater equity, freedom, and democracy. As resistance grew, laws became more draconian and successor National Party regimes increasingly resorted to violence, house arrest, imprisonment, torture, and assassination to keep apartheid in place. Nongovernmental human rights organizations estimate that as many as two hundred thousand South Africans were arrested between 1960 and 1992, the majority of whom were tortured while in detention. Moreover, in most cases whole families and sometimes entire communities were affected, as well as individuals. State violence during apartheid permeated every aspect of non-white South Africans' lives, from the direct brutality of illegal detention and torture to the daily injustices of separate facilities, pass laws, and segregated residential areas.

Unequal access to education, health, and economic opportunities left the overwhelming majority of blacks in grinding poverty with few prospects to better their situation. Apartheid policies segregated students from elementary school on up, allocated resources unequally among various racial groups, and offered better quality education to the white minority. State expenditure for white children in 1985 was estimated to be seven times higher per child than the expenditure for Indian, mixed race, and African children.[8] Even after universities began to lower the color bar, the number of black students who were academically qualified (not to mention financially able) to pursue higher education was limited by the earlier lack of a fair educational infrastructure, a factor still true now in the post-apartheid era.

Moreover, apartheid policies continue to be reflected in continuing economic divisions. A household survey conducted by the Community Agency for Social Enquiry (CASE) in 1994, the year of the democratic transition, of a nationally representative sample of four thousand households in

South Africa found that close to two-thirds of all African households (more than three-quarters in rural areas) had monthly incomes below the minimum living level (then R900) and nearly one-fourth monthly incomes of only R300. In contrast, two-thirds of white households reported incomes of more than R2000.[9] Approximately two-thirds of the African population lived in overcrowded housing without electricity, clean water, or sanitation. Only twenty percent of African households reported having a water tap inside the home compared with nearly one hundred percent of whites.[10] As more recent figures from the 1996 census indicate, a slow rate of economic growth has made it difficult for the Mandela and Mbeki governments to overcome these economic divisions. In 1996, forty-eight percent of employed African women earned R500 or less per month, whereas sixty-five percent of white men earned more than R3000.[11]

Moreover, the implications of apartheid spread well beyond inequalities in access to resources and political power to exacting a psychological toll. Claims of white superiority and black inferiority, which undergirded the system, have left a legacy of deep social divisions, psychological scars, and distrust between groups. As Bernard Spong observes,

If people do not meet one another as equal human beings in all areas of life they do not know or understand one another. This simple implication of apartheid meant that there were two nations within one. Black and White lived apart from one another except in the workplace where White was legislated to be in the superior commanding position. Apartheid laws supported a societal mentality of "us and them." Inferior resources lead not only to poor living conditions and a lack of prospects for improvement but also to a mental state of superiority and inferiority. White training and education was toward an automatic understanding of oneself as a cut above the rest of society. Arrogance creeps into such sensibility very quickly. On the other hand, inferior status in the social order leads, especially with constant conditioning, to an acceptance of oneself as less than fully human.[12]

Although the divides between perpetrators and victims and between the beneficiaries and the exploited of the apartheid system were the major fault lines, they were by no means the only social and political divisions bequeathed by apartheid. The apartheid policy of divide and rule set supporters of the Inkatha Freedom Party (IFP), a Zulu-based political party, against those who identified with the African National Congress (ANC), which had a multiracial and multiethnic base. From the mid-1980s many black townships and the KwaZulu-Natal region erupted in black-on-black violence fostered by the apartheid administration and a mysterious so-called "Third

Force" that apparently had Inkatha connections. These conflicts continue to simmer in some areas.

There are also other continuing political divisions. Differences in political strategy during apartheid created friction between the ANC and more radical black political movements. The Pan Africanist Congress (PAC) and the Azanian Peoples Organization (AZAPO) disagreed with the ANC over the appropriate racial basis for an anti-apartheid coalition, whether to seek a multiracial or exclusively black African membership. Then after Nelson Mandela's release from his long imprisonment neither the PAC nor AZAPO supported the ANC's policy to negotiate the dismantling of the apartheid system with the ruling National Party government.

Historically a small minority of the white community, primarily drawn from the English-speaking population, opposed the apartheid system and supported the goals of the ANC. Currently the white community is divided between those supporting democratization and others unable or unwilling to adjust to the new society.

The Public Role of South Africa's Religious Communities

During the apartheid era, religious bodies played significant roles both as supporters and opponents of the apartheid system. The *Truth and Reconciliation Commission of South Africa Report* identifies religious communities and leaders, particularly Christian churches, as falling into three categories: some were supporters of the apartheid system, others were opponents, and a third group were victims of oppression.[13] The actual relationships were, however, more complicated than this triune classification. Members did not necessarily support the official policies of their denominations. Thus some denominations contained both supporters and opponents of apartheid. Moreover, many religious bodies were ostensibly apolitical, taking no official position on apartheid initiatives, but by so doing in reality supporting the status quo.

The Dutch Reformed churches, particularly the largest of them, the Nederduitse Gereformeerde Klerk (NGK), served as pillars of apartheid, actively promoting and supporting the apartheid system. These churches were infused with a conservative theology that preached it was contrary to the laws of God for whites and blacks to be put on equal footing or even to have close social relationships. The belief that people of different races should be kept apart motivated the NGK to establish separate churches for its converts and eventually to advocate for the political process of separate development. Like the apartheid society, the structure of the NGK was officially segregated. It set up parallel religious structures for whites, blacks, coloureds (persons of mixed racial backgrounds), and Indians. After 1948, when the Afrikaner-dominated National Party came to power, the NGK urged the government to implement the policy of apartheid and actively supported the adoption of many of the laws that were central to the system.[14] During the half century of apartheid rule, the NGK conferred its blessings on the system, offering biblical sanction and theological justification for the practice of racial separation. Until 1986, when the NGK Synod began to distance itself from an active defense of apartheid, the church functioned *de facto,* if not *de jure,* as an official state church, with considerable benefits accruing from this role.

Other religious communities also gave the apartheid state tacit support through such means as propagating theologies that neutralized dissent and/or promoting obedience to the existing political leaders. The Apostolic Faith Mission and other conservative and pentecostal denominations constitute examples. Various right-wing Christian groups like the Christian League of Southern Africa, the Catholic Defense League, and the Anglican Reform League also played important supportive roles.

In contrast, some religious communities and ecumenical bodies opposed apartheid's principles and policies, most notably the South African Council of Churches (SACC). Under apartheid the suppression of opposition political parties and the incarceration of major black politicians left a void that the SACC and some church-related voluntary organizations tried to fill. Many of the progressive denominations approved official statements and resolutions critical of apartheid. Others sent petitions and letters to the government on a range of issues, and some sought to intervene behind closed doors. Some faith communities, undertook marches and acts of civil disobedience to express opposition to specific apartheid policies and requirements. For example, local congregations deliberately flouted laws by establishing multiracial congregations. And a few appealed to international partners to press for economic sanctions and disinvestment from South Africa.[15] Despite the violence of the apartheid regime, the anti-apartheid movement was remarkably nonviolent, partially as a result of the influence of the religious community. In addition, the SACC served as a liaison to agencies in the international religious community involved in the anti-apartheid movement.

The SACC and the more progressive Christian churches suffered for their activism. Their activities were disrupted, their leaders persecuted, and in a few cases, their land and assets seized by the apartheid regime.[16] Not infrequently, the government and its allies tried to discredit them with propaganda. A bomb was planted in the SACC's headquarters, and the Southern Africa Catholic Bishops' Conference was set alight.

Nevertheless, religious opposition to apartheid, much of it emanating from the SACC and a few multiracial denominations of British origins (Congregational, Methodist, Anglican, and Presbyterian) tended to be expressed more through the drafting of official statements and the courageous leadership of a few individuals than through the sustained commitment and mobilization of members. Indeed, the 1986 *Kairos Document*[17] drafted by a group of progressive black theologians criticized these churches for issuing condemnatory statements without undertaking effective action. Although the most severe criticism in that document was directed at the Dutch Reformed churches for their "state theology" that officially supported apartheid, the *Kairos Document* also characterized the group of denominations that had prided themselves on their progressive stance as guilty of adhering to a "church theology" based on "cheap" reconciliation. It argued that authentic reconciliation could only follow white repentance and a clear commitment to fundamental change. According to its drafters, "No reconciliation is possible in South Africa without justice."[18] The pejorative "church theology" designation sought to challenge these denominations to a more activist stance, referred to in the document as a "prophetic theology," characterized by solidarity with the victims of apartheid and partnership with their struggle for a just, democratic society. Nevertheless, only one denomination, the Congregational Church of Southern Africa, endorsed the document in its entirety. While the *Kairos Document* may be considered unduly harsh in its critique of mainline churches, the religious leaders of several of these denominations have subsequently been self-critical about their records under apartheid.[19]

The impact of apartheid on the religious community is important to note. The Dutch Reformed and conservative denominations were not the only ones with racially segregated structures. The Baptist churches were racially divided as well. Despite their official opposition to the principle of racial segregation, many Protestant congregations were racially homogeneous. Sunday was and continues to be the most racially divided day as people tend to remain in their various racial and ethnic areas for church. Even when denominations were officially multiracial, white congregations and clergy usually benefited from having far more resources at their disposal. Moreover, many of the religious bodies, particularly local congregations, were internally divided into supporters and opponents of the apartheid regime. Frequently, proposed initiatives to express opposition to apartheid policies generated controversy. As the Truth and Reconciliation report notes, "Different interests, perspectives and world views were represented—often within the same faith tradition. Likewise local churches and similar communities contained victims, beneficiaries and perpetrators of apartheid."[20]

As the political transition became more likely, some religious actors sought to prepare for and encourage a democratic future. The National Peace Accord was launched in September 1991, with the active involvement of the SACC, to help promote an ethos conducive to a democratic transition. When political compromise seemed elusive, members of the religious community helped to bring politicians back to the negotiating table. When the TRC was established, the religious community also sought to be supportive. The SACC characterized the TRC as "an extraordinary act of generosity by a people who insist only that the truth, the whole truth and nothing but the truth be told." It anticipated that through the TRC "the space is thereby created where the deeper process of forgiveness, confession, repentance, reparation, and reconciliation can take place."[21]

Consistent with the public and political role of the religious community, religious thinkers and clergy held key positions in the TRC: Chairman, Deputy Chairman, four other Commissioners, and the Director of Research. And given the charismatic presence of Archbishop Desmond Tutu as the Chair, theological formulations and religious liturgy were interwoven into the TRC process, particularly its public hearings. The Christian atmosphere and discourse of the TRC, and particularly Archbishop Tutu's frequent framing of issues in terms of repentance and forgiveness, was applauded by some South Africans, for whom Christian ideals had served as an ethical critique of apartheid, but it was distasteful to many others. This latter category included some of the Commissioners and staff of the TRC as well as some academics, victims, and victim advocates. These multiple voices are reflected in the TRC report.

Recognizing the public role of religion in South African society, the

TRC held a special hearing on the role of faith communities during apart-heid. One of several such sectoral hearings, the faith communities hearing took place in East London in November 1997. The TRC received more than sixty submissions from a wide range of religious communities. Some thirty groups testified during the three days of hearings, as well as individual staff and leaders. The submissions and testimonies at the hearings formed the basis of a chapter in the fourth volume of the TRC report.

The TRC's Efforts to Promote Reconciliation

Given South Africa's history and the events leading up to the establishment of the TRC, the mandate assigned to the TRC to balance truth-finding with promoting reconciliation made a great deal of sense. A wide variety of reli-gious and secular thinkers emphasize that forgiveness and reconciliation re-quire coming to terms with the past, not attempting to forget or repress it. Establishing a shared truth that documents the causes, nature, and extent of severe and gross human rights abuses and/or collective violence under an-tecedent regimes is a prerequisite for achieving accountability, meaningful reconciliation, and a foundation for a common future. As Archbishop Des-mond Tutu stated in the foreword to the Commission's five-volume report, "Reconciliation is not about being cosy; it is not about pretending that things were other than they were. Reconciliation based on falsehood, on not facing up to reality, is not true reconciliation and will not last."[22]

But what seems appropriate in theory may not be feasible in practice. Truth commissions, including the TRC, function in situations where the legacy of conflict has resulted in deep social divisions and sharply conflict-ing and contested versions of the past. In such situations, it is difficult for any single body to succeed in establishing a shared truth or promoting rec-onciliation, let alone both. Moreover, the requirements of these two goals may be in conflict. While truth-finding and the formulation of a shared his-tory likely are prerequisites for long-term nation-building, the process may not be conducive for promoting forgiveness and reconciliation, at least in the short term. At the least, the examination of gross human rights viola-tions risks reopening deep wounds and thereby exacerbating societal divi-sions. Moreover, as the TRC experience showed, both the process of truth-finding and the conclusions drawn can be contentious and leave actors holding a wide range of perspectives deeply dissatisfied and thus potentially more divided. Conversely, the desire not to harm prospects for national reconciliation may influence the manner in which a truth commission accumulates evidence and shapes its findings.

The only other predecessor truth commission with the twin objectives of establishing truth and working toward reconciliation was the Chilean National Commission on Truth and Reconciliation. The Chilean Commission framed its task as "a truth for reconciliation."[23] While its focus was on investigating and determining the truth, it understood that this truth had a clear and specific purpose: "to work toward the reconciliation of all Chileans." To that end, the Commission sought the advice of a broad range of groups of victims' relatives, human rights agencies, professional associations, and political parties regarding how the Commission could best reach the truth and thereby aid national reconciliation.[24]

In contrast, the TRC Commissioners understood their mandate as pursuing both truth and reconciliation. To do so successfully at the least would have required a clear conception of each task and a sense of how they interrelate. However, the TRC did not have consensus on either the nature of the reconciliation it was mandated to pursue or the relationship between truth-funding and reconciliation.[25] As the TRC report notes, "The overarching task assigned to the Commission by Parliament was the promotion of national unity and reconciliation. Debates within and outside the Commission demonstrated that the interpretation of this concept was highly contested."[26] Complicating the task of the TRC, reconciliation was not well defined in the National Unity and Reconciliation Act of July 1995, which established the body, and thus it was not clear what the mandate entailed. Understandably, the TRC's leadership, both Commissioners and senior staff, had problems deciding how to proceed with this obligation. Moreover, the TRC was inclined to focus on other things, particularly its public hearings and amnesty process. It was not until much later in the TRC's life that the Commissioners turned their attention to the subject of reconciliation.

Piet Meiring, who served as a member of the Reparation and Rehabilitation Committee of the TRC, indicates in his interview in this volume that about halfway through the life of the TRC "a long, drawn out argument" developed among the Commissioners over the nature of reconciliation, its needs, and what the TRC should do. He alludes to the many debates among them and to their failure to resolve the very significant discrepancies in their perspectives. These ranged from the politico-judicial or legal minimalist position of the lawyers and politicians that equated reconciliation with the end of overt conflict to those of Archbishop Tutu and some of the other clergy and committed Christians in prominent positions who insisted on a religious approach to reconciliation.

The TRC never resolved differences in viewpoints on reconciliation. As a result, Commissioners and staff often pursued very different approaches to reconciliation. Depending on who was taking the initiative, the public interface and sections of the final report of the Commission sometimes conveyed religious perspectives and linked reconciliation with interpersonal forgiveness. At other times the TRC reflected a more political and judicial concept of reconciliation. The dominant role of Archbishop Tutu meant, though, that the religious understanding of reconciliation often trumped other views.

The TRC also had a "particular difficulty of understanding the meaning of unity and reconciliation at a national level."[27] During its life, the TRC slid between a variety of approaches, variously prioritizing reconciliation between political parties (the African National Congress vis-à-vis the National Party), reconciliation between races (blacks and whites), and reconciliation between victims as a group and the structures of the state.[28] Much of the time, though, the TRC individualized issues of reconciliation, just as it individualized its interpretation of responsibility for violence and abuses, and thus neglected the national and community dimensions. Both the TRC process and the final report focused on reconciliation between victims and perpetrators, interpreting it as little more than forgiveness, rather than the more complex and ultimately significant topic of national or political reconciliation. The section on reconciliation in volume five of the TRC report devotes most of its space to anecdotes recounting specific instances of reconciliation between victims/survivors and perpetrators.

Quite ironically, in view of the religious imagery and public witness of the Commission, the final volume of the TRC report alludes to the "potentially dangerous confusion between a religious, indeed Christian understanding of reconciliation, more typically applied to interpersonal relationships, and the more limited notions of reconciliation applicable to a democratic society."[29] It then goes on to observe that the model of confession, repentance, and forgiveness is central to religion but raises questions about its applicability and relevance to South Africa's situation.[30]

The Issues and Approach of This Volume

The interviews that follow and the essays interpreting them seek to illuminate a number of issues:

(1) *How should we understand the concept of national or political reconciliation and its requirements?* In an earlier article I conceptualized reconciliation as a process of developing mutual accommodation between antagonistic or formerly antagonistic persons or groups so as to establish a new relationship predicated on a common shared future.[31] In addition, I suggested that there are six requirements for reconciliation. The first is discernment, preferably by a body with official status, of the truth about the extent, causes, and perpetrators of the violence and abuses in the past. The second is open and shared acknowledgment of moral responsibility by those who inflicted the harm and others who were complicit by their silence and failure to oppose the wrongdoing. A third requirement noted in this earlier work is a willingness to let go of the past and not seek vengeance. The fourth is achieving justice, specifically a measure of appropriate redress. The fifth requirement is commitment on the part of all parties to repair and reestablish their relationships. I suggested that the sixth and final requirement is to create and sustain a network of understandings and relationships necessary to shape and support a new and common future.[32] To what extent do the interviews identify similar requirements? How do they assess the process of reconciliation along these dimensions?

(2) *What are the differences and similarities between religious and political approaches to reconciliation?* I have previously suggested that (national) reconciliation may be understood as a social and political process with religious and theological dimensions.[33] Even if this characterization is correct (and I am currently less inclined now to stress the religious foundations and connections), reconciliation should be understood as a social and political process. Nevertheless, this was not the approach of the TRC, which frequently conflated theological approaches with political requirements. For this reason, it seemed relevant to ascertain whether a wide cross section of religious leaders viewed the challenge of national reconciliation as requiring religious or political initiatives or some combination thereof.

(3) *Does national or political reconciliation require forgiveness between former victims and perpetrators?* The TRC process and its final report place an emphasis on the importance of forgiveness, frequently appearing to

equate interpersonal forgiveness with reconciliation. Accordingly, the title of the Archbishop's memoir about the TRC is *No Future without Forgiveness.*[34] The five-volume TRC report recounts many dramatic and heartrending stories of forgiveness and reconciliation between victims and perpetrators. Some of these anecdotes are repeated in the memoirs and articles written by Commissioners and staff. Often they were the stuff out of which the media, particularly foreign journalists, fashioned their coverage of the TRC. Nevertheless, the relationship between interpersonal forgiveness and reconciliation, particularly among communities, is unclear and likely to be quite complex. Quite conceivably, national reconciliation among communities and formerly antagonistic political forces may be able to go forward without or independent of interpersonal forgiveness between former victims and perpetrators. Alternatively, national reconciliation may be a prerequisite for interpersonal forgiveness.

(4) *What is the appropriate role of religious actors in a truth commission process?* As noted, the prominent role of clerics in the TRC had no precedent in any other truth commission. How do members of the religious community view this experiment? Do they believe that the leadership role of religious figures shaped the TRC, and if so, in what way and with what kinds of implications? Overall, do they believe that the presence of religious thinkers and clergy strengthened the TRC process, and if so, do they recommend that other countries emulate the South African model?

(5) *How do religious leaders assess the contributions and limitations of the TRC?* Given the active role of the religious community in supporting the establishment of the TRC, how do various religious leaders evaluate the TRC? Do they believe that the TRC fulfilled its mandates? What do they identify as the TRC's major contributions and limitations?

(6) *What kind of initiatives are contemporary religious communities taking to promote reconciliation among their members and in the wider society?* Under the best of circumstances, the TRC could do no more than establish some of the preconditions for reconciliation and take some initial steps. As widely noted in the literature, reconciliation is a long-term process, not an act or a single event. Of the various institutions in South African society, religious communities seem best suited to carry the process of reconciliation forward, both within their own denominations as well as in the wider society. Nevertheless, it is not clear that local congregations or wider religious bodies are actively involved in promoting reconciliation. What kinds of programs and initiatives are various faith communities undertaking? And what

factors are shaping the level and type of reconciliation initiatives of various faith communities?

NOTES

1. Conclusion, Interim Constitution for the Republic of South Africa, Act No. 200 of 1993. Loosely translated, ubuntu is the recognition of a common humanity.

2. In a few situations, nongovernmental organizations and church agencies have also sponsored the work of unofficial truth commissions.

3. Priscilla Hayner, "Fifteen Truth Commissions—1974 to 1994: A Comparative Study," *Human Rights Quarterly* 16 (1994): 607.

4. Preamble, "Promotion of National Unity and Reconciliation Act," 1995, Republic of South Africa, *Government Gazette*, vol. 361, no.16579.

5. On this point see Everett L. Worthington, Jr., "Unforgiveness, Forgiveness, and Reconciliation and Their Implications for Societal Interventions," in Raymond G. Helmick, S. J., and Rodney L. Petersen, eds., *Forgiveness and Reconciliation: Religion, Public Policy and Conflict Transformation* (Philadelphia & London: Templeton Foundation Press, 2001), 161–182.

6. Mohammed Abu-Nimer, "Introduction," in Mohammed Abu-Nimer, ed., *Reconciliation, Justice, and Coexistence: Theory and Practice* (Lanham, MD: Lexington Books, 2001), x.

7. In South Africa, the faith community encompasses a wide diversity of religions and denominations, including numbers of very different Christian churches, African traditional religious groups, Islam, Judaism, Hinduism, Buddhism, and the Baha'i faith. Christian churches have particularly played important public roles. The selection of interview subjects reflects both the range of religions and the disproportionate influence of the churches.

8. F. Wilson and M. Ramphele, *Uprooting Poverty: The South African Challenge* (New York: W. W. Norton and Company, 1989), 273.

9. The Community Agency for Social Enquiry, "A National Household Survey of Health Inequalities in South Africa" (The Henry J. Kaiser Foundation, 1995), 11.

10. Ibid., 10.

11. These data are from Statistics South Africa.

12. This statement was part of a longer document of written reflections provided by Bernard Spong via email in December, 2001.

13. This section is drawn from the characterization of the role of the faith community during the apartheid period in chapter 3 of volume 4 of the *Truth and Reconciliation Commission of South Africa Report* (Cape Town: CTP Book Printers [PTY] Ltd., 1998).

14. "The Story of the Dutch Reformed Church's Journey with Apartheid: 1960–1994: a testimony and a confession," General Synodal Commission of the Dutch Reformed Church (Nederduitse Gereformeerde Klerk), July 21, 1997, section 2.5, <http://www.ricsa.org.za/trc/drc_sub.htr>.

15. For a description of these activities, see "Faith Communities and Apartheid: The RICSA Report." The text is available on the web site of the Religious Institute on Christianity in South Africa (RICSA) in the University of Cape Town's Department of Religious Studies <www.ricsa. org.za/trc>. The RICSA report was commissioned by the TRC and is loosely based on submissions and testimony that took place in conjunction with the 1997 faith communities hearing conducted by the TRC. The text is also reproduced in James Cochrane, John de Gruchy, and Stephen Martin, *Facing the Truth: South Africa Faith Communities and the Truth & Reconciliation Commission* (Cape

Town: David Philip Publishers, and Athens, OH: Ohio University Press, 1999), 15–77. The discussion of faith communities as opponents of apartheid is in pp. 45–57.

16. See "Institutional Hearing: The Faith Community," *Truth and Reconciliation Commission of South Africa Report,* vol. 4, 59.

17. *The Kairos Document: Challenge to the Churches,* rev. 2nd ed. (Johannesburg: Institute for Contextual Theology, 1986).

18. Ibid., art. 3.1,9.

19. The submissions and testimony of the Catholic Church and several of the more progressive Protestant denominations to the faith communities hearing conducted by the TRC were self-critical about the failure to be more activist during apartheid. The full written submissions are available on the web site of the Religious Institute on Christianity in South Africa (RICSA) in the University of Cape Town's Department of Religious Studies (or at least were so at the time of writing): <www.ricsa.org.za/trc>. See also the initial RICSA report of the faith communities hearing written for the TRC. The text is available on the same web site, and it is reproduced in Cochrane, de Gruchy, and Martin, *Facing the Truth,* particularly pp. 41–43, 48–58.

20. *Truth and Reconciliation Commission of South Africa Report,* vol. 4 (Cape Town: CTP Book Printers [PTY] Ltd., 1998), 59.

21. "The Truth Will Set You Free" (Johannesburg: South African Council of Churches, 1995).

22. Archbishop Desmond Tutu, "Chairperson's Foreword," *Truth and Reconciliation Commission of South Africa Report,* vol. 1 (Cape Town: CTP Book Printers [PTY] Ltd. For the Truth and Reconciliation Commission, 1998), 17.

23. *Report of the Chilean National Commission on Truth and Reconciliation,* vol. 1, Phillip E. Berryman, trans., published in cooperation with the Center for Civil and Human Rights, Notre Dame Law School (Notre Dame, IN: University of Notre Dame Press, 1993), 24.

24. Ibid., 24–25.

25. For a discussion of this issue, see this author's chapter, "Truth Commissions as Instruments of Forgiveness and Reconciliation," in Helmick and Peterson, eds., *Forgiveness and Reconciliation,* 247–268.

26. *Truth and Reconciliation Commission of South Africa Report,* vol. 1, 106.

27. Ibid., 108.

28. See this author's evaluation and critique in Audrey R. Chapman, "Truth Commissions as Instruments of Forgiveness and Reconciliation," in Helmick and Petersen, eds., *Forgiveness and Reconciliation,* 247–268.

29. Ibid., 440.

30. *Truth and Reconciliation Commission of South Africa Report,* vol. 5, 442.

31. Audrey R. Chapman, "Coming to Terms with the Past: Truth, Justice, and/or Reconciliation," *Annual of the Society for Christian Ethics* 19 (1999): 235–258.

32. Ibid., 245–248.

33. Ibid., 246.

34. Desmond Mpilo Tutu, *No Future Without Forgiveness* (New York: Doubleday, 1999).

INTERVIEWS

Conducted and edited by Bernard Spong

෯෯෯

A S WE NOTED EARLIER, Bernard Spong conducted the interviews in this volume over a period of twelve months beginning in August 1999. The same instrument was given to each person, and is provided here to guide the reader in the responses recorded in the following conversations.

The experience of the Commission illustrated the difficulty of understanding the meaning of unity and reconciliation at a national level. They also highlighted the potentially dangerous confusion between a religious, indeed Christian, understanding of reconciliation, more typically applied to interpersonal relationships, and the more limited political notion of reconciliation applicable to a democratic society. (TRC Report 1.5.19)

What is your understanding of the concept of reconciliation? How closely is it tied to the need for acknowledgment of wrong on the one hand and forgiveness on the other?

Is there a difference in the religious and secular approaches to reconciliation?

What is needed in South Africa to achieve reconciliation?

This task was necessary for the promotion of reconciliation and national unity. In other words, the telling of the truth about past gross human rights violations, as viewed from different perspectives, facilitates the process of understanding our divided pasts, whilst the public acknowledgment of untold suffering and injustice helps to restore the dignity of the victim and affords perpetrators the opportunity to come to terms with their own past. (TRC Report 1.4.3)

To what extent and in what ways has the TRC contributed to national reconciliation?

To what extent have white South Africans come to accept personal and social responsibility for apartheid as a result of TRC hearings?

To what extent have the survivors of gross human rights violations benefited from the TRC?

Was it helpful to have a considerable number of religious persons on the TRC which was a national government appointed body?

Different interests, perspectives and world views are represented—often within the same faith tradition. Likewise local churches and similar communities contained victims, beneficiaries and perpetrators of apartheid. Reconciliation within such communities could have a leavening effect for the whole of society. From them should flow a source of renewal extending to the entire South African society. (TRC Report 4.3.3)

What can and what does the religious community do to foster reconciliation? As far as your specific faith group is concerned, are the commitment, energy and resources available? Or are there other priorities?

What is the task of the religious communities at this time in South Africa?

Have you any comments on the possible granting of a blanket amnesty?

Any other comment on the reconciliation process?

PROTESTANTS

ℐℐℐ

BAPTIST CONVENTION OF SOUTH AFRICA

Wednesday, August 25, 1999

There is no theological or even human way of forgiving if the people just say, "I want forgiveness but I do not want to say that I have done anything wrong and I am sorry."

ℐ

THE BAPTIST CONVENTION grew out of the struggle against apartheid. The Baptist Union stance of being a-political was seen by many black Baptists to give support to the apartheid government. A new society was formed to bring together those of a Baptist persuasion who wished to express their abhorrence of apartheid. One of the first acts of the Convention was to join the South African Council of Churches, which the Union had left because of its anti-government stance.

I met with their General Secretary, the Rev. Frank Makoro, and the Director of Church Development and Ministerial Services, the Rev. Ramakatsa Mathibedi.

WHEN WE TALK OF RECONCILIATION, the first thing we must address is the question of acceptance of the wrongdoing. That means taking responsibility rather than shifting blame somewhere else.

Reconciliation is a process. It might start with someone who has been wronged or with someone who is willing to accept the reality of the circumstances and to address the problems which have taken place. Reconciliation happens where two or more than two people become aware of a problem and they are willing to address that problem.

In religious terms it is necessary first of all to recognize all people as the creation of God and equally deserving of respect and dignity. Within the church it is very important that this Christian-centered doctrine is propagated. It is heretical for us to hold different theological definitions that separate people according to their pigmentation. The church has to reconcile in terms of teaching the truth and addressing the realities of the past and their effect on the present.

IN SOUTH AFRICA we need people changing their mindset. This includes an awareness of wrong having being done and the willingness to do something about that wrong. We have to accept that some of the wrongs might have been done in a context in which it was not seen as wrong, but now the circumstances and the environment allows people to see things from other perspectives. We believe that we should all be willing to learn and to say that even though in the past I did not understand things this way now I see that this was wrong and unacceptable. I am sorry for what has happened and for what I did or did not do. I am now willing to do something to ensure that I create an atmosphere in which others also feel that they are part of the creation of God.

THE TRC HAS DONE A LOT OF WORK in that it has helped people—even those people who wanted to pretend nothing wrong had happened—to come to a place where they realize that something wrong has been done. It has helped people who were never heard before to admit that something wrong has been done and that we need to create an atmosphere in which others will be able to live as human beings. So we do believe that, to a certain extent, the TRC has helped.

Another TRC achievement is the fact that it disclosed the brutality of the apartheid regime. And it has informed some of the relatives about the mysteries surrounding the disappearance of their loved ones.

THERE ARE SOME WHITES who have come around to accepting that something evil happened and are ready to do something to address those wrongs. At the same time, there are many more who are still say-

ing that they had nothing to do with what happened. They say that somebody else did it and they must take responsibility. This is not a helpful attitude.

It seems that some older people tend to justify even the atrocities of
apartheid as if there was divine approval. Some people were misinformed
by their cultural backgrounds and their beliefs. They believed that apartheid
was divinely ordained, which is not the case as far as we are concerned. It is
absolutely wrong and unacceptable for people to justify killings of innocent
people as if God ordained it to happen.

All people are equal before God. They have the same rights. Now older
white people have resistance to change. It seems that it is easier for younger
people to accept the reality of what happened, and they are willing to be instruments of change in that regard. But the fact remains that some white
people, because of their particular kind of background, still find it difficult
to accept that apartheid was a sin against humanity and that the oppression
was wrong.

THE TRC HAS REALIZED that most of the black people who were
involved in the struggle reacted out of frustration and desperation.
They were forced by circumstances, and the TRC has exposed how an unjust policy oppressed people.

A benefit for the victims is the confirmation in the TRC of what happened under apartheid. Many people now know what happened to their relatives. That, in itself, is helpful.

We strongly believe that South Africa has a long way to go in terms of
compensation. When you look at the victims you see people in wheelchairs
and others who have lost limbs. Then there are the families of those who
died. Much has still to be done to help these people. They have not benefited directly yet in that area of compensation.

The government needs to call upon business, call upon the church, and
call upon civil society to bring them together to see what can be done for
the victims. Perhaps the church would be a neutral body that could best be
used by the nation as the vehicle of assistance to the victims. There are many
victims who suffered under the apartheid system, people on both sides of
that struggle who need help.

IT WAS HELPFUL to have religious leaders on the Truth Commission. Their religious background was very helpful in that they understood the concept of reconciliation—not only the Christians but people from other religions as well. They all understand that if two people do not see eye to eye it is necessary that they go through the problem, find each other, and admit his or her fault to the other, and then find the way of coexistence and continuing in life together. It was very helpful to have people with an attitude that was not seeking for revenge but to find a solution to the problem.

FIRST OF ALL, many religious leaders have to put right the preaching of the past. Whatever misinformation we gave to our people in the past, we have to address that and correct it. All those who were involved in proclaiming the theology of apartheid should admit that was a heretical approach. That is the first point of departure. And then also those who believed that they could use their physical strength to remove the apartheid regime from power should also realize that during that process innocent people were victimized. And then from there, after acknowledging our responsibility, we can be in a position to sit around the table and say we learned from the past and now we have to go forward as one people, as equal people.

This has to happen. But sometimes it becomes very difficult because one can have the will and desire to see it happening but you find that an atmosphere is not created in which it can take place. We can talk from experience as church leaders who are trying to get this to happen even after the downfall of apartheid. In the church you still find people who want to think in terms of superiority and inferiority. We say no, let's look to each other as people who are made in the image of God, accepting each other regardless of the pigmentation of our skin, and then we can move forward. We come with that attitude, that heart and that spirit and still find that there is resistance. You still find that desire to cling to power. The church has to fight that spirit.

THERE ARE TWO MAJOR BAPTIST GROUPS in South Africa, the Baptist Union and the Baptist Convention. The two organizations have traveled a long way, and we have done a lot of things in trying to bring the two together. But our perspectives on certain issues and our understanding of certain issues are different.

These differences arise in our theological understanding. We, as people who come out of the struggle, have our own understanding of certain theo-logical issues. Unfortunately, those who come from the previously advan-taged, who even at this point are still advantaged, see things from a different perspective. The emphasis is different.

We know that if you look over the country there are many people who are suffering. Because of apartheid they are where they are economically and educationally. It is necessary for them to be helped. When people say, let us address issues of the soul and not social issues as well, we have to respond to say that our approach is holistic. We are not only talking about a heart or spirit or soul here, but we are talking about a person who lives somewhere and who has to eat. We are asking a question: Why is this person living like this? These are some of the differences between us.

There are talks going on between us and we are hopeful about them. We have come a long way, from being hostile to each other to a position where we can gather together in the same room and talk about issues and differ without being hostile to each other. We have come to a place where we allow each other to see things differently.

There was no need in the first place to have segregated theological training colleges. For people who are the witnesses of Jesus Christ there is no justification for segregation. Disparities were made, even in terms of de-signing the curriculum. Another thing is the empowerment of white pastors on the one hand and the approach in which Africans were treated in the church on the other. Church leaders were treated as inferiors by their white counterparts. This is unbiblical and cannot be accepted within any Chris-tian circle.

As a result, the Baptist Convention rightfully took its stand around the acknowledgment of all people created in the image of God and deserving of respect. This is our approach. Unless the two major Baptist groups realize that everyone is equally important before God, there can be no glory for the Baptist witness in South Africa. It does not matter whatever kind of philo-sophical teachings we espouse; we must acknowledge our equality and ad-dress the key areas of human development. Baptist Union and Baptist Con-vention should realize that the time has come to be a true witness together for Christ. We must use all our resources and assets together as one people. Then the world can realize that we really know God.

We need to be very careful of a sort of window-dressing type of recon-ciliation where we stand and hug each other and we say everything is okay. We must not say we are reconciled while attitudes remain intact. Reconciliation must not be something that is external, but it must also be internal. When we say, "You are our brother," it must be from the heart. Something within us should say "Amen" to that.

So that is the kind of situation that we say we need to create. It must not be just for the sake of standing before the press and having pictures taken and then when we go back home we say this was a sham, it was not genuine and there is nothing to it. And when we go to our meetings we still have white meetings and black meetings and justify them because of our cultural differences; meanwhile deep down in our hearts, we know we do not accept these people as part of us. These are the challenges.

We hope the Baptist Union is hearing us. Only the results of our talks will tell. We wish the Baptist Union to realize the importance and the fruitful contribution that the Baptist Convention is involved in, especially toward the evangelization of the world. The Baptist Convention is no longer a national Baptist Convention but a world Baptist Convention. We have been admitted and been given international platforms. This is not the case in the present Baptist Union. This international recognition has really advanced us, and we wish some other African pastors who are in the Baptist Union could understand that they are being left behind while the Baptist Convention pastors are at a very advanced stage. However, we would not want to advance our Baptist Convention pastors only. We want all pastors, including both black and white Baptist Union pastors, to be exposed to the international way of doing Baptist things and to receive recognition. This is our desire, to let all the Baptist groups be exposed to the global Baptist family in which the Baptist Convention is now at the forefront.

We have been involved in discussions with the Baptist Union, and there are certain individuals that we have seen changing from what they used to be to being something that we believe is what God desires from us as Baptists. These are from the Baptist Union, and we thank God for these individuals and the sacrifices they are making to try and foster the spirit of reconciliation and unity. But there are those who still feel otherwise. Sometimes you find that, even though you may desire the right thing, those in power will ensure that it does not happen. That is the situation. There are those who have come a long way and there are others who cling to the past.

We have learned a lot through the Baptist Convention. We have developed because we have been in partnership with the South African Council of Churches and its member churches. We have had international exposure. Our theological understanding has developed.

We needed to stand alone to develop ourselves and then be able to face the Baptist Union. We cannot accept that someone else defines our ideas and our feelings. This has been the case in the past. Even our respective languages were undermined and altogether written off from the constitution of the country until 1994, when they were legitimized again. It is very important that people have a platform on which to define themselves and their destiny.

BLANKET AMNESTY is a definite no-no. We are talking about helping both the victims and the perpetrators. People have to be brought to a place where they realize they have done something wrong and accept the responsibility for all the hurt that they have caused. Then the victims can say that they forgive them.

There is no theological or even human way of forgiving if the people just say, "I want forgiveness but I do not want to say that I have done anything wrong and I am sorry." There is no truth in amnesty given to people like that. People need to say, "I am sorry I have done something that is wrong."

General amnesty does not help the perpetrator and does not help the victim. The victim may say that because amnesty is given so easily I will take my own revenge. We do not want people avenging for themselves, but at the same time we do not want the perpetrators simply sitting back and receiving amnesty as if nothing had happened. That is not acceptable.

GOD STARTED RECONCILIATION. He provided reconciliation through Jesus Christ. It is within that context that we should operate with one another. God is a God of justice. That justice and judgment is out of love. This is the context in which reconciliation has to be understood.

It is our hope and prayer that as we go along the victims and the perpetrators will find each other, and also that the government, civil society, and the religious communities will find a way of helping those who became victims of our past. We must offer something that will help all people face the future with hope.

The South African Council of Churches (SACC) is the national ecumenical coor-dinator of inter-church debate and action. Through its membership of 24 churches with one observer-member (the Dutch Reformed Church which re-joined the SACC after the end of the apartheid era), the SACC represents the majority of Christians in South Africa. The SACC was the leading source of reli-gious opposition to the apartheid system. It is now engaged in trying to shape a new mission to assist in the reconciliation and reconstruction of the nation.

DR. BRIGALIA HLOPHE BAM

Friday, August 27, 1999

So the hopes and expectations to this day in South Africa about the church are really very high. But I am beginning to feel, as a church person, which I am, that we are not living up to the hope and we are not living up to the expecta-tions.

☙

DR. BAM is a dedicated lay member of the Church of the Province of Southern Africa (Anglican) and a former General Secretary of the South African Council of Churches. She is the present Chairperson of the Inde-pendent Electoral Commission and President of the Women's Development Foundation.

YOU CANNOT EXAMINE the present response of the church lead-ers to the Truth and Reconciliation Commission without remembering that the churches were very much involved in its establishment. Also, and this is very important, the government had high expectations of the part the church would play in the Commission and that the churches would also play a leading role in reconciliation even after the Commission had finished. This was said to us by the then Minister of Justice just before the Commis-sion membership was announced.

You have to add to that the fact that Archbishop Desmond Tutu was chosen to chair the Commission because he had been a very well-known figure, a world figure in his own right. Such a person was needed. But we must understand that Desmond was actually chosen mainly because he was a leader of the church.

The panel that chose the members of the Commission looked to the leadership of the churches. After the panel submitted its list of names the government chose a Methodist bishop, Dr. Khoza Mgojo, precisely because they recognized the importance of the Methodist Church and its large membership throughout South Africa.

YOU WILL ALSO REMEMBER that we tried to have conversations with the Dutch Reformed Church separately because we knew that a number of people who were labeled as perpetrators were likely to come from them. And you will also know that one of the reasons we recommended in the committee Professor Piet Meiring was precisely because we knew that there needed to be an outreach, a very concrete outreach, to the Dutch Reformed Church. I think we need to say quite openly that President Mandela on several occasions said to me, "If we are talking of reconciliation in this country there is no way we can talk about reconciliation without involving the Dutch Reformed Church." They have a strong following. They are influential. The Dutch Reformed Church members are worshipers who look to the church for guidance. There is no doubt about that.

Mr. Mandela was so close himself to people like Professor Johann Heyns.[1] And he is the one who said that Professor Heyns and Professor Meiring should go to the Afrikaans leader, Eugene Terreblanche,[2] and speak with him. President Mandela, we must give him the due, realized that discussions on reconciliation were closely related to the Dutch Reformed Church. And that is why, for instance, he asked us, when we submitted our suggested list of members of the Truth Commission, whether the moderator of the Dutch Reformed Church was on our list. Of course he could have appointed him if he'd wanted to, but there were other representatives of the Afrikaans community and the Dutch Reformed Church.

It is very important to recognize that these things were a pattern as part of the hope around the setting up of the Truth and Reconciliation Commission.

WHAT I AM NOT SURE OF MYSELF is whether as churches in South Africa we have lived up to the hope that had been invested in us—the hope that we would in fact be very enthusiastic, the hope that we would be active.

I am sure that in their minds the government kept thinking of the Dependants' Conference[3] and how active we had been through all those years and the courage that the churches had shown on the "Standing For The

Truth"[4] programs as well as what we did for the returning exiles. So we had a history of leadership and active service of the people.

I never sensed, even as the General Secretary of the South African Council of Churches, that there was the same enthusiasm when it came to the Truth and Reconciliation Commission. We complained during the time of the hearings that the response, even to go to listen to testimony or to be present to support the victims, was very, very low. I felt that our churches lacked enthusiasm. I do not want to pass judgment, but it is a fact that very few church leaders or priests or pastors attended the hearings.

It seems that we, as churches, are running away from the new issues that we have to face, especially real reconciliation, and we are spending energy on survival. But on the current issues of today we are lacking visibility. We are not heard or seen to be active by the public in South Africa.

YOU MUST NOT FORGET our running around in the negotiation process and our running around, which is not documented, on forming the Peace Accord. All the mediation and persuasion was behind closed doors, and so most people do not realize the part the church played in those things. In fact we gave birth to the Peace Accord, not the politicians or business people.

I am persuaded that one of the reasons I was appointed to this position, Chairperson of the Independent Electoral Commission, was not only confidence in me as a person; it was the confidence this nation has in the churches. In the elections we appointed many pastors and priests and lay church leaders to be what we call Provincial Electoral Officers, which is a very important position in the whole process of elections and democracy, because the people had confidence in them. We had no objection on any name of church people that we brought to the table. But the communities rejected many other names, and many were rejected by the political parties.

It seems that the expectations of the public in South Africa are very much upon the church and its role in our nation. I was acceptable because of my background in the church. It is that which gives me credibility and acceptability. I worked for the churches, I worked for the SACC and, therefore, the door is open. These expectations of the people of South Africa run right across the board, and there I am talking about our divided society of black and white, young and old. They all have so much confidence in us as the church.

So the hopes and expectations to this day in South Africa about the church are really very high. But I am beginning to feel, as a church person, which I am, that we are not living up to the hope and we are not living up to the expectations.

I SENSE THAT WE ARE NOT ABLE to deal with the issue of reconciliation in our own churches. If you look around in our denominations, look around in our programs, you will see that most of us do not have identifiable programs on reconciliation. We have not had any restructuring in our churches to help reconciliation happen in its broadest form, not only for the victims, but for all of us as a society and a people to discover each other, to heal each others' wounds, and to appreciate the other person.

My contact now that I live in Pretoria is with many persons who speak Afrikaans. They are all Dutch Reformed Church members and it is clear on our part that as neighbors we genuinely want to discover each other, we want to talk to one another, we want to find a way of saying, "Where are you? I am a South African too." But we are lacking an institution like the church to make that possible, to help it happen. The pastors are not trained to deal with this kind of need.

WHEN I WAS WITH the World Council of Churches I dealt more with global things. Then when I was with the South African Council of Churches I was very much involved in national issues. Now I have moved to a local parish. I attended a synod on behalf of that local parish this July. The Archbishop, because of the concerns we have that as a Church of the Province we are not doing much, decided that outside the formal channel of the meeting he should invite Dr. Barney Pityana (Chairperson of the Human Rights Commission) to give direction to the people of the church, which through its own leadership has had a reputation since the days of Archbishop Selby Taylor. But after our discussion with Barney I did not feel that the Church of the Province had a vision on how we deal with the issue of truth and reconciliation.

We have to take courage as denominations to look into our own denominations and begin where we are with our own members. When the churches made submissions to the Truth and Reconciliation Commission in East London, there were certain commitments made. They were not recommendations in a formal sense, but we had ideas about what we can do within the church itself, within our denominations. It seemed to be recognized that we need to go through our own histories and deal with that first, face-to-face, in the very churches we belong to. I do not think that we can go out to the world to assist the world in dealing with reconciliation if we do not first deal with it within the church.

We are the best people to begin the process because we have a given audience of people who have a common identity. This is true in any church, whether it is Methodist, Congregational, Presbyterian, or Independent. We have a given group of people with a similar commitment, and one of the things we believe in as Christians is precisely reconciliation. I think we must open our own doors and say in the church, "What is it that we could have done ourselves?" and "What is it that we need to do now among ourselves?"

Some churches have tried this in the East Rand. But in general we have not engaged as individuals within the church and given people an opportunity to talk about their pain, or whether we are ashamed of what we did or didn't do, or that we were afraid, or tell of our anger or our own racism or our own manipulation. I feel we are not doing enough for ordinary South Africans to provide the forum for healing, for confession, for reconciliation.

WE SHOULD USE THE WORSHIP, the liturgy, the meetings, our synods and presbyteries, and the many church conferences. We have youth groups and we have women's groups, which are usually very strong. In these we have many women who are mothers and wives: wives and mothers of people who were perpetrators, and wives and mothers of those who were victims. Some who didn't know that they were mothers of perpetrators are having to face that only now. We must start, to use the jargon, on a micro level before we say we can do big things for the nation of South Africa.

That is where we must start. We should start discussion groups in some of our churches. We have Bible study groups in some of our churches, and we have people of the two sides, but we have not given them an opportunity in a church setting to tell of their pain or of their shame. We need to pray with them and to pray for them. This is what we are best at. But we do not seem to do it. I hope I am wrong.

COUNSELING IS ANOTHER THING we are best at, but it seems that we are not in a position to counsel so much because of the depth of the sensitivity, the sense of shame, the sense of guilt and of anger. We must start at the local level with the people. We can have symbols on a national level, but reconciliation has to happen between people at a local level. I have thought about this a lot, and we should have thought this through differently when the Commission began.

Some churches have set up what they have called Reconciliation Funds. That is a very interesting concrete thing that they do. I have a recollection that they are more of service and welfare and not so much of reconciliation—people doing service for the poor and then you are not into reconciliation.

FOR ME, AS A CHURCH PERSON, I am overwhelmed by a sense of failure. Somehow during those hearings we didn't seem to be able, as churches at that time, to influence each other or to plan together what to do next. The South African Council of Churches established a program with great hope, but it has not been effective. Maybe we were wrong in the timing. The churches do not seem eager to engage in reconciliation.

THE TRC CERTAINLY DID A GREAT JOB in revealing the truth. They did what I would call phase one and that was to hear the truth, to meet the victims, and to hear the victims. I would say that one of the most valuable things about the TRC was the restoration of the dignity of the people who before were "no-persons." It was important to allow them to speak and tell of their pain. That was something very important that was achieved. But reconciliation is for us as a people and as a nation to learn to live with each other.

IT IS VERY HARD FOR US TO MEASURE reconciliation among us. How do we know about the anger, the shame, and the guilt? What way can we measure it? Do we measure it on an individual level, or do we measure it on a national level? It is difficult, especially if we never meet to talk about it. How do the churches know how their people feel? Have we, both black and white, engaged in conversations?

We are not dealing with it. If you take our own city churches we have to ask why it is that all the whites have moved away. Why have we not talked to one another? Or used the opportunity to worship with one another? Whites will talk about the worry of driving in the dangerous center of the city and the crime. They do not say that they do not want to be with black people. We are not even honest with one another.

But perhaps we are putting too much on ourselves. We expect too much of ourselves. When I think of Europe and remember going there in the late sixties I was amazed at the attitudes, the anger that still remained toward the Germans. At one time, unknowingly, I proposed that we should have a German president in my department and people said, "Brigalia, are you out of your mind?" Now this was in 1968, more than twenty years after the war finished, and yet that anger and hatred were still there. I remember being told by a Norwegian only two years ago that they could not speak yet about reconciliation. One of their representatives told me, "I now have courage to speak about these things because I went to South Africa. I can report about the TRC and for the first time challenge my Norwegian friends as to whether we had forgiven the Germans."

We are a young country that has taken this step to seek truth and reconciliation. Maybe we should not be too hard on ourselves. We tend to say as South Africans that we have accomplished so many miracles. We have had a settlement that is not revolutionary, we have produced Mr. Mandela, we have not had a war, and we were recently told at the Independent Electoral Commission that this is the first time since 1957 that an African country has had elections that are not disputed. We broke a record of not one single dispute.

So we expect always to be the winners, and maybe because of that we begin to overestimate ourselves. How can we really expect South Africans within the space of ten years to all be reconciled when the rest of the world still nurses anger and hurt from fifty and sixty years ago?

BUT THAT IS NOT AN EXCUSE TO DO NOTHING. We must work hard at reconciliation, especially in the churches.

NOTES

1. Johann Heyns was a Dutch Reformed Church leader who was one of the church leaders to be involved in the church interventions in the negotiation process for a democratic South Africa. Prof. Heyns was shot at his home by an unknown gunman thought to be against the movement of the Dutch Reformed Church into cooperation with ecumenical agencies.

2. Eugene Terreblanche was a leader of the extreme right-wing movement AWB (Afrikaner Weerstandsbeweging).

3. The Dependants' Conference was a program of the South African Council of Churches to give financial and other support to anti-apartheid activists detained for their stand and to their families.

4. Standing For The Truth was a religious program of protest against apartheid in the latter part of the 1980s.

DR. WILLIE BOTHA

Wednesday, March 15, 2000

What is needed in South Africa is that we must try and get into the shoes of the other people. The oppressors must get into the shoes of the victims and get an idea of what they experienced. Perhaps also the victims need to see something about the oppressors who were saying, "This is for God and country," and "We must stop communism at all costs," and "We did this because we are soldiers of the gospel in South Africa to protect the church against communism." That is what they heard in the church. That is what we told them to believe.

❦

THE DUTCH REFORMED CHURCH (DRC in English or NGK in Afrikaans) is the major church of the Afrikaaner people. Its theological support for the system of separation of the races practiced through apartheid made it an outcast in the world church. It was expelled from the World Alliance of Reformed Churches at the same time as apartheid was declared a heresy. The DRC has now returned to the ecumenical fold and is an observer member of the South African Council of Churches.

The DRC remains white in membership. Talks are taking place between it and the Uniting Reformed Church of Southern Africa, which is made up of its former mission "daughter" black and coloured churches.

Dr. Botha is the Information Officer of the Dutch Reformed Church. We met in his office in the church's imposing synodical building in Pretoria. Perhaps it was the obvious signs of packing and restructuring that helped create an impression of change. The building seemed to be trying to speak of power and spoke only of a poignant sadness of what had been.

WHEN I HEAR the word *reconciliation* the first thing I think of is reconciliation with God. I think that is how we reformed people are trained. Despite what we are and what we did there is forgiveness, and God through Jesus Christ reconciles himself with us. I think that is where some Afrikaans people would say "full stop." That is what reconciliation means according to scripture. God forgives us, and there is no need to go further or ask forgiveness from any other human being.

That is the first thing—God stretched out his hand in love despite what I did. But more and more we are looking to 2 Corinthians that commands us to a ministry of reconciliation with others. We must convey reconciliation between people as well, despite what they or we have done. As the Lord was prepared to forgive us, so we should forgive each other.

That points to the difference between religious and secular reconciliation. Religious reconciliation is the message of love shown in Jesus. Secular reconciliation is about personal advantages.

I have heard experts say that reconciliation should start with the victim. The victim should move to the perpetrator. That is not very easy. It would be wonderful, but I would not expect the victims in this country to do that. I think that will only be the grace of the Lord if somebody would be prepared. I cannot expect it, but it would really be a boost for reconciliation.

I think the oppressor is in a better situation to start the reconciliation process by asking for forgiveness. Perhaps even to save his own skin! At least, he should also be prepared to move. Many of the oppressors fear what the reaction of the ones they have wronged might be. They ask themselves if they dare to approach the victim after the dreadful things that have happened, and expect of them any mercy. Perhaps that is why many of them do not make a move to reconcile.

We recently had a conference of some NGK ministers to discuss reconciliation and poverty. There was group discussion and report back. Some people said things like, "I am not a racist" or "I was still young in those days of apartheid" or "These things happened a long time ago and I am not responsible. It is the military people and the cabinet members. I do not feel guilty." I did not expect to hear that after the Truth and Reconciliation Commission, but it was there. Immediately after that you also had reaction from some of the younger guys saying, "I do not look at the history of the country when I think of reconciliation. It is a command of the Lord in his Word and, therefore, we must reconcile." Some said, "It is an order and I have no choice. I have to give everything to enhance reconciliation."

That conference was held in Pretoria with dominees in the Pretoria area. They had a similar conference in the Northern Province, and the men there said, "You people from Pretoria do not know the context we live in here in the platteland. It is difficult to talk of reconciliation in our situation."

THINGS ARE CHANGING, but very slowly. It seems to me that it is not as easy as we expected. The people were not helped by the media or even by the church to accept the Truth and Reconciliation Commission.

Right from the beginning the Afrikaans media were not very positive about the Commission. They reported in a negative way. And the Church Executive was advised by some political leaders in our churches to keep away from the TRC. So we did not encourage our people to attend the hearings or become involved in any way. Our people were completely divided with the majority feeling that they did not trust the TRC. It was only later when some of our leaders became involved and the church agreed to make a submission to the TRC that our people began to take the TRC seriously and positively.

Months after the TRC started, most people still said that what was said at the Commission was not true, it could not have happened. It took at least a year for people to realize that it actually did happen. People, especially religious people who attended church every Sunday where they heard the Ten Commandments and the need to love your neighbor, found the stories about the atrocities very hard to bear. A sense of shame for what had happened began to develop.

Afrikaner people, in my view, do not easily concede their need for forgiveness. There is a tradition about being strong and tough. At a recent meeting one dominee stood up and said, "We are not sissies you know. We do not cry about everything and we think the TRC sobbing is not in our culture. They killed my grandfather. It is a tough country and we carry on." We say especially that men do not cry. We must be strong and we do not easily show our feelings in public. The TRC at times seemed to be staged, and this was irritating and off-putting.

WHAT IS NEEDED IN SOUTH AFRICA is that we must try and get into the shoes of the other people. The oppressors must get into the shoes of the victims and get an idea of what they experienced. Perhaps also the victims need to see something about the oppressors who were saying, "This is for God and country," and "We must stop communism at all costs," and "We did this because we are soldiers of the gospel in South Africa to protect the church against communism." That is what they heard in the church. That is what we told them to believe.

THE PEOPLE WHO SUFFERED should be compensated. I do not know how but there must be a return of that which was stolen. I think that in some way there should be compensation. Perhaps by an extra tax from those who were oppressors? I would be happy with a percentage of tax to really help do more for the people who suffered. And I am concerned about those who suffered but did not appear before the Commission. Some kind of general and worthwhile compensation should be made.

THE TRC DID HELP some people to accept that these terrible things happened, and they now feel they must do something about this. And many of them are prepared to do their part to help the victims. That is the one thing. The other is that the example of the people who went to the TRC and spoke the truth is a good thing. That is good for Afrikaner people, as we do not easily come and confess. People say that if I confess it is on my knees before God and not anywhere else. We do not easily confess in front of other people, despite James saying that we should confess to one another.

It did us Afrikaners good to see some of our leaders confess—such as Minister Vlok, for instance—and that was good. At the beginning there were problems, but he eventually needed to come out with what was in his heart. I wish everybody did that.

Then there were the examples of those people who accepted the confessions and when people embraced each other. They too moved it seems and went from saying we will never forgive to eventually embracing the other. That is a wonderful example. Not many of us would do that. When the victims forgive the oppressors it is by grace.

The TRC was also a channel for some people who sat with stress and anger and hatred to release it and let it come out.

SOME WHITES HAVE BEEN HELPED to accept their culpability, but I would not even want to guess what percentage it would be. It is likely to be a small minority. Some people still say that it was not the truth at the TRC. They focus on a small thing that is obviously not true, such as the numbers of people involved or the date of an event, and use that to say the whole thing was not true. I fear that even in the end they would say there was obviously some truth but not a lot of truth. That is what I hear.

People did take notice of the TRC. The media made it impossible to escape. And even if they did not want to read about it they did, and watched the news even though they did not like it. I think some of our people watched perhaps because they feared what might come out. They were frightened it might involve people they knew, even members of their own family. Afrikaans people felt they were involved whether they wanted to be or not.

I do not understand why they did not attend the hearings. It seems that we were not prepared to make an effort to attend. We wanted to watch from the outside.

I think that for the Afrikaans people, they are just so busy keeping themselves going. People are turning into themselves, and their concern is about their work and their families. And they are afraid of affirmative action. They were dead against it when it was first introduced, but many are accepting it now. But the response is to look at themselves and their own needs.

It is very difficult now to talk about "the Afrikaner." This is one of the major changes that have taken place. Individualism is growing, a feeling of no matter what synod says or leaders say, so what? It is interesting, for instance, to see how people voted. They decided for themselves. Peer pressure is not as important now as it once was. We were used to very strong leaders and we just followed them. This has changed. People are possibly more mature. They decide for themselves.

There is a debate about who are Afrikaners. It is now so difficult to qualify. There is one Afrikaans radio station that talks about the Boere Afrikaners and not just the Afrikaners. That is a certain group of conservative Afrikaners. And some coloured people say that they use the Afrikaans language and attend NGK churches, so that makes them Afrikaners.

BLACK PEOPLE? How will I know what value the TRC had for the victims? It did seem to help those many people who wanted to know the truth about their loved ones and how they died. They wanted to know the truth about what happened, and the TRC helped them. I do hope some healing came out of this.

My own daughter was killed by her husband, who then took his own life. What exactly happened there I do not know and I do not want to know. I never wanted to know. The loss was enough. But others say that they lost their children, and they want to know exactly what happened. I can understand that people feel that way, but it is not my way.

MY FIRST RESPONSE to having religious people on the TRC was to say yes of course. People have confidence in church leaders. I thought that helped a lot. White Afrikaner people respect the people of the cloth, and I fear that if the TRC consisted of lawyers and business executives it would not have worked so well. I think it was a good thing. When you talk about finance or art or business, do not get too many ministers there, for what do they know about that? But when it comes to creating the atmosphere of trust and talking about reconciliation it is a good thing. Afrikaans people at first did not appreciate Desmond Tutu too much, but he grew in stature and I think many people learned to respect him. I think there was a lot of appreciation for his integrity and his sincerity. Yes, it was good to have religious persons on the TRC.

I do think that some Afrikaner people who are not church people would ask, what do these dominees know about these things? They should not be there. It should be a strictly legal process. These people would say that the religious leaders are too soft on the people who appear before the Commission.

WE SHOULD DO MUCH MORE than we are doing. In the Afrikaans sector we reach large numbers of people every Sunday. One person worked out that on one Sunday we have more of our people in church than a whole year of Currie Cup rugby matches! That is a large number of people. We do have large congregations, as can be seen by the cars parked outside the churches every Sunday. So we have the opportunity to teach and we must use it. Some do. But I fear that the majority do not. I am not sure.

Our General Synod appointed an ad hoc committee on reconciliation. This is a very unusual event in our church. That committee is coming up with recommendations. And it is surprising that in places such as the Northern Transvaal Synod they worked on this issue. They worked throughout the province in regional meetings to talk about reconciliation not just as a subject but also in regard to what they can practically do in their congregations and in their towns or suburbs. So there are some things that are starting.

We talked about poverty at a conference, and I said that our church is not doing enough. Somebody said it is very clear that you sitting up there in the offices in Pretoria, you do not know what is going on in the congregations. People are working on these issues. So the General Synod is talking, and a report is compiled and decisions will be taken. At the local level things are already happening. And that is where it has to happen.

We should do more. One problem is that our church is a white church, and we do not have enough contact with other people. We have missionaries, but generally an NGK dominee and his people would not know what is going on and what it is like in the townships and rural communities.

I have already mentioned the need for compensation of the victims. I think the government should do more on compensation, but we are talking about what we can do. We did talk about having one Sunday where we take all the offerings and make it available for some or other project of reconciliation. But what can that mean in relation to the whole problem? Poverty is so serious, and what lasting value would our two or three million mean in that? Very little, I am afraid.

I do not know what it is like to be a victim and therefore feel unable to say what should happen about blanket amnesty. I expect that it would make some feel cheated. If the majority of the victims can say blanket amnesty is good, then I would support it and say it is wonderful, but it is not for us to say.

෴ ෴ ෴

THE REV. JAMES BUYS

August 21, 2000

I have heard comments made that South Africa is most divided on a Sunday. People are still racially divided and churches remain racially divided, so that whatever has been said about the church's contribution to the reconciliation of society remains subject to the ability of the religious community itself to deal with the kind of racial divisions that still exist among them.

෴

WE WERE VERY KEEN to obtain a voice from the Uniting Reformed Church. This interview was conducted by Mr. Paul Haupt, a staff member of the Institute for Justice and Reconciliation, in Rev. Buys' Cape Town office. The Rev. James Buys is the Moderator of the Uniting Reformed Church.

I THINK THE COMMISSION quite rightly concludes that within the religious community people often refer to reconciliation in terms of interpersonal relationships and that is as far as it goes. My own personal understanding extends beyond that to the concept of reconciliation within the framework of the act that brought the TRC into existence. It wishes to deal with the past, the conflicts of the past, gross human rights violations, and to see how, within a legal framework, it can bring South African people to a point of dealing with that past and abuses in a way that restores relationships between races and also between the people and institutions of government.

IF I COULD FOR A MOMENT use the distinction that may apply within the religious community with distinction to how it applied to the TRC. Within the religious community I think the values are being driven by religious values. Within the Christian community it's a concept that grows out of the redemptive act of Christ in dying and thereby reconciling people with God and people with themselves. And also the extension of it by looking at the reconciliation among people would amount to the acknowledgment of wrongdoing, the seeking of and the granting of forgiveness.

Within a broader, political context I think one would find a legal framework of the acknowledgment of wrongdoing and the granting of amnesty. But apart from the legal framework of the granting of amnesty I think the concept of reconciliation and forgiveness in society also implies that the victims of those gross human rights abuses, in terms of attitude and general understanding, afford the forgiveness needed to make the process complete.

Yes, I think the difference, as I understand it, most probably comes from the premise, the one being driven by religious values and the other by the legal framework in which the government sought to promote reconciliation and national unity in South Africa.

I THINK ONE WOULD NEED to approach the question of reconciliation in South Africa on a broad front. One cannot deny that part of reconciliation relates to interpersonal relationships—the victim meeting with a perpetrator, having to deal with what's happened in the past, and having to forgive. But it extends beyond interpersonal relationships; it also includes reconciliation of races that have been kept apart by apartheid, of races that have been the victims of abuses by the government, and the discrimination involved in the apartheid society.

So one would need to approach the whole concept of reconciliation on different levels. There is the interpersonal level, of the institutions of society vis-à-vis the different race groups in this country as they have suffered under the apartheid government. But one would also need to look at how the current government deals with the legacy of apartheid, which to my understanding cannot merely be the kind of reallocation of resources in terms of current priorities. It would also need to deal with the ways and means of correcting the imbalances—an act which in itself may be discerned as some form of reverse discrimination, as has been the case with affirmative action. But those, I think, are also necessary. Without that kind of correction on the part of government and its organs I do not think that reconciliation can in fact be promoted.

Prior to the TRC I think one of the debates we had in the country had the potential of a Nuremberg trial, of actually bringing charges against individuals as far as they could be identified for their actions in the implementation of apartheid. The government, to my understanding, wisely chose to follow the path of the TRC, which in terms of its three subcommittees I think attempted to deal with some of the problems relating to past actions. On the one hand, the families of victims merely sought to know what had happened without necessarily seeking a further compensation. For them merely the fact of what has happened was sufficient to start to deal with at least some of their pain. As such I think that part of the hearings has helped many people to know what has happened precisely to family members.

On that level the perpetrators of human rights violations had the opportunity to come clean, in the sense of their own acknowledgment of what they have done and the extent to which they participated as individuals and functionaries in the various institutions of the former government, in some cases on their own and in some cases under direct instruction from immediate superiors, even as high as cabinet members, who caused people to act in a particular fashion. The acknowledgment of wrongdoing, I believe, is not only helpful for the sake of the people against whom they acted but also for their own healing, to come to terms with their own past.

The more difficult part concerns the whole idea of compensation, since in some cases people have viewed compensation as an inherent part of the process of reconciliation, of correcting what has been done to them. The extent to which the TRC has not succeeded in convincing the government or securing the release of sufficient compensation has left some people dissatisfied with the way the process has gone.

Others are also of the opinion that, apart from compensation, the mere acknowledgment of ills should not necessarily have led to amnesty. Rather, some people should have been taken up into the formal process of being charged and convicted, and only after conviction should forms of amnesty been considered. And in dealing with it in this fashion they felt that having criminal convictions against people would have had an effect on how we restructure South Africa, especially taking into view the conviction that people with criminal record, among others, should not hold public office.

Reconciliation and conciliation? I think reconciliation itself is when people come to grips with the past, whereas conciliation refers to the ongoing process.

I THINK IT WOULD BE difficult to speak in general; the one thing to recognize is that the white community in South Africa is not homogeneous. And often because of their own political past and support for different parties they need to be understood to have different positions, even in regard to apartheid.

Now as far as the Afrikaner community is concerned, I believe the TRC has only had a limited success, as with the coming forward of certain individuals who spoke vicariously on behalf of the Afrikaner people but who were not necessarily representative of the Afrikaner people generally taking responsibility for what has happened in the past. One would ask, what organ is there to really be representative of the Afrikaner community? I think not much because of the division that exists within the Afrikaner community itself, from the more right-wing to the liberal.

The one group that could have played a much more significant role in trying to move the people to respond in a different fashion is the Dutch Reformed Church: the religious community of the Afrikaner society, the church. For me it was significant that the Dutch Reformed Church, among others, did not choose to make a submission regarding the past but rather bypassed the past and spoke about what they understood their role should be in the future. The Afrikaner churches still predominantly remain as separate entities and have not in any way transformed, as one has seen in some forms of transition in the South African society with the scrapping of the apartheid laws, the integration of schools, changes to the labor law, equity, etc. I doubt whether one can adequately identify an organ representative enough to speak on behalf of the Afrikaner people. And I think that is one of the weaknesses. With regard to the English, more liberal side of society, one has seen some sign of acknowledgment of what has happened, while oftentimes keeping the Afrikaner government responsible and showing a misunderstanding of our apartheid history and how far it extends back even with regard to the role of the British, English-speaking people in this country.

Another point I need to make is that I believe that some groups of people within the white part of our society literally felt that one should not have made a point of going into the past in such great detail. Many felt that after the elections of 1994 the past should be forgotten and we should just go on to rebuild South African society. I think that is a fallacy. We cannot continue without adequately dealing with what happened under the apartheid government.

I HAVE ALREADY MADE some reference to what I believe were some of the benefits. Corporately speaking I think that people were vindicated in terms of what was said about what happened to people and the role of the apartheid forces. Often we were ridiculed in terms of what was happening or demonized and called liars, but we were vindicated in the issues that were raised. That was one area of benefit.

The second one that I spoke of earlier—of the need for individuals to know the truth and to have the mere opportunity of hearing what has happened out of the mouth of the victims or out of the mouth of the violators—has in itself I think contributed to healing individuals and society.

A third area should have been compensation. Many people felt that the process stopped short and did not answer the real needs of the people. The organs of civil society tried to promote the process of reconciliation, such as in the religious community, by having services of reconciliation, trying to bring people together, counseling people—both victims and perpetrators—to try to come to grips with the past, and using religion as a tool in promoting reconciliation.

I MAY BE BIASED IN SAYING YES it was good to have religious people on the TRC. I believe that it did benefit in a sense where the concept of reconciliation and the kind of values that drive it, morally and otherwise, aren't necessarily present within other disciplines or within the organs of state, as they exist. While organs of state may deal with confession and forgiveness in a legal framework of formal hearings and formally dealing with processes, I believe the religious community brought on board the kind of values that impact on attitudes of how people can respond to the experiences of human rights violations. So I may be biased, but I do believe they bring along certain values that may have helped.

In general, because a great number of people in this country acknowledge that they are religious people, I believe the religious communities did make a point of seeking to deal with the counseling of people, seeking to create opportunities for victims and perpetrators to meet in a process of healing by using occasions of worship to help people reconcile with one another after what has happened. I think these were all important occasions within the religious community, although I believe the standing of the role of the religious community cannot be limited to the TRC processes only. I have heard comments made that South Africa is most divided, on a Sunday. People are still racially divided and churches remain racially divided, so that whatever has been said about the church's contribution to the reconciliation of society remains subject to the ability of the religious community itself to deal with the kind of racial divisions that still exist among them.

WHEN WE COME TO OUR OWN particular denomination, it was precisely our acknowledgments of the impact of apartheid, not merely as an ideology but how it was supported religiously, that made us feel we had no choice but to actively work toward church union—bringing together especially, in our instance, the black African and so-called coloured African together into the uniting reformed church. This is not, I think, sufficient as yet in promoting unity as a religious community, but I think it is a start. And the extent to which the message we carry is credible is dependent on the kind of healing that is required in the religious community in this country.

I think we do not have the commitment of resources within the church toward the work of reconciliation, and I say this because I believe that since 1994 the religious community has been overtaken by the processes within the country as a whole. They have gone so far that I don't believe the religious community has been able to deal with the kind of claims to time and energy and resources needed to take up the various aspects that contribute toward the transformation of our society, whether it be in terms of its impact on political processes, in terms of democracy at work, and even in terms of national and global issues like debt relief—or even, I believe in this particular case of reconciliation, in following up the TRC process with a process of maintaining (if one can call it that) a campaign for reconciliation in our country.

One of the weaknesses comes from the fact that before 1994 the religious community, in a sense, played a vital role in being the voice of the voiceless and in taking a lead in opposing the government in South Africa and at least being a conduit to assist people to act against apartheid. But after the elections of 1994 the church, and most likely the rest of civil society, has been dis-armed by having a democratic government and less of a broad community-based action in dealing with what was happening.

The opportunity does not exist to impact on public policies. Opportunities do exist, but there is a sense in which the skills and the energy to do them are missing. That is one of the key weaknesses of the church in defining and understanding its particular role post-1994 election. Many felt that the job is done and we can now leave politics to the politicians and we have no more roles to play there. I find this a pity, as I do believe we still have a role to play. Take the question of morality. The government cannot legislate morality. The religious community with its values instills or promotes the standards of morality that are supposed to undergird the transformation of society.

IN TERMS OF PRIORITIES I think the churches have identified certain priorities jointly, but whether they can cohesively maintain them I don't know. The Jubilee 2000 is one of those—the debt crisis, the question of globalization and economic justice, the question of the integrity of creation as regards ecological questions. One can see a national and international move in remaining aboard and bringing in religious perspectives in these debates. Nationally I think that many of the people in religious communities, especially the black ones, struggle especially with economic issues, the question of resources, the question of adequate leadership, to take forward whatever they have in terms of their ministries and campaigns. Another one I need to add in relation to the debt issue is the one on poverty, which is also a priority in this community.

Let me take the one thing: the Jubilee 2000. The area in which the church and broader religious community can forward these aims lies predominantly in advocacy and consequently challenging government by way of a broad-based campaign in the way it deals with the debt crisis in the global context on the one hand while also realizing that our debt crisis is somewhat different from the rest of Africa or other third world countries since most of it is internal debt. We can challenge the government on its own understanding and how it deals within the budgetary framework with the debts that take up about twenty-two percent of our annual budget. Within the ecumenical movement we, after two sessions of debate with the minister of finance on the budget, would go into coalition with other organs of civil society and seek ways of promoting and putting onto the agenda at the beginning of next year an alternative budget to that which was presented by the minister of finance. This is just one of the ways of saying, "Listen, here we have a debt crisis with this taking up so much of our annual budget and therefore limiting the kind of economic resources which should become available to promote quality of life, public growth and employment for people." So that would be one way of dealing with it.

On the level of morality, the debates we had with the previous President and the current one on crime, violence, and corruption in society are once again entering into areas of interaction between religious communities and government. So, for instance, the year before last it was the religious community that invited all political parties to a conference at which a code of conduct was presented to sign giving public acknowledgment that they undertake to act in a particular way in terms of the office they hold in governance. At the same time, they would agree on a secondary level to promote a code of conduct which is supposed to gather response from all sectors and spheres of South African life in order to get a broad-based response in terms of how they will act individually and corporately. So that is another area in which the religious community has to promote the values it holds. With regard to the issue, for instance, of globalization, the religious communities, especially the ecumenical movement, have been part of the whole campaign in dealing with some of the free trade agreements and with the World Trade Organization, and in dealing with the International Monetary Fund and campaigning for a more equitable economic structural order, if one can call it that.

I think the one thing one needs to say of the task of religious communities in general right now is they need to transcend the kind of divisions that still affect the behavior of individuals. Oftentimes the kind of exclusive nature of sectors of the religious community leads to general intolerance and enforces certain attitudes and forms of discrimination, such as the denial of rights. I would think one of the greater challenges would be whether the religious community in this country can transcend those differences by acknowledging the kind of general issues of humanity of tolerance, respect for life, promotion of values of morality that in themselves may promote the kind of society one would like to have. One has to acknowledge that apart from people as working people the next closest grouping of organized groupings would be the religious community. It therefore has a structure, which may have a greater impact if it is effectively used.

I DO NOT BELIEVE we should even consider the granting of blanket amnesty. The issue I have heard being raised concerns certain individuals or members of parties or former institutions who have missed the deadline of appearing before the Amnesty Committee of the TRC and thus have not acknowledged what they have done in the past or have not adequately confessed to what has happened. People now seek to cover those areas by way of a blanket amnesty. I think blanket amnesty without dealing with the details of different individuals or organs or parties would be contrary to the spirit of the TRC. It seeks to evade the truth and is a denial of the rights of the people to know what has happened and in the current processes of the way it should be dealt with. Personally I am not a supporter of the idea of blanket amnesty.

Would you be happy if they approved blanket amnesty for all who have applied for amnesty?

No, I would not. I think that the process as it stands allows for the nature of the evidence presented to be tested, and that to me is important. People who have held back important information would benefit by that kind of blanket amnesty.

The following two interviewees are both members of the same downtown Methodist Church in Johannesburg. These discussions did not follow the general pattern. I asked them both, on separate occasions, to speak about the transformation of their specific congregation.

PROF. TREFOR JENKINS

Friday, May 12, 2000

With some, I am sure it was incipient racism that came to the surface in that situation and they felt threatened.

TREFOR JENKINS is a well-known human geneticist. Originally from Wales, he has lived in Johannesburg since 1963. He is one of the few remaining white people in the Central Methodist congregation.

WHEN WE CAME to Johannesburg in 1963 we went to the closest Methodist Church because of our tradition of attending Methodist churches. It was an exclusive white congregation with a typical cross section of white South Africans at that time. There was a certain restlessness with some of us in the congregation wanting integration. It was not a popular ideal, and we had to work hard to maintain any kind of contact with Methodists of color.

I remember, for instance, that an African congregation of black fellow Methodists used the church for their own afternoon service each Sunday. When neighbors of the church in that affluent white suburb objected to the singing, the trend was to withdraw permission for this to happen. Some people even invoked the Verwoerd law that a population group that was not resident in that area should not use a church. Some of us then went to the various neighbors in the area to canvass their views and were impressed that some Christians, of various churches, were opposed to it while some Jewish families agreed to the use of the church by blacks.

In the early seventies we moved home and started to worship at the Civic Methodist Church under the leadership of the Rev. (later Bishop) Peter Storey. Things were very different because of his style of leadership. There were seminars on faith and race and issues of that nature. When Civic united with Central Methodist and Peter Storey moved as minister we automatically moved also. That is where the sea change took place. This was largely because of Peter's efforts in the early eighties. A positive effort was made to bring people together. The congregation, however, remained ninety-five percent white.

There was a gradual change in the late eighties as more black people came from distances to worship at Central. Most of the white congregants traveled from the suburbs. The residences in the city were becoming black, and some of these also began to join us. It gradually transformed until now when it is ninety-eight percent black.

Our first black senior minister was the Rev. (also later Bishop) Mvume Dandala, and he tried to maintain a balance and did his utmost not to frighten away white members. We have seen the most dramatic change in composition to the predominant black congregation during the leadership of Bishop Paul Verryn. I think it is most interesting that Mvume was trying to follow Peter's tradition of a city church and, although there were activities such as Bible studies and prayer meetings, there was a strong attempt to keep it a city church, which as far as I am aware tends to be an anonymous church where people come from a distance only for the worship. The church life is in serving the city area, often with professional leadership, through programs and ministries. There is something different about a city church.

Bishop Paul Verryn brought with him an experience of Soweto and the community type of church life. This, together with a change in the style of worship, has frightened away the most significant number of whites. It seems to me that whereas the previous ministers certainly had a component of the community ideal, they acknowledged that the only contact that we had with a significant number of the congregation would be at the Sunday service and at the time of fellowship afterward. Paul wants us to be much more of a community and, whereas that is highly commendable, I think he has great difficulty in maintaining this because of the large turnover in people. Central still tends to attract visitors; most of the congregation travel from various parts of Johannesburg and Soweto, and it is difficult to attract people to Bible studies and building people up in the faith. Many liked the anonymity of the city church. There is difficulty in getting leaders to come forward to grow in leadership roles, and I can only put that down to the fact that people come from a distance. I have not got any actual figures, but I do not think the majority come from the flats around. They come from the suburbs and from Soweto.

Central was a white church and has become a black church. How we overcome that division and polarization is difficult. It has to be done gently and slowly because of the sensitivities of people. If people have been worshiping in a particular way for forty years and are then suddenly confronted by this dramatic change—it was a dramatic change—a major exodus is understandable. In this case it was a major exodus of white people.

Some people said that it was becoming too black, and some said that they did not like the singing and format of the service with hymns in a number of African languages. And there were also the very long services. Many people didn't mind an hour or an hour and a quarter, but when it became two to two and a half hours it was too much. With some, I am sure it was incipient racism that came to the surface in that situation and they felt threatened.

The move within the church has been African and not coloured. I would think that in the days when the congregation at first was mixed in any way it would be coloured people. I think it is fair to say that many of the coloured people who were worshiping at Central left with the whites. I think that is true.

The choir was vast majority white, for example. Paul made it clear that he found the big church organ behind him and its dominant role in worship inhibiting. He used the term domineering. He prefers unaccompanied African singing and African spontaneity in worship away from the organ and western music. Some of the choir people who liked their singing as they had done it over the years felt they were being swamped, so better to go and join another choir in a suburb where they could sing the music they liked. The choir became increasingly black and came down to only two white members out of the forty or so. One of the last two left recently at age ninety, and the congregation honored her and put on a wonderful demonstration of her commitment. The old congregation would not have done it. This was an African celebration, and they showed how much they appreciated the perseverance of this white member who stayed so long.

I always feel extremely welcomed by the black congregation. I do not feel alien. It is an interesting experience to try to put myself into a position of a minority, which may be a bit masochistic, but then that is how it was for blacks in a predominantly white congregation. I can only hope the pendulum will swing again and we will find ourselves in a position of greater balance and able to share the treasures of the different kinds of worship.

I have not been able to find a niche for myself in the church as it is at present. I still attend and support but do not feel I can be enthusiastic about the church. I am getting older and my family challenge me about going into the city center for weeknight meetings where some of our people have been mugged. That maybe is rationalizing. Maybe it is just that one's enthusiasm drops off.

The white people do not sit together. We are so few and well dispersed and, yes, I think we might tend to speak together, but we also greet and speak with the people who sit in the same area of the church each Sunday. I am most likely as close to them as to the small number of whites who are there. I do not think there is clannishness.

There is an attempt to make the service open for all. The sermon is in English, there is always an English reading, and many prayers are in English. So apart from some prayers, the *Te Deum* and Lord's Prayer and most hymns, English is the predominant language. I do not think it is a language thing. I feel I can partake pretty thoroughly in the service. I can put up with the long service and manage that. My wife does not like the long service, however, so I sometimes compromise and we go to the early service at 8 A.M. That is all in English with communion and the congregation of about forty or so will be equally divided between black and white. It is a shorter service with hymns from the Methodist Hymn Book.

The evening service is a different set-up. It is a younger congregation of about forty or so, and there one sees both white and black very closely integrated in a singing group and worship team. That is the hope for the church. It certainly looks much more integrated.

If I were the minister I would try to sound out the people as to what they are uncomfortable about and try to ensure a continuing mix of people. We need to actively go to the people who have left and try to devise strategies to do what we can to make it a mixed congregation because I do not think anyone wants a one-race congregation. Blacks do not feel good about whites leaving. I feel sure Paul doesn't but I have not tackled him head on about it.

I believe that the church structures can help in reconciliation. Long before the TRC I certainly felt that being a member of a place where church meetings consisted of black and white people was very helpful. We were formal and the regulations concerning meetings were a unifying force. We grew in respect for one another. It was a model of parliamentary debate procedure. I felt privileged to be in a situation where one was on equal terms, and it is sad so many white people have not even yet experienced that and got to a position of respect, let alone reconciliation. I would not imagine you would be reconciled to other people unless you have a mutual respect for one another.

I think the institution of the church, the organizational side of it, must have improved relationships between members of different racial groups. Now if on top of that you have a unifying force, the object of your worship, it must enhance that even more. I would assume that a congregation that is racially mixed must be conducive to reconciliation.

The Truth and Reconciliation Commission would not be achieving its goal if it remained a high-profile TV show: the reconciliation process has to be taken into the communities, including the churches. We started off doing that, and we certainly held some services dedicated to reconciliation. We still have services on the theme, but we have not done enough to try to realize the goals of the TRC. It is not too late to go back to that. At the last, of course, it means a drawing together of the individual members. The sad thing is that there are not a lot of white people anymore at the Central church.

Presumably we are aiming for some stage where it will not be reconciliation but just forging of friendships. Reconciliation is putting right some undesirable experience of the past where people have become estranged or opposed. Though I guess there will always be situations where some human beings are in opposition to other human beings in South Africa, we will hopefully get to a stage where reconciliation is no longer the major issue.

The church should facilitate this kind of meeting. We are not being encouraged, there is not enough leadership encouraging the people to work at reconciliation. The churches, ours included, need to be working on a reconciliation program. Preachers should be preaching about reconciliation and transformation, and I think that perhaps transformation might be a less difficult term to use. We need to be turning to each other and not always because of estrangement. Transformation may not be as threatening to people.

People assume reconciliation is an apology for all the wrong things they have done, and they are not convinced that they did wrong. So if they are not convinced, they cannot be on the path to reconciliation, but if you are talking about transformation you are saying that your whole outlook, attitude, and concerns in the present must be different, must be changed. It is not looking back. To talk about transformation is looking forward and reconciliation is looking back. We would say in order to go forward we must acknowledge the past, but people do not see the second and they are resentful or naïve not to be aware of their wrongdoing. Certainly I agree that unless you acknowledge the wrong you have done it is difficult to transform.

MS. LINDI MYEZA

Tuesday, May 23, 2000

We have been singing their (white) songs but they will not sing ours. They make no effort. Some even say anyway when they do come and we sing they think it is for their entertainment. We do not need to entertain them!

Ms. Myeza is one of the "Mothers of Soweto," having taken part in the maternal-type leadership of that huge complex during the apartheid days. She is a committed member of the Methodist Church and a strong supporter of the ecumenical movement.

I STARTED WORSHIPING at Central as far back as 1978. That was when the Rev. Stanley Pitts was there. When he left us and the Rev. Peter Storey took over I was brought in to help in a program aimed at peace and reconciliation called "My Brother and Me." That was the first program to look at our divisions and try to help people understand what was happening around us and claiming us.

We say as Methodists we are one undivided church, but we were divided according to our color and our domicile. Peter then invited me to be employed full-time for a while to travel around to various white churches to say what it meant to be a mother from Soweto. To talk of those mothers who had to leave a child as early as four in the morning to go to town to look after a white madam's child. To tell what it was like to go along the bus route. You can never be on time because so many buses are half-empty, but you cannot ride on them because they are for whites only and your buses are full and you are late and you get hell from the madam. So I was asked to come and educate white Methodists about what it means to be a black mother from Soweto. Our concept was that you get to a kitchen where you find two women who have been together for twenty-five years, and they tell themselves that they know each other very well. But madam does not know that this "girl" is not just a pair of hands but she is a leader in her own right in the church and the community. She is articulate. But according to the madam, because she has got to be looking after her children, she is just a subservient person who cannot do anything except what she is told.

So I had to go to various white Methodist churches to talk about this and got a very good response, I must say. But I was only visiting and not invading them! There were some times I remember very well, especially with young people. I remember asking some white children and black children to touch one another on the head. One white boy said that he had never been so close to a black before and that he had goose flesh when asked to touch, but it was so soft and gentle that he will never see black people the same way again.

I was worshiping at the Central Church. I was the only black member. I would get into church and the whole choir was white and the whole church was full of white people. I was the only single black among this sea of whites. Come Holy Communion I wasn't sure whether I should go forward or not so I just sat there. I wondered what the whites would say. But one day I just got mad and went to communion. The heavens didn't fall and there was no negative response from the whites at all.

In the early eighties other black people started to attend. Some came because they were disgruntled by their churches in the townships. Others were people who heard from me about the good preaching. They said they would like to come along but it is a white church. I told them that it is their church so come along. A number of them came because of that. Then there were a number of people who were now leaving townships to come and live in town, but they still went back to the townships to worship there. When I asked them why they were not attending in town, they said that the churches in town are still white churches. I would ask what they meant and be told that they are still singing as if they are in Kent, where John Wesley comes from. And they told me that though the preaching is good they were used to the fiery type of preaching and interpreting and lots of talking and being able to shout "Amen" and respond when you want to. These white places, they said, are cold and so that is why we go back to the townships.

So I said it was high time to get the choir singing some things in other languages. We targeted the choir as the first place of change. Most of the new black members in the choir were not necessarily Methodists. Mvume Dandala was now minister, and he would recruit people he met to come and sing to change the choir. The twist from white to black started in his time. It was still predominantly white, but the number of blacks was growing very fast.

Whites began to move out because the whole spirit of the singing and style of worship was changing. The African beat was moving in. They left also because the services took longer. They were used to worship that lasted from ten until eleven. So when they had to do our thing where you just start and end when you end—that irritated quite a number of people. At the same time, some blacks were irritated and asked why the preaching was still in English when there were fewer and fewer whites.

We still have it in English because we are more of an international church, with a lot of visitors and people who have been out of South Africa for some time. We have people of many different languages. And because the services are longer anyway we felt it was faster to just use English and everybody can hear. But it has put off the people who like to worship at two in the afternoon. They come in as early as ten but sit on the pews outside the church itself, and when I ask why they sit there they say its because of the white people. Then I ask them to show me the white people and they say but you still preach in English. They have their own service in the afternoon in Xhosa and Sotho and they feel comfortable there.

But the singing in the main service has become very Africanized. We even Africanize the various songs from Kent. We sing Wesley hymns in our own languages. We use different hymnbooks in the different languages of English, Zulu, and Sotho. We have told the minister it is important to introduce the vernacular songs and so now three-quarters of our songs are in the vernacular.

We now have a women's Manyano. There was no Manyano. We do not meet on the traditional Thursday afternoon. We meet after the Sunday service. We have to maintain that city church idea that people come for Sunday and then go home till next Sunday. They stay far away and some are working and cannot make it during the week.

Bishop Verryn is trying to get a more community-type church but it is not easy. Even many of the black people do not feel gelled, except on Good Friday when we have the long seven words service according to our tradition. Apart from that it does not work. It is a central city church. We need to realize that all the people who come to Central do not come from Johannesburg. We have people from many of the suburbs and townships and even from Krugersdorp and as far as Pretoria. These are black people who travel because of the particular worship at Central. They say it is different, for they say that as much as we are bringing the "pepper" of African worship we are not bringing the type of township worship. It is unique.

It is unique in the sense that it is a mobile church. There is nothing to pressure you. We want to build a community church, but it is not easy to do that because people are moving around and you get very few who are there all the time. And most of the people like it that way. They want to come to church, enjoy the worship, and go home. It is an open church and very relaxed.

Financially we have the tithing but we are also bringing in *Rona,* which is the old tradition where you have mission month when you give as much as you can during that whole month. We do not have a special month but we do have the spirit of *Rona,* and when you give you come up and say, "I give this ten Rand because I thank my parents for what they did for me" and that kind of thing. We feel that makes it more unique because whereas in the township *Rona* has its specific time and it is only those who understand it who join in, we do it at any time in the worship itself.

Quite a number of the black people say it is such a pity that whites have left. It would have been very good if they stayed. That is why they are so appreciative of people like Muriel and Tony who stayed on in the choir. They will say it is such a pity that they are missing this worship that comes from our traditional Methodism. It would have been very good if they could have had a chance to learn our songs when we have been singing their songs for so long. I do hear those vibes. We have been singing their songs but they will not sing ours. They make no effort. Some even say anyway when they do come and we sing they think it is for their entertainment. We do not need to entertain them!

Nevertheless, I must commend Bishop Paul, who has made great efforts and is being envied by many and now they can sing the long *Te Deum,* the famous *Siyakudumi sa tixo.*

There is an "us and them" feeling. Worship is central to our faith and yet we are separated by our traditions and cultures, and change for many people is problematic. We ought to try and be inclusive and accommodate but the whites are not there to accommodate. That is why it is such a problem. That is what makes people to say what a pity that they are missing out.

You know there are some people who attend the ten o'clock service but who go to the communion at eight o'clock. They say, "We miss our white friends and this is a chance to meet with them there." Amazing. It is a comforting feeling of the need not to lose each other.

We had quite a number of coloured people and they seem to have moved out as well. It is not just the worship. I spoke to some of them about it. Some said that they had been in this church for a long time but now they no longer see their black friends and white friends together at the church. Others said that they go near to where they stay or that they have children and there is a Sunday school. Others said they did not feel they belonged, they felt uncomfortable. When asked where they worship now they say they visited traditional coloured churches but still did not feel comfortable so they now go to Bryanston or Berea. I find that interesting.

It is a very sad reflection on what apartheid did to us. It shows apartheid did succeed to divide us and to divide us in the church. It is as if it planted deep-seated divisions and attitudes and a feeling of exclusiveness. That is within the church and it is very sad.

We need to share our traditions. We need to support one another. Churches are closing in upon themselves and we are more divided than ever. I look at the whole area of the ecumenical movement and see that people have folded to themselves. We have to acknowledge our differences but they must not keep us apart.

BISHOP MVUME DANDALA

Friday, August 27, 1999

If my son, my uncle, or my brother died because he wanted reconciliation between black and white people, the best way I can honor that person is by walking toward the reconciliation that that person fought for. Now we are not doing that in our country as far as I am aware. We need to do this with more power than we have done up to this point.

༇

TO GET TIME with this incredibly busy church leader is a difficulty in itself. He is not only the Presiding Bishop of one of the largest Christian denominations in South Africa, the Methodist Church of Southern Africa, but also President of the South African Council of Churches. I managed to grab some minutes between a breakfast meeting for Methodist leaders and a SACC committee.

CLEARLY IN THE SOUTH AFRICAN CONTEXT, given the kind of history we have had, I do believe that reconciliation should mean—in fact this is what reconciliation should mean anyway—the acceptance of one's past, particularly the wrongs and the shortcomings, and then a search for forgiveness. In religious language, the acknowledgment of one's sin is a very critical factor in reconciliation, and it is that which will lead to the possibilities of better relationships between people and between communities. I do believe very firmly that there is a place in any reconciliation process for each individual to actually sort himself/herself out in order to be part of the healed community.

But having said that, it needs to be said with equal vigor that when we talk about reconciliation, particularly in a context like ours, it cannot only be an individual thing because of the way we dealt with one another as communities. Therefore there has to be a fair amount of collective acknowledgment of collective sin, collective shortcomings, and the ability for people to deal with those things that still divide us as communities.

I do also believe that as a Christian when we talk about reconciliation, we are not talking about something that is acted out only by the one who has caused harm or wrong. It requires, as well, a lot of sacrifice and giving up of oneself on the part of the person who has been wronged.

Therefore it poses a very crucial question, in this instance, for those who have been victims of the past injustice. How can we even allow reconciliation to happen given the kind of things that have happened among us? Of course, if we go to the scriptures we find reconciliation as Christ represents it. Christ did not exact a price from those who had committed evil for them to be reconciled with God. He took the suffering upon himself, and that is the model that is presented to us by the Christian faith. At the same time, the Christian faith also says that if you are coming to the table of the Lord and you remember that you have something against your brother, go and put that right before you proceed in trying to do good with God. These two positions have to be held together with one another.

So here are two difficult positions that we have got to search between in order to find a way forward. One thing that is not a compromise when people talk about reconciliation is that, whatever is done, there must be one clear goal in mind. That is the goal of being united with your brother and sister. It is never for the purpose of exacting vengeance on the one who has wronged you.

I THINK there is much that the secular society can hear and use from the religious experiences of our people. Let me acknowledge first that, as we have seen through the Truth and Reconciliation Commission, people were traumatized, people were destroyed, and their lives and their homes were destroyed. These are not simple and easy things we are talking about. We are talking about things that have broken people at the nub of their being, at the heart of their being.

Yet there is something that is honorable that I for myself believe needs to be lifted up a little more than it has been done so far. And it links very directly with Christ's approach to his own self-sacrifice.

Many of our people, particularly young people, died at the hands of the apartheid regime. We can be very angry that they died so young and find it very difficult to be reconciled with people who supported the old regime. I don't believe that we can arrive at reconciliation if we do not help the communities of those who were struggling against justice to understand and accept that the lives of our loved ones were not taken from them. They themselves, like Jesus, laid their lives down. In other words, rather than allowing ourselves to act like something could be done that could make up for their lives, we need to be working in the development of processes where we are going to say together: here are our heroes who laid their lives down for a higher goal and an honorable goal.

I think that South Africa's fear of creating heroes is robbing us of an opportunity to focus on what those heroes were giving their lives up for. Now, since freedom in this country, I have watched very closely and I have come to the conclusion that we have decided, as South Africans, to get on with life as if all is well. I don't think so. I think all will be well, not only for us but also for our young people, if there are processes that highlight the high goals of honor, the high noble goals for which our people laid down their lives. We have got to build liturgies if need be, build activities that seek to say thank you for these lives.

Now, I don't think that there is any amount of money that can make up for that kind of recognition. But I am afraid that we have tended to see everything in materialistic terms, so that we are denying ourselves an opportunity of creating a joyous excitement in people as they search for reconciliation. If my son, my uncle, or my brother died because he wanted reconciliation between black and white people, the best way I can honor that person is by walking toward the reconciliation that that person fought for. Now we are not doing that in our country as far as I am aware. We need to do this with more power than we have done up to this point.

THAT IS ONE SIDE when we talk about those who were victims. But on the other hand, I do believe that there is much more that ought to be done by those who were associated with the perpetrators. Somehow, we are allowing issues like fair distribution of resources just to be political factors. So when people talk about equitability at the level of schooling, public schooling, in our country we immediately ask, "Why should you drop the standard for me?" We have not got to a point where we ask, "If you do that do you realize that you are sharing with your brother or sister who suffered because of where you are?" And, "How can we help you to find joy in actually sharing that as a way of saying 'let us find reconciliation together'?"

If it is only the formerly oppressed who will seek to exact that out of those who had benefited, then it ceases to be a path to reconciliation. It becomes, instead, a spiral of fighting with one another. I do believe that this is a critical role, for bodies like churches to help people who come from the communities that consciously or unconsciously benefited from apartheid to actually say: "How best—not how can I make up for the past, but how

best—can I share what I have which I received at the expense of other people? I may not have been in the forefront of doing that deliberately, but I
have benefited from a situation that was meant to benefit me at the expense
of other people. I need to be helped to actually find honor, to discover nobil-
ity in learning to share that privilege." I have not heard many of us in the
churches, and anywhere else for that matter, talking meaningfully about this.

Now one can say that perhaps the business community has tried it
when it has promoted things like black empowerment and so on. But we do
know that there are all kinds of questions around that. I would say, for myself, if we are really keen to make a contribution that leads to reconciliation,
it is not enough to let us make a few black millionaires. The question is: how
do we redesign our economic activity in ways that will give opportunity to
the least of our people to be able to compete and find their own way into the
front line of economic activities like everyone else? I think that what matters
here is the spirit in which we do things.

I DO BELIEVE that the church has got to be a very key player in this. I
am not saying only the church can do it, neither am I saying that the
church is the best place to do it, but I am saying that the church *must* do it.
It does not have an option.

There is something that bothers me greatly when I look at our churches. When you talk about reconciliation you will find churches that have the
means are happy to say, "Give us a disadvantaged community that we can be
twinned with and in that way our people will be encouraged to give." While
we may argue that twinning churches is the best practical way of sharing resources, I do think that there are dangers. One of the key dangers is for people who give to be unaware that in fact what they are doing is just pleasing
their consciences again instead of looking for something fundamental that
is going to transform the position of the people that they are linking up
with and transforming themselves as well.

Now, I want to encourage the church to look at all kinds of ways by
which it can mobilize resources, mobilize them in ways that will allow them
to flow to poorer communities, the communities of the disadvantaged, in
ways that are not going to give profile to the giver but rather give profile to
the reason for giving, which is moving people toward reconciliation. That to
me is a key thing.

Now, in my own church we are battling with that. We say to people, "Let
us look at common ways where even the poor will give." Say for instance

you are establishing a foundation for development. Don't let us say, "Let the white people put in money there because they did this and that to the black people." Let us say, "Let all the people of South Africa put in something for the benefit of us all," so that even the poorest of the poor can have an opportunity to put in his/her one cent if need be. And let those who have bigger means give out of their wealth so that we can say *together* we did this and *together* we are healing our land. These are some of the things that are crucial.

I THINK THE TRC WENT A LONG WAY in helping people to actually see what they have been doing, to help us as people see what we have been doing to one another. I do know that people are coming up with all sorts of arguments: "This was not entirely legally correct," "It was not tested," and so on. The truth of the matter is that there are things that are undeniable. They happened in communities, and the TRC gave people opportunities to share the way they perceived things and, whether we like it or not, perceptions are facts. They might not be what I want to believe actually happened, but if the other person believes that this is what happened I have an obligation to work with that person to ensure that it is corrected and we get to the truth.

I do believe that the TRC went a long way in showing people what kind of perceptions are there in the community and what kind of actual things happened in the community, things that need to be dealt with. I do believe that it went a very long way in taking people toward reconciliation. At least you know what you are dealing with. That is the first thing. But where I believe that we could have done a little more, and I don't know if this should have been the task of the TRC or whether it should have just been left to other people, I do believe that we should have worked harder in bringing together those people who genuinely carried a deep sense of guilt for things that they were made to do. We have to find a way to take those people to the communities that suffered so that together with those communities they can find a way for their healing.

Now this could be done in all sorts of ways. It could be done liturgically, and it could also be done through some practical acts. All in all I am just saying that actions that help people to give back to communities are crucial and must have a key part in the process of reconciliation.

It will take more than that to arrive at reconciliation. For instance, you remember the stories of how some of the security police acted. I have in mind a person like Captain Nieuwoudt in Port Elizabeth. I read a story of how he visited the Mtimkulu family and how one young member of the family was so distraught that he hit Nieuwoudt over the head with a vase and made him bleed. The best part for me in that story is that it was actually Mrs. Mtimkulu who jumped out to embrace Nieuwoudt and to protect him from this anger. I think this is what it takes to find reconciliation, because whatever else may have been happening in Mrs. Mtimkulu's heart, suddenly her humanity said you cannot allow any harm to happen to this man. That is what we need to be working toward with our people. I think that because, of course, it is very delicate, very sensitive, very difficult, we have tended to avoid it.

I think the churches can help in this, but my greatest fear is that churches have not equipped themselves to do these things. But I think we need in the churches to equip ourselves to do these things more and more. I do want to believe that the churches can rise to the challenge. But bodies like the South African Council of Churches and others have got to work hard on how to help local churches to actually find the courage and the capacity to do this. It is the local church at the end of the day that must do it.

We must have a proper design and a proper plan at an ecumenical level where we all come together and say that this is what we want to do. But frankly it is not resolutions at that level that will do it. It is the ordinary worshiper who will take it upon himself/herself to go out of his/her way, individually and collectively with others, to bring that kind of healing and reconciliation on the ground. I do believe that to be the greatest service we can offer this land.

DR. WOLFRAM KISTNER

Wednesday, August 18, 1999

Rightly the TRC report says that reconciliation is not a cozy term. It is a concept which, on the one hand, brings people together, but on the other hand, it brings about conflicts with all structures of excluding people, or trying to exclude them from access not only to the kingdom of God, but also from access to justice.

DR. KISTNER is a Lutheran theologian. He is a former Director of the Justice and Peace Division of the South African Council of Churches. Quietly spoken, he suggests rather than states his position. We met at his home in a Johannesburg suburb.

I THINK there is a difference between a religious and a secular approach to reconciliation. This is recognized in the Truth and Reconciliation Commission report. But at the same time there is a very close interrelationship, and the religious concept of reconciliation is a far more comprehensive one. If you use the term *reconciliation* it very often seems to have different connotations.

You have reconciliation in the religious sense, where you think about repentance, forgiveness; about making a new beginning; about restitution.

Whereas reconciliation in a political sense could include negotiations as part of reconciliation, but they are not necessarily always part of true reconciliation, because you can have negotiations in a situation where beginning negotiations is a betrayal of reconciliation. This depends very much on the political and economic context of that time.

The word *reconciliation* has been used politically. And it had been used to cement, or to bring about certain reforms without changing the fundamental power structures. And therefore religious people rejected it. Not by all church leaders, but at least by many concerned Christians it was rejected, and also by some of the church leaders.

For instance, in South Africa, the churches were involved in the publication of the *Kairos Document* where we said "No reconciliation without repentance." But very shortly after that time, Nelson Mandela was released and the negotiations started. Then later when Nelson Mandela came with his concept of reconciliation—that was negotiation. This is the same Nelson Mandela who had initiated the armed struggle. He had wrestled with Albert Luthuli about this issue. Albert Luthuli was a man of nonviolence, but after Sharpeville Nelson Mandela had argued that we couldn't contain the violence. It is obvious it can happen to our people at any time, and the responsible way now is to engage in armed struggle.

Now in that situation you could not speak about negotiations. Neither Luthuli nor Nelson Mandela. But in the new situation in 1990 negotiation was a beginning, paving a way toward reconciliation, but it was not reconciliation itself. You get people sitting around a table who were enemies, who had fought against each other. You talk to people who have probably been very much involved in very serious human rights violations. And they didn't talk about how to deal with the past, with the matter of confessing and forgiving. But each one tried to get the most out of the other. Nevertheless, that was a way of reconciliation. So you can say that the word *reconciliation* is used in a political sense for such negotiations.

Thus, I think, there is a difference between the religious and political concepts of reconciliation.

You could also speak about reconciliation in the juridical sense, where you say in order to get reconciliation there has to be some punishment. And that's a different sense again. The juridical system is concerned about compensation for an evil deed—not so much about the person. Something bad has happened, and for the sake of society it must be seen that there will be punishment. But it is not so much concerned about the perpetrator or the victim.

All these are valid aspects of reconciliation, but they are not reconciliation in the religious sense.

There is also the very important economic dimension of reconciliation. And I think that has a lot to do with biblical understanding, because in the Bible, the whole question of debt in forgiveness originally has an economic meaning. You find it in the text of the Lord's Prayer: "and forgive us our *debts.*" This is the Matthew text, at least. That has very often been neglected. We have had political reconciliation held up as the element that is still outstanding in South Africa. I can't see that there will be reconciliation if the people who have suffered for so long remain in a situation of poverty, or the majority of them, as is still the case.

Now, the TRC report says that there was a "difficulty in understanding the meaning of reconciliation at a national level." And it "also highlighted the potentially dangerous confusion between a religious, indeed Christian, understanding of reconciliation, more typically applied to interpersonal relationships."

Here the Commission presumes the Christian understanding of reconciliation mainly as one of interpersonal relationships. Now, it may be that it is the generally accepted understanding of a Christian concept of reconciliation. I have doubts whether it is the biblical understanding. It may be very widely accepted among Christians, but I think in the Bible reconciliation has real structural implications. The concept of reconciliation as used by Paul comes from a political context originally: overcoming barriers or bringing together again parties who have been hostile to one another in an act of diplomacy and arriving at a settlement. Paul uses that picture in a religious sense to illustrate reconciliation. It is a reconciliation which has been achieved by bargaining, which pertains to the world, the whole world.

It has an anti-Roman Empire stance. The Roman Empire offered peace in its own way, a forced reconciliation under which all its people lived, but now here is a different understanding of reconciliation, a gathering together of people of Gentile and of Jewish background in a new fellowship which brings about peace in a very different way than the Roman Empire. This Paul offers as a model of peace and reconciliation. And it has very strong structural implications, not merely interpersonal. Paul speaks about it as a beginning of a new creation.

It has an individual dimension too, but primarily it is a communal concept. You can't exclude the individual; that's very important. But, in general, in church circles it is very often seen merely as an individual experience, and the structural implications have been neglected. I would put the primary emphasis on the communal aspect, realizing at the same time that you can't separate the individual from community. They belong together.

In South Africa it has much to do with the unity of the church. In the struggle against apartheid this was very important. When Dr. Beyers Naude was inducted as the Director of the Christian Institute, his sermon was on the basic text in 2 Corinthians, "reconciled us to himself through Christ and gave us the ministry of reconciliation." But this was reconciliation as the beginning of a struggle against structures of irreconciliation, of exclusion. Rightly the TRC report says that reconciliation is not a cozy term. It is a concept which, on the one hand, brings people together, but on the other hand, it brings about conflicts with all structures of excluding people, or trying to exclude them from access not only to the kingdom of God, but also from access to justice.

The message to the people of South Africa in 1968 was the same. It had to be. It was the beginning of the church's struggle, challenging the state on the basis of the concept of reconciliation.

And later at the time of the *Kairos Document* the struggle was intense. There was a state of emergency. So there was another dimension, another religious dimension, that was emphasized. That was reconciliation at the human level. But the other aspect was not so much emphasized, because we were in an intense conflict. The context changed the emphasis.

From the outset all human beings rely on a reconciliation that has already been achieved in Christ, and that is the basis for our struggle for reconciliation. It is a comprehensive understanding of reconciliation that empowers us to take up the struggle against structures of irreconcilability. But at the same time it is this which empowers us to aim at the liberation also of the oppressor. And that aspect becomes very important after the change in power, because then you get the temptation for the people who have been oppressed for so long, simply to move into the positions of power of people who were the oppressors. And that is a different aspect of it. One always has to be aware of the danger that something of the oppressor is alive in all of us and, if we get the chance, we can do the same.

TO ACHIEVE RECONCILIATION in South Africa it is necessary for what has happened to come out. The unknown should not remain hidden, because it is necessary for the people to get rid of the burdens of the past and be able to make a new beginning. I think it is necessary in those disclosures not only to recognize the things that happened to individual people but what was wrong with the political and social structures of the time. What has to change?

All of that depends on the people. Will the people who were responsible for maintaining the system recognize their responsibility? And not only their responsibility for very bad things, such as human rights violations, but for many of us—the majority of whites and including many many blacks—how we tolerated what happened and did not have the strength to resist. This is an indirect participation in injustice that has scarcely been addressed.

It was not the task of the Truth Commission. It is the task of the churches. We must be careful to focus only on the very bad crimes that have happened, where people were tortured, but not on our allowing this to happen. All those things could not have happened if there was not a lot of indifference to what happened to other people through fear and so on. I think that area is still outstanding, and that is not a task of the Truth Commission, that is the task of the churches.

Every Sunday we preach about guilt, confession of guilt, forgiveness, reconciliation, making a new beginning, as part of worship services. And again here you have a close link between political reconciliation, national reconciliation, and reconciliation in a religious sense.

THE TRUTH AND RECONCILIATION Commission made a very important contribution in paving the way toward reconciliation:

disclosing what has happened is its main contribution. There is nobody who can now say that they do not know what happened, and it has given wide publicity to it, at a very early stage after the event. Compare this with Europe—how long did it take until things came out there? Here, at least the sin of what has happened is known. Not everything that has happened is known. But we have an insight into the apartheid system and the crimes that have happened. We know that if it would have come to the crunch even worse things could have happened, such as mass destruction and poisoning of people. All sorts of things could have happened, not only to individuals but also to communities. In that respect the Commission has made a very great contribution.

That was the main emphasis—to disclose the truth. But also it has even transcended its terms in trying to promote a better understanding between victim and perpetrators and to facilitate forgiveness wherever this was possible and people were prepared. But that of course was on a very limited scale. But it was important that it happened.

And I must say that to keep such a commission together was an act of reconciliation in itself. The Commissioners were people of such different backgrounds, ideological backgrounds, religious backgrounds, and it was a tremendous achievement and was in itself a model of reconciliation. And I think that was something very good.

And one of the most important contributions in my view is that the Truth Commission has put on the public agenda issues like guilt, forgiveness, repentance, and restitution. The issues, which we preach about in church, have become public issues. That also is very good.

There is a lot of criticism of the TRC. But I think the TRC had to act within a legal framework which was set for it and which imposed limitations on it. Its witness has been worthwhile. Our legal system cannot handle those same issues. The legal system is geared toward punishing offenders who are individual offenders and guilty of punishable offenses. It is not very appropriate or well equipped to deal with offenses where a large section of society is indirectly implicated and shares responsibility.

The societal responsibility has come out very clearly. The community bears a large share of the responsibility for the way in which people were educated, indoctrinated from youth onwards.

And it has brought out the weakness of the churches. If you want to get a good insight of what sin means, what forgiveness means, what repentance means, you could go to the Truth and Reconciliation Commission. But if you go into a worship service there are very few worship services where you could get such good instructions. I know of pastors who took a confirmation class to the Truth Commission, and I think they were right to do that. But it shows the weakness of the churches.

Every Sunday we preach on these topics. We pronounce forgiveness at the beginning of the worship service, but it is in a very formal way. The Truth Commission says that there can be no new beginning without disclosure. But what has been disclosed there in our worship services? We simply pronounce forgiveness. In some churches there is a confessional, but it is very formal and very generalized.

It is said that it was partly the churches who insisted there could be no new beginning without disclosure, and an acceptance of what has happened. But what do we do in our worship services? How is the celebration of Holy Communion related to this? Or our understanding of baptism? Formally it is there, but only formally. I believe it shows that these things have to be corrected in church life.

It is my impression, I couldn't prove it but it is my impression, that at no time since the time of the Reformation have these issues been highlighted so much in public. At the time of the Reformation it was the public issue of indulgences and all other issues arising from that. At no time since then has this come up so clearly as a public issue. Through the Truth Commission all these topics have now been highlighted in the public domain. It is a challenge to the church, and it is a challenge to the state and to the judicial system.

Our judicial system is very much focused on the individual and on the deed, not on the perpetrator or the healing of the perpetrator, and certainly not on healing the victim. And that is a weakness. I would think that in the long run one of the most important contributions is the attempt to deal with the perpetrator and victim. This is important not merely in South Africa, but on a global level. We need to work anew on this because in many countries nowadays you have internal wars and nobody knows how to deal with the issues. Politicians are helpless, and when they are completely helpless they appeal to the churches. They call for some input on morals.

But not only the politicians and the legal system cannot deal with these issues. The traditional church systems and church structures are not adequately equipped either. Psychologically, are we trained for helping traumatized people?

All these things have come out through the Truth Commission. There is a need for cooperation between Christians with a variety of skills. It demands an ecumenical endeavor to deal with these issues, and in exploring possibilities in different countries. I would think in the long term that is the main contribution.

In the short term, I think it is too early to decide whether the TRC has contributed to national reconciliation. In one way it has, but whether this will have a long-term effect depends very much on how living conditions change for the people. Will there be some type of help for the victims? Up to now we don't see any, or very little of it. This is not a matter for the TRC. This question should be directed to the nation as a whole.

The legislation says that the perpetrator is not expected to make any restitution. The state is expected to do that. Now that might have been necessary for the sake of a compromise, but it was a compromise. How much are we, all the people who have benefited from the apartheid system, prepared voluntarily to contribute toward the economic reconciliation that is so much needed? Actually it is too early to answer that question. It depends on what the churches are going to do, on what the education system is going to do. There are a variety of participants, and that question should be asked in ten years time.

I WOULD THINK WHITE PEOPLE couldn't ignore the truths that have been revealed, but that doesn't mean that they accept responsibility, and I don't think that has happened on a large scale. There are people who are very deeply hurt; they have been very deeply affected. On the whole, I think, the white community has tried to overlook the hearings and its implications. And in that respect it is necessary for the sake of the process of reconciliation that not only should there be an economic contribution so that economic conditions can change, but I think that it is necessary that people share responsibility for what happened. For the sake of healing the wounds, their confession is necessary. I do not think that has happened to a large extent.

In our congregations it has happened partly, but I do not think it is deep enough. For it to really happen you need encounters with the victims, and that has to be facilitated. That has started on a small scale in some churches. We have a minister who tries quite a lot in that respect, but this is still a long process that we have to go through.

There have been such confessions in the Truth Commission, but I don't think it is the best platform for that to happen, particularly if you have television. You need another setting for this type of healing. Yes, something happened in the Truth Commission, but the real work now must be picked up in the religious communities. You need a different setting.

FROM THEIR OWN STATEMENTS we know that many of the survivors who have had a chance to give evidence have felt that it was a healing experience. Sometimes they met the perpetrators and found that to be a great help. But you also have the survivors who have rejected the whole process, and they have valid reasons for doing that. But even if they rejected it, it has mobilized them—they are no longer passive—and I think that is a positive step. There is at least dispute about it and that is good.

It's also good for the churches and for the TRC to face this dispute. A perpetrator who acknowledged what he or she had done, did not keep anything back, and could prove there was a political motive could get amnesty. But that amnesty very often is confused with forgiveness. And the question is whether an amnesty, even an amnesty with such crimes, should be given without some type of restitution.

It is highly questionable in a religious sense for people just to be forgiven and not to be asked to do something in return. You can't impose it, but I think it is part of the healing process. Though we are Protestants, I must say there is some truth in the Catholic understanding of confession where if you make your confession, something has to be done. It is not a condition, but you are called on to be aware of the pain you caused and express your remorse. That has not been taken into account. It could not be taken into account in terms of the legislation, but I think it is a real theological issue for us all and it is neglected.

I THINK THAT, IN ONE WAY, the Commission could not have functioned without religious people, not only Christian but also committed religious people from other religions. It would not have worked out without the person of Archbishop Tutu.

To me, this raises the question of whether a model of this sort can be transferred to another country. South Africans in general are a religious people, and I am not sure whether you could do something similar in a rather secularized country. Europeans are often very optimistic, saying that this is the way it should be done in their country. I don't think they can do it in the same way.

On the other hand, I must also say that there were elements in the working of the Commission that made it difficult for people. This happened where there was a transition from a pastoral style of procedure to a more legal procedure. For instance, in the hearings what was done very well was the pastoral way of taking care of people who have undergone very deep emotional pain and are still in that pain. They were given a calm setting where they could speak. But at the same time the legal demands were of such a nature that if in that hearing somebody is named as a perpetrator they must be informed that his or her name name has been mentioned. That person then has the right to question the victim. In that legal procedure you expose the very same people to further victimization. True, their emotional report may not be completely exact. Whether your son has been stabbed three or seven times doesn't make a difference. It is your experience and that is the truth. But then from the other side you could legally say, this is not a reliable witness. I don't think that fits together, and it must have been very painful for those people.

It must have been very painful for the many people who did not get to the hearings at all. Some would make a statement and then get a notice that their suffering did not fall within the terms of reference of the Commission. It is as if they have not suffered. And, of course, there is the fact that structural human rights violations have not come to the hearing at all. I mean like forced removals and so on.

So there are some very serious weaknesses. But you also have to remember that this was a compromise. Another possible mistake was made in the beginning by raising too high an expectation with the slogans about the healing of the nation and "The truth will set you free," which had a religious connotation. Well, where do you get the truth? Whether that was good, I doubt, because expectations were raised that could not be fulfilled, and it was clear from the outset that they couldn't be fulfilled.

On the other hand, there were also pragmatic considerations for the religious membership. I don't think the Commission would have got the huge support, especially from outside the country, without people like Archbishop Tutu.

WHAT CAN THE RELIGIOUS COMMUNITY DO? I think first of all it has to reexamine its worship practice. Why is it many of those perpetrators of the worse crimes have participated in worship services? What did they hear during the apartheid regime? It is true that the churches have submitted confessions, and I think in a way they were honest, but they didn't answer the questions such as, what are we going to do? How are we going to repair the damage? And I think that is outstanding.

I would think that in the normal worship time teaching is an important aspect, education is an important aspect, and a lot of that can be done in the church. We must also try to promote encounters between perpetrators and victims and also make every church member aware that this is something that has happened in this country and we all somewhere share the responsibility. We must help them see that communities suffered and all of us share responsibility as members of communities. We need to reread the Bible, in view of what has happened. And there I would say that it would be very necessary to take account of the economic dimension of the Bible.

What does the Torah say in the Old Testament? What is it about? It is about guidelines for life, derived from the fact that God has liberated his people from the house of bondage. What are the implications of that? And then it is spelled out, and one of the central points is the Sabbath, taking care of people who are nobodies; the slaves have to rest; animals have to rest; there is need for good working conditions; work is not the highest aim; do not judge another person. Everything is to live together to God's praise in God's place. Even nature has to be given a rest, and so there is the seventh year, the Sabbath year. You also have to have rest. And it speaks of procedures where an economy leads either by its structures or by the greed of people accumulating wealth just for themselves while others get poorer—that that must be addressed at intervals.

Of course you can't apply that directly. But these were guidelines, not only in opposition to the accepted and normal behavior of the people who had power, but also to demonstrate an alternate way of behaving. That is what the churches have to learn. How do we offer to the world in which we live alternative patterns of living together and sharing together? And sharing includes the spiritual experiences and material resources, and the church has tremendous resources, both material and spiritual, tremendous spiritual resources.

I often go to the East Rand where you have workshops of victims coming together, people traumatized through violence. A lot of those crimes have happened in the time since the change, during the transition. There were conflicts between different political groups, but often between members of the same political group.

They are very poor people, and many of them have had little in the way of education. It is a state-sponsored healing center with support from private organizations. And every time toward the end the people start a worship service. And I even have had experiences where a choir was invited. And the choir was made up of young people who had been involved in gangs like self-defense units. These were gangs that had their own territory to defend. Initially they did not trust one another and didn't even know one another's names. They were simply invited to play every week, meet in a social way, and from their playing a choir developed over a number of years.

When they came to this meeting where victims are engaged with other victims in mutual healing, they began to sing, "My heart is heavy, I have killed somebody." You could see from their faces that this is not simply an invented story. It is true. The leaders have not been trained psychologically. They are simply trained on the spot and through experience. I asked one of them, is it not possible that some of these people have killed children of the very people you have here together as victims? She replied that she did not know, it was quite possible. And here at the end they all have worship together, and sing and dance.

On a national level we say that there is no reconciliation without disclosure. It is a very general statement. There are other ways too. If you insist on that as a rule nothing will happen. The police never get the truth about the crimes that have happened. The truth slowly emerges as the people first of all meet together. The simple act of meeting together is already part of a reconciliation process. And thus we have to be very careful not to say this is the only way of doing it. It may be necessary on a national level, but there are many other smaller steps that are very helpful, and I think the churches could get involved in these.

I go as a visitor to participate. Usually you have a time when you meet with a partner and share your experiences. As they talk you learn theology from these very simple people. I am amazed at how much Christian foundation there is. You would never go away without a prayer. Most of them are Christians, and different people lead in prayer. Many come from independent churches. I find it very remarkable.

On one occasion, I remember, they made drawings. They were asked to make a drawing in the form of a pathway to describe what had happened to them in the last few years. In most of them there was a grave for almost every year. We have had experience of one particular bereavement, and you wonder how these people manage so much grief. And at the same time there is a tremendous spiritual resource among those victims. There is a strong resilience we often forget. We emphasize the suffering, and there is the tremendous spiritual resilience.

I think churches could link congregations with different experiences so that people could know and learn one from another. Very often you would not get a whole congregation, but if you get small groups that will have an effect on that congregation. And the link meetings can share success stories as well so that we encourage one another.

Is it possible to start something new in which we help people who are aware of the situation and are doing their best to know that there are many others who are involved in something also? We sometimes feel that the church is doing nothing, but there are many church people involved in many ventures—but they are isolated. We need to link them up so that they can strengthen one another, to feel that they are not alone, and share not only their failures but also their successes. And give hope to one another.

These are some of the things that need to be encouraged in our churches.

THE REV. WESLEY MABUZA

Thursday, March 2, 2000

Another thing is that it seems that many white people are refusing us the right to feel bad about the past. It is very painful. White people keep on saying, "Now look at this President Mandela. He comes out after twenty-seven years in prison and is not bitter and you should be like that." You refuse us the right to feel pain, and you are pushing us too quickly to forget. It is another perpetuation of oppression that you even deny my feelings.

THE INSTITUTE FOR CONTEXTUAL THEOLOGY (ICT) is suffering like many other organizations from a lack of continuing financial support. Wesley Mabuza was its dynamic and outspoken director at the time of our interview.

THERE ARE TWO TYPES of reconciliation. There is the one where reconciliation contains the acknowledgment of wrong by one party and forgiveness by the other. The other one is where one party gives in: that happens when someone feels that to go on with the other person or group is much more valuable than not to go on. This is the path, I believe, that was taken by the ANC leadership. I heard someone say that negotiation is a sign of weakness. Whether that is true or not, I do not know, but it shocked me. But I did say deep down in my heart that both parties had lost. The government lost the will to govern, and the ANC liberation movement knew it would be difficult to beat this machine. So it became a case of, "let us go on and see where it ends."

And now we have government leaders saying, "we were not ready." So I think there was that element that they both agreed to negotiate, to reconcile if you like, because they knew there was no winner. It was not a win-win situation but a lose-lose. It ended up in the watering down of many things so that our oppressors received golden handshakes; there were the sunset clauses, high pensions, and guarantees for civil servants. These things are still tying down people up to today. But you look at it and say, "was there an alternative?" And the alternative was blood. Hardheadedness does not do anyone any good. But we must be clear that when we actually accept that the alternative is ghastly and we take another route, our so-called reconciliation comes from accepting a utilitarian position.

IS THERE A DIFFERENCE between secular and religious reconciliation? Yes and no, in the sense that in religion there are certain binding imperatives because you have chosen to be religious and to be bound by them. On the secular side it is really a question of what gain is there for me in this whole thing, and if reconciling with you does not make me to gain anything, then I can just go on and not bother.

But I need to say that this idea that there is secular on one side and religious on the other is a western approach. For us it is an *ubuntu*[1] situation. Whether you are religious or not, what is the human thing to do in this situation? From the African mind I would have problems with this demarcation. I would say reconciliation is reconciliation.

Interestingly, a lot of Christian principles were already contained in our culture. For instance, when two people were fighting with sticks, the one who won took the one who had been beaten to the river to go and wash his wounds. That is restoring the dignity of the person. So the question is not whether it is religious or secular, but does this reconciliation restore the dignity of the person who is hurt and the one who is asking for forgiveness?

For me Christianity resonated so much because of the way I grew up at home. It was not based on Christianity, but when I began hearing and understanding what the Bible says, it was no different to what I had been taught in my home. It was part of life. I think this is why a majority of Africans tend to be Christian, not because of the missionaries but because it gels with who we are. I sometimes think we understand Christianity more than those who taught us!

That is why for me it is sometimes sad that we do not get a chance to lead these churches. The white leaders prefer people who think like them, even if they are of a different color. This is sad because we are losing a lot. Our people need to know that Christianity is not a thing that was "out there," but it helps to bring out those valuable things that were already in us.

ANY EXERCISE IN WHICH WE AIR our past can only be good. This is what happened with the Truth and Reconciliation Commission. The extent is a different matter. But I think we have to establish that the fact that South Africa was looking at itself in all its ugliness was good. There should be no doubt about the usefulness of that exercise. The exercise itself, the shocks that came out, the traumas, they have all helped. It is very rare that you can have a national examination of the psyche of a nation. I would not detract from the tremendous power that process had for many individuals and for the nation.

But because of the nature of the negotiations there were certain limitations placed on the Commission that allowed people to run away from the ugliness and pain they had caused.

An exercise of this nature can only scratch the surface. It is too much to have expected in that limited time with those limited resources to have done all that is needed. However, I was disappointed with our South Africans for overrating ourselves in the sense that I am still unhappy that the very people who were actors in the situation sat on the TRC. Some people see this as good, but I see it as a sense of national arrogance. I think, as a keen person on justice, I would have been happier if an international body sat on the TRC.

How do you become objective in a situation in which you were so thoroughly involved? What does it do to you when you have to turn against some of the things you said during the struggle? The government has appointed you so you start changing your tune. Some of the people sitting there, others could go to them and say, "but this is what you did," but you couldn't because there they were sitting as if they didn't do anything. Those very people themselves needed healing. Most of them were either on the left or on the right, but they were involved. I understand the idea of the wounded healer, but I thought this was too far and too quick. They could have been there on an advisory capacity but not as Commissioners.

I am not in any way questioning the integrity of the people who sat there. I am talking about the principle. I do not say this from a position of righteousness, as I did allow my name to be nominated for the Commission. But I realized as it went on that I am deeply wounded and in need of healing. And yet who healed them? How are they now? What damage has been caused?

MY EXPERIENCE OF WHITES is that on a scale of ten I would give a mark of three. I think this is one aspect of the failure of the TRC, not to be able to bring whites to a place of offering the hand of friendship and asking for the forgiveness that we were just willing to offer. It was unfortunate that whites spoke as individuals and would usually say, "I never participated" or "I was following orders." But as a collective I would have thought whites would have looked at what was done in their name and actually plead for forgiveness. It would have helped so much, even with the crime that is happening now. If only there had been a collective voice saying that we as a white group recognize what happened and we are asking this country to forgive us so that we can move on together. That is still lacking.

And the subsequent reinforcement of the apartheid mentality that we have experienced from some white people who say, "Now we can go and play rugby, now we can play international cricket without any problem, wherever we go we are acceptable, we have lost nothing and we are still where we are economically" is very hurtful. We have a sense of being cheated.

We were being cheated, and our white counterparts, with whom we very much want to live, are still cheating us. And, by the way, we would also like to acknowledge a lot of the good they have done, but they are not giving us that opportunity. They are not giving us the opportunity to look at that good because as long as someone gives the appearance of being superior you withhold that acknowledgment. So there is a lot of damage really. I would give three out of ten because we have not felt this outgoing spirit on the part of whites. Yes, a number of individuals, but not as a whole people.

Another thing is that it seems that many white people are refusing us the right to feel bad about the past. It is very painful. White people keep on saying, "Now look at this President Mandela. He comes out after twenty-seven years in prison and is not bitter and you should be like that." You refuse us the right to feel pain, and you are pushing us too quickly to forget. It is another perpetuation of oppression that you even deny my feelings. We thought whites would have understood that such a long and sustained period of oppression should have done a lot of damage. Instead they expect us to smile and say we are fine. It seems that the government wants to push us as well. They say we should not be thinking that way now but you should be thinking in this other way. I resent this. I resent being told how I should feel and think.

People have a right to feel the way they do until you show them the benefit of what is happening. We were pushed into so many things, and even today this is still happening and this scares me. When you start talking about retaining a colonial mind and people tell you that you are talking an old language, it scares me. If reconciliation means you must keep quiet, you must not say there are shacks and must instead talk about informal settlements, use a euphemistic term, you scare me because you are saying I must no longer look at a thing as it really is. I must try and sugarcoat the pill. We are not going to have a proper diagnosis of what is happening in the country if we carry on like this. Let us continue to say the things we used to say until we remove them. Let them hurt us and challenge us.

It is not helping white people by keeping quiet. I expected white people would have thought that they had all the benefit of oppression, whether they liked it or not or whether they chose it or not, and would want to do something in return. I really want to appeal to white people that they do not blame us for the way we feel. Do not deny us the right to feel this way. Just remember we never experienced what you experienced. We have had years and years of oppression. We do not like it when we are told how we must feel. It reminds us of the olden days when whites used to say, "These blacks are happy, man!"

TO SOME EXTENT THE PROCESS, especially individual cases, has helped blacks. I do not think many people would have been healed without the TRC. The confessions and the information about the burial places of sons and husbands have helped. The TRC has done a lot of good work, and I hope that those who were affected are building on it.

However, as a people that pain is still there. I was disappointed when Archbishop Tutu said to us after our presentation at the hearings in East London, "You guys are still angry." I did not expect this from him. Who wouldn't be angry? God forbid that we should not feel angry at acts of injustice. I still feel very strongly that we have not arrived.

The other thing that makes me *very* angry is that we could have gone very far by now. The oppression of blacks is similar to the oppression of women by men. If a family harnesses all the powers of women and men, that family becomes powerful. It is the same with our nation. If we harness the powers of both black and white together we can be powerful. But we continue to limp along on the issue of color.

When we take advantage of our power as men we are losers in the process. That is what has happened for our nation between whites and blacks. South Africa lost the wonderful leadership and participation between white and black. If Nelson Mandela had been allowed to lead at the time he was taken to jail, if Steve Biko had been allowed to do the conscience cleansing as he was doing, how very powerful this country would have been. I am angry at our failure concerning what we could have been.

Perhaps we are too late, but, please God, let us cut off competitiveness and unnecessary arrogance and remember we are human beings destined together. We will make many mistakes together, but let us remember the positions from which we come. Let us try as if we really want to reconcile and be honest with each other. Let us remove the masks that we are wearing and speak the truth.

There is so much that can still be done for the victims. There were many who were hurt in a particular way, but there is a sense in which the whole black race was a victim. I think we still need a dose of actions that are going to restore our dignity as a people. There is a great need for reparations, but there are things that do not need money such as the acknowledgment of another person's dignity.

What we need to do is organize civil society as we did in the past. We know from our experience the value of having many nongovernmental organizations. People say to the ICT that they are giving money to the government and we should ask them for funds. How can we be an NGO and ask for money from the government? Then we would become a government agent, a GO! We need to encourage each and every effort that is trying to assist in transformation. Many NGOs have closed. Why? I think that has made our country poorer.

I FEEL VERY STRONGLY that churches need their own TRC. It was fine to have religious people sitting on the Commission, but their own organizations need to look at themselves closely. That time for submissions from religious groups was not enough. The leadership should not have been the ones to speak there. It should have been representatives chosen by the people. Some good things were said, but a lot of it was parading our good works and a little bit of giving away something by saying we are sorry for not doing more. The only church that was there rightfully was the Dutch Reformed Church because they did not have any alternative other than to plead forgiveness. But most of the churches have not looked at themselves in a mirror, and my fear is that they do not want to look at themselves in the mirror.

What should religious communities do? They should look at themselves. I am asking the hierarchy to ask the people how they see them and to accept it. There is no way the religious community can take part in reconciliation and transformation when it itself is not transformed, when it is not reconciled. We are still divided on racial lines. And we have forgotten how to work ecumenically. Is it no longer important that we are divided denominationally? Does it no longer matter that we pay lip service to the ecumenical movement?

And in the churches themselves, does it not matter that much as many churches are trying to have integrated circuits and parishes, the economic side still dictates the situation? So the religious community, especially the majority Christian community, has a lot to do to reconcile with itself first.

And we need to look at the training of ministers. When churches do try and be colorless in regard to stationing, it is without any kind of preparation. And those ministers end up as a kind of sacrifice. We have so many people in our churches, and we need to retrain the ministry to help them in the present situation. We still have ministers who want to teach their people what is right and what is wrong instead of empowering the people to discover for themselves. I detest the continuous patronizing in ministry that our churches seem to dish out to congregations. The religious community has a lot to do on its own. Never mind what it can give to the country. If it can get right it will automatically get the country right. I am not so naïve as to believe that the hierarchy of the churches will give away power to empower the people so easily. The pretense that churches are places where there is justice and we know what justice is about is a pipe dream and the sooner we acknowledge it the better.

We need a TRC for the churches with an international panel in which the hierarchy sits as the accused. And the people must speak. The churches continue to treat their people like Sunday school pupils instead of helping them get their own lives into their own hands. The churches give milk instead of meat. It does not augur well for the future. We are not creating mature Christians in South Africa. We are doing more harm than good.

What about the Institute for Contextual Theology? We are asking ourselves many questions about a theology of empowerment and a theology of transformation. We can see a need for the retraining of ministers in the light of our present situation. We would like to contribute toward a new understanding of ethics and action. We would like to contribute to moral regeneration, not in a cheap moralizing way but in bringing out the consciousness and awareness of people in terms of the powers within them to actually act in such a way that does not only benefit them but the whole country.

ICT is able to organize trainings in the different regions to help persons discover themselves, have an identity. We will be embarking on a huge conference/seminar in which we will be trying to determine the psyche of the South African nation. What is the soul of the nation? We know there are white people and we know there are black people and among them there are certain non-negotiables, but what are the things that make them both South African? We want to highlight these, and this is where ICT can play a role.

NOTE

1. Ubuntu, which can be translated as the achievement of personhood through relationships with others, was a term championed by Archbishop Tutu in the TRC and used as a rationale for a restorative approach to jurisprudence.

THE REV. CHARITY MAJIZA

Tuesday, August 24, 1999

So you have the element within the churches, the denominations, that reflected apartheid legislation where whites and coloureds and blacks had to worship differently, that even in our new open situation a lot of people still want to go on in the old way, their own merry way of separation.

Rev. Majiza is a minister of the Presbyterian Church. She was in exile in Scotland and Australia for eighteen years before returning to South Africa in 1997 to be the General Secretary of the South African Council of Churches. It was in this capacity that she spoke with me in her Johannesburg office.

M Y CONCEPT OF RECONCILIATION comes from the Christian understanding, of course, and the fact that there is a prerequisite for reconciliation and that is to confess. And then after one has confessed that which has happened, whether it is to another individual or to the community, there has to be some repentance or remorse that is actually evident to show that the person is not just going through the motions by saying that he or she is confessing. That then opens up the possibility of reconciliation. Reconciliation is not easy. It is a very costly business.

Even God himself through Jesus Christ, as we look at it as Christians, paid the costly price of the death of Jesus in order for us to be reconciled to God. To be reconciled to one another is very costly, and I think that this is a very important ingredient in reconciliation that we need to understand. We cannot just gloss over it in South Africa, as it seems some of the people would like to do.

Repentance and forgiveness are essential elements in the reconciling act—very much so. It will be more effective and more meaningful. It would mean much more to the person, for instance, who has been wronged. And often it is not simply a matter of judging one of the people concerned, because sometimes in a situation both parties have contributed toward that which has created a rift between them. There is a need for both parties to come to terms, with both parties being honest in looking into what has happened. Then the whole question of reconciliation becomes possible.

I also believe that the term *reconciliation* is a very Christian or a biblical term. I do not think it belongs to the secular world. At the same time, I am not advocating a position that this is to be clearly monopolized by the churches, but I think that the depth of it could be missed if it is not looked at from its roots. Remember that reconciliation has to do with atonement, which reconciles us to be at one with God and that is a very costly business.

It is very difficult to know how we in South Africa move forward to reconciliation. The churches, for instance, went to confess at the Truth and Reconciliation Commission in 1997, but we have not been quick, as churches who have confessed, to actually move on from there. And this shows how difficult this whole question of reconciliation actually is in South Africa just now. There is confusion about which way to go.

There are those people who are in a hurry. They say that this is the past and we need to move on. They say that it has been ugly, as it has been portrayed to us on television, but that we are on the eve of the new millennium, of the twenty-first century. Why don't we just forget in the interest of the new nation and go forward as it is? But some people still want to know and some people still want to deal with this ugly past. They want to go into it and examine it and say that we cannot move forward until that has happened.

And others feel pressured to forgive very quickly. We tend to forget that some of the people had closed this chapter and got on with their lives and then the TRC opened up the old wounds. People all of a sudden are actually finding out about the circumstances under which their loved ones have died or how they suffered. They, therefore, still need to take time to look at this and it cannot be hurried.

The churches, actually the pastors, priests, and ministers, need to be very much aware of this. We can't just say to people, you are a Christian therefore you have to forgive. We have to travel with the people and to be patient with the people. It is a bit like grief: some people can get over their grief in a year or three years, but other people need ten years, while other people live their whole lives as if their loved one had never gone. Therefore we cannot say to people, stop what you are doing, and you know you should have got over it by now. We cannot do something like that because we are all different and our thresholds are quite different and that is where pastoral care on the part of the churches is so important.

ABOUT THE TRC and its work, well the hub of the matter is that actually the Truth and Reconciliation Commission should not really have been called a reconciliation commission at all. I do not believe the TRC could be concerned with reconciliation except that the TRC primarily was concerned with getting at the truth, which is a first step.

Now, it is debatable whether we have obtained the whole truth, only some of the truth or only a small part of the truth. I think that the miracle about the TRC, how unusual it was, its uniqueness, is that, unlike in any other countries, this has been an opportunity by this one organ of the nation to help us to have glimpses of some of the things that have happened. This gave us a general picture of the nation at that time, but as you know, not everybody had an opportunity of going to the TRC to tell their own stories, and there is still a lot of listening that has to be done.

The TRC was concerned, as I have said, about getting at the truth so that we can hear it and share it. But the work of reconciliation, as I said at the beginning of this conversation, is the work primarily that belongs to the church. The concept is a religious one. And not just the church but other religions also have to look at this and help the nation toward healing. This healing is going to take a long time because the wounds that have been opened took a toll on the people and the people, have to deal with this in their own time.

So the Truth and Reconciliation Commission was one organ, one possibility, but much more has to be done. The government had to do something in order to try and bring the nation together and also to try to make sure that people feel that something is being done about what has happened to them. But it is debatable whether, because of amnesty, the carrot of amnesty that was given to the perpetrators to come and talk about what they have done within the political framework of that given time for them, whether that augers well for the victims.

I have a debate in my mind about that. I have to ask myself, if it were not for the carrot of amnesty would those people have come forward to say this is what I did during that time? Or would people have got on without knowing what happened to their loved ones?

The other thing that concerns me about this is that it almost feels like the perpetrators have won twice. They have come to talk about what has happened to them in the past—I am not saying that was easy for them to do, but they have come to talk about that—and they knew what the end results would be. They knew that if that the Commission believed them they would be granted amnesty and off they would go and they would move on and carry on with their lives. But the people who are victims, those who have been on the receiving end, on the other hand, they are not able to move on. There is the whole question of restitution and compensation. It seems as if it is neither here nor there and, even if we know that nobody can compensate for a life that is gone, the concern remains that it seems as if people who were the victims have to be easy in terms of forgiving and then there is nothing that comes to compensate them on their side. Those people who ask for amnesty, their lives go on untouched. It was a cathartic experience for them in which they say, there it is, we have put in on the table and therefore we can now go on with our lives. But, on the other hand, the people who were victims are still dealing with this new wound that has been opened, and their lives have not improved at all. They still continue to live in poverty, often because the breadwinner of that family is gone.

HAVE WHITE PEOPLE accepted responsibility? I was talking earlier about people hurrying on to the future. There are some excep-
tions, but it seems that many do not want the past to be raised again.

We are into the second term of our new democracy, and we need to be
getting on with building South Africa. But there are deep psychological
scars that hinder even the best, the strongest people, to go forward with
what they are supposed to do.

I feel that when we talk about whites—it is terrible to talk in these terms
but for the sake of clarifying things we must use them—when we talk of
whites within one denomination it seems that there are problems.

How do we reconcile people and make this country work when people
are not together? There are congregations that were previously white and
that are now changing because of the possibility for black people to live in
the city. The blacks can now come and worship in the same building. Have
you noticed that there is a white exodus and large numbers of white have
moved out of those congregations to other suburban churches where they
know there will not be many black people coming in? Now, if we can't worship together, where is the hope for the church?

The church is looked upon as a healing agency and a hope for the nation, that it will bring people together. But now people move away, and you
still find those congregations that are predominately black and others that
are white. These are the questions that I have in my mind about what do we
mean about this reconciliation and hurrying away from the past. Is there a
fear that if people spend too long a time together they might talk about
these things, raise questions? Therefore to avoid raising the question or the
issues of the past, in order for us to be healed together, people—white people—are shying away or moving away so that these questions do not arise.
As you know, there is nobody in South Africa today that would say they
once supported apartheid!

But, of course, we do have a remnant; we have those people—white
people—who were involved in the struggle, people like Beyers Naude and
Archbishop Hurley and many others we know who suffered with us
through this kind of choice during the apartheid times. Those people were
not treated very well in their communities, and some of them have still not
been fully reconciled within their churches. They are still part, if you like, of
the black population in the eyes of those other people.

So you have the element within the churches, the denominations, that
reflected apartheid legislation where whites and coloureds and blacks had to

worship differently, that even in our new open situation a lot of people still want to go on in the old way, their own merry way of separation. An attempt to deal with this does not seem to be made.

But also within some white congregations on their own, those people who dared to question the apartheid laws and how they were contrary to the gospel, those people are not yet fully reconciled to their own churches. And those churches are where they could speak to their own group of people about what it was like for them and now in a free society they could help the people access information and make new interpretations. And I sort of feel that the opportunities of change are being passed by, or are passing us by as churches. We need to start talking about this.

I THINK FOR THE PEOPLE who were victims it was very comforting to have a number of religious people on the Commission. The South African Council of Churches talked about the ministry of accompaniment when people were there before the Commission.

It must have been comforting for people who had to share their painful stories to see Christians there. To see a person like Archbishop Tutu, who had been with them in the struggle, was a strength for them. They would find comfort in the fact that they would be listened to very carefully because this person has traveled with them. And many other members of the Commission were part of that as well.

I ALSO THINK THAT in an ironic way it shows how South Africa in a sense has been a Christian country. We came to know through the Truth and Reconciliation Commission that there are other religious people who are not necessarily Christian. These people also made their own confessions about how they participated in the struggle or failed to do so.

There is a new hope in this country. Even if the country is eighty percent Christian, we have a new constitution that is opening up opportunities for us as faith communities to begin to talk to each other, albeit that we probably don't know how to do that because of our ministerial formation in the past. Our ministers have been trained in a strictly Christian manner. We did not have things like the phenomenology of religion or the sociology of religion to help us understand other religions. Perhaps there was no need for it in the past because it was just accepted that we are a Christian country. But now the challenge is that we cannot just exist as if other peoples' faith or other faith communities did not exist.

And we also know that, like in the Christian community, there were certain individuals in other faith communities, as reflected in the present government, who were part of the struggle. I think we need to find each other in South Africa, whether between blacks and whites or within the black community or within the white community or within the Christian community, and also across our faith communities. If we want a changed South Africa and a new South Africa that reflects its entire people, we need to tackle these issues.

MAYBE PEOPLE WHO DO NOT BELIEVE in anything, do not belong to faith communities, maybe they would have felt that the number of religious people on the Commission was heavyhandedness on the part of the faith communities. But the term itself is, as I have said, a religious term. And most people recognize that the church was a leading force in the struggle. Therefore I am not surprised that the people who were part of the TRC were drawn from faith communities because they took the lead while the whole political opposition was in exile. I saw the religious membership of the TRC as a natural progression.

I BELIEVE WE CAN NOW BEGIN to analyze the Truth and Reconciliation Commission, including its composition or what happened to it and what happened to the people who came before it. When the report of the TRC came out—it came out on October 6, 1998 and was handed over to the President—I deliberately did not want to deal with the question of reconciliation there and then. For one thing there were political parties such as the ANC and Mr. de Klerk of the NP who wanted to question the TRC findings. And it was so shocking to realize what we, as South Africans, had done to one another that I thought that if we can have a space and a cooling off period, so to speak, it would be best for us. When the passions are not so high about certain things and people have a time to think through the report, then we can begin to deal with it.

So it was only in July that we started having our very first reconciliation workshop to do with priests and pastors. Not everybody had a time or chance to go to tell their stories to the Truth Commission but, at the same time, all of us are carrying wounds about apartheid. People may have not been tortured, people may not have been jailed, but people have suffered in the way apartheid was legislated. People were forced to live in certain areas, were told who they should be friends with, who they should marry, what type of school they could attend—and it was a poor system of education if you were on the bottom line, like African people.

Now there are so many people within the churches that are aggrieved about what has happened, but they have never had the opportunity to deal with this. That is why I have said that we must help priests, ministers, and pastors in their liturgies and in their way of preaching to incorporate this whole notion of where we have been and where we are now and look at how we can begin to open up and deal with the issue of reconciliation. This has to be done first within the church's worship, and then flowing from that kind of preaching and liturgy comes the pastoral care that has to reach out to our people.

People should not feel that because nothing dramatic happened to me I have to keep quiet. Those same people are living in poverty because of the apartheid legislation. I think there are many people like that: people who never had something dramatic happen to them—or even some of those where it did happen to them. They never had an opportunity to go and present themselves to the TRC. Some of the people may feel left out by that. Or others may feel that if there is compensation it will be for those who went to the TRC. What about the rest of the people who might feel that they deserve compensation as well? That might become something to divide people and alienate them from the work of the TRC.

I DON'T THINK THE CHURCHES are doing much. I am not saying that nothing is happening. There may be things that are happening here and there. There are trauma centers, for instance, but there are not enough of them, and I think we need to establish more of those where people can come together and examine the past.

I think there are quite a number of things that churches can do, of course. Our liturgies can help us to deal with this. Our pastoral care can help us to deal with this. But also, at the same time, we should be opening spaces where people can come and talk about what has happened to them and how we can deal with it. But also I don't believe that the whole question of reconciliation can only be tackled in terms of people coming in and confessing what they have done or what they have not done. I think there are other positive ways that can help us, especially as churches.

For instance, the skills in our churches are not the same. There are those people who were previously advantaged by their education while there is a lot of paucity in the black education. I would imagine, for instance, that it would be a very satisfying thing for somebody in the white part of the church to share their skills with others. A psychologist, for instance. We lack those in the black community. How about a black clergy person gathering people in his/her congregation to come and share with one another? A layperson from a white congregation can come and help to facilitate in that group and empower the people there. I think that that kind of thing can help build trust among people and also empathy. People may not fully understand what has happened to other people but are able to enter into the pain of the other through this kind of contact. I think that's one of the things.

When we look at skills such as accounting, people could offer those to smaller congregations or groups that have been formed. You do not have to be a qualified accountant to do bookkeeping for some group of people and also in the process have an understudy to teach them the same skills. So I feel that there are other things that people can do which are positive and are affirming for both people. There are black people out there who need to know that there are white people who actually care for what has happened to them, who are sorry and who would like to help. I think those are some of the resources that have not yet been tapped within and among churches.

IN REGARD TO THE POSSIBILITY of blanket amnesty, I think that in a sense we cannot go on forever and ever digging up the past. I think there is enough there for us to work on and there is enough to enable every South African to look at himself/herself in this mirror of what we are and what we have been and what we have done to each other.

Yes, there will have to come a time for amnesty, but we cannot put a time on this kind of thing, as I've already said in regard to grief, because here we are talking about people's lives. Maybe we will have an opportunity to say we have to stop looking at this. That time is not now.

When we are talking about the amnesty in itself we need to remember the victims. Take a case in point, the bombing of the South African Council of Churches. We were very much concerned that the truth should come out. We were never people who were looking for retribution because we believe that vengeance is of God and not ours. But there is a very thin line between justice and vengeance, and sometimes because you have experienced the pain that kind of line can be blurred somehow. And so we are also of the opinion that the people who have been granted amnesty and who have spoken about what has happened should not just let it go or end there. It is important that they should meet with the people they harmed.

This is so necessary in all the cases. The perpetrators need to be helped to see the damage they have done to others, and that happens only, of course, when the victims can feel open to this kind of meeting. I think that if the perpetrators don't get to see the damage they have done to people, then it becomes a theoretical construct and people cannot understand fully. And I think that it is very important for the victim, if the victim would like to do so. As I have said earlier, sometimes a person who is a victim feels that he or she is more hard done by in the end and is not getting anything, and yet here there are people going along with their freedom.

I think that it is a question of justice. We will need to be clear on how that amnesty is set up as well as how we will make sure that the dignity of these people who were the victims is assured.

THE REV. BASIL MANNING

Thursday, June 10, 1999

I am not sure that I believe that the saying of "I am sorry" there [at the TRC] contributed to national reconciliation. I see the issue more holistically than that. We need housing, services, and infrastructure. You cannot fix that with a TRC, but it does need to be fixed, and one of my basic problems with the TRC is that it did not go far enough. It was not just about a government that used excessive force but the way in which it dehumanized people, both white and black. We have not even begun to touch the tip of that iceberg in terms of the damage it has done to us.

BASIL MANNING calls himself a black person of mixed descent as one of his attempts to make new definitions for our changing society. He is a minister of the United Congregational Church and the full-time Chairperson of the Centre for Anti-Racism and Anti-Sexism and a freelance trainer and consultant on these same issues.

FOR ME THE CONCEPT of reconciliation is obviously very much tied to the acknowledgment of wrong on the one hand and forgiveness on the other. But for me it is more than that. It is more than saying I am sorry; it is the *doing* of I am sorry. It is this that is making the task of reconciliation so difficult for us in South Africa. There has been a lot of saying I am sorry, but there are too many reminders of the past that create leftover feelings even for someone like me. I have worked on it, and I still have leftover feelings that make reconciliation with others extremely difficult. I find this especially so with those who do not own the fact that there were great benefits to be gained by apartheid.

For instance, if I go into Parktown, Greenside, or Houghton and then I go into Sebokeng or Soweto I am struck by the stark realities in terms of lack of resources, lack of infrastructure, and lack of services. Things that are taken for granted by white people are not available for so many black people at all. I turn on the radio and hear people complaining that the grass verge on their pavement is no longer being cut, and then I see other people who do not even know what pavements look like, let alone tarred roads. Then the leftover feelings become strong and I find it very difficult.

This is why I feel so strongly about the fact that the Reconstruction and Development Programme (RDP) was replaced by Growth, Employment, and Redistribution Strategy (GEAR). I think the GEAR process of economic growth followed by employment and redistribution will mean that the rich will still become richer, and only when they feel they are rich enough can we think of creating employment and redistributing wealth. If we had stayed on course with RDP, and done this much more vigorously, I think we would have begun to address some of the things that make for reconciliation.

I believe the change from RDP to GEAR happened because it is a self-imposed structural adjustment program. It is the equivalent of the Economic Standard Adjustment Programme in most of the countries to the north of us and also in Latin America. It is fundamentally being in tune with the World Bank and the International Monetary Fund. It was realized that if we do not do certain things now they are going to force us to do them in the long run, so let us do them now and not let them be imposed from outside.

In a situation where there is already large-scale unemployment, the retrenchments that are going on are quite devastating. This large-scale adjustment is taking place within the country so that some people will make bigger profits but employ fewer people. It is having the same effect in South Africa as it has had in other parts of the world, where basic essentials such as education and health care are the first to be cut. The poor who are dependent on these services are the ones who suffer.

THE TRUTH AND RECONCILIATION Commission went part of the way toward reconciliation but not far enough. It focused only, and understandably so because of limited time and resources, on the excesses of the regime. But where will the truth be told about what Bantu Education did to the majority of black people in this country? Where will the truth be told about the deep feelings of thousands who were humiliated and hurt by what was done to them under the pass laws? How will we heal the damage that was done to so many people by the Job Reservations Act and the inequity in pay and conditions? If South Africa was a television set that was smashed and we could take it to the repair shop and have it repaired we would be far ahead, but the harm that has been done has divided our society and deeply hurt so many that it cannot be repaired so easily.

In the work that I do with different groups I recognize that reconciliation is very difficult unless we work through the truth that needs to be told of the pain of the past which still remains to contaminate our present. When the truth is told there are people who say, "O come on, you are going over the top now, this could not have happened. It was not so bad." We need to own that it did happen, and it damaged us all in the process.

So what needs to happen, for me, is that the physical reminders of the things that make it more difficult for me to forgive need to be addressed and need to be addressed quite urgently. And there is need for ownership of the fact that unless we deal with the past it is the past that will continually affect the present and the future. White people have to actually acknowledge that it did go wrong, and we need to look at why it went wrong. They need to own up to what was done, not necessarily by all the people themselves, and that all white people did benefit by it. They need to own that fact so that a re-meeting can take place, not on the basis of "let's forget everything and move on" because we cannot do that, but on the basis of a search for equity.

That is what I mean of the difference between the saying of "I am sorry" and the doing of "I am sorry." And the question of who will do the "I am sorry" makes it more complicated. Is it the new government that will do that? They cannot. Or do we need some other symbolic things on the part of the beneficiaries of apartheid that acknowledge that past and help to rebuild?

I suppose Mr. Mandela's answer would be to say that he is working on that and getting companies that did make big bucks out of the exploitation of others to build schools here and do that there. Maybe that is helpful. The people who are doing it are those who benefited from apartheid. But the question on my mind when I see it on television is to ask if this is just a paternalism that is continuing or whether there is some real ownership of doing this because of the legacy of the past. Are they saying, "We are doing this because we acknowledge we did benefit and because it is about time that we make some reparation for what happened in the past"? I do not see those elements coming through. Maybe it is happening in the background, but all we hear is about how fantastic it is that these people have provided so many millions. It could be happening for the wrong motives and actually not helping to achieve reconciliation.

THE TRC WAS NECESSARY. I get a lot of flack in the workshops I run with people asking what is the point in raking up all this stuff from the past, why not just leave it. That is, of course, mainly from white people. The divisions are still there. Why can we not just get on? But I feel it was necessary. If it was necessary for nobody else it was necessary for the victims, people whose close relatives died under mysterious circumstances. It was necessary from a cultural perspective so that people were able to receive the remains of their loved ones and go through that emotional healing necessity of providing a decent burial. Knowing what happened was also very, very important.

I am not sure that I believe that the saying of "I am sorry" there contributed to national reconciliation. I see the issue more holistically than that. We need housing, services, and infrastructure. You cannot fix that with a TRC, but it does need to be fixed, and one of my basic problems with the TRC is that it did not go far enough. Apartheid was not just about a government that used excessive force but the way in which it dehumanized people, both white and black. We have not even begun to touch the tip of that iceberg in terms of the damage it has done to us. But as a concept I think the TRC was right.

It helps to realize the benefits of that process when you visit other countries and wonder about their situation. The United States will remain a racist society until it has a process where it owns up to the fact that it was built on the blood of at least fifteen million Native Americans and there has never been any kind of acknowledgment of that. The United Church of Canada has said they are sorry to the First Nation people of Canada for their involvement in the residential schools through which the children of Native Americans were assimilated into Canadian society at the expense of breaking up families. Interestingly enough, the First Nation people of Canada have acknowledged receipt of the apology, but have also said we are not accepting it yet: we want to see you apologizing in your behavior, so we will let you know when we accept your apology. We need something like that here is South Africa: we acknowledge that you have said you're sorry, but we need to watch you and see before we accept your apology.

WHITE PEOPLE ARE MOVING, albeit slowly. The emotional temperature of the workshops that I run on racism today is very different from three years ago. Whether that is the contribution of the TRC or of several things I am not sure. We say to the white people that they need to tell us what we need to do as black people. Mandela was imprisoned for twenty-seven years, and he comes out and leans over so far backward and puts all his effort into reconciliation. Then come the first democratic elections and everybody believes the country will go up in flames. It did not, and the international press comes and leaves soon because there is no story of violence.

And then people said it would come at Mandela's inauguration but it didn't happen. Instead, some of us were in tears as *Nkosi Sikelel'i Afrika* was played on the grounds of the Union Building. Then it was going to happen when Mandela leaves, and nothing happened because to all intents and purposes Thabo Mbeki has been executive president of this country for the last three years at least. Now people are saying it is going to happen when Mandela dies. So there is still an element of that kind of thinking, even when we say to them that if we as black people really wanted to reverse the situation we could have had one session of Parliament and passed one law that said wherever it says "white" change it to "black" and wherever it says "black" change it to "white." But we did not. Instead, we set up a culture of human rights with a Human Rights Commission, and we are setting instruments in place to ensure there is no discrimination.

Why then, we ask whites, do you still think that we want to kill you or drive you into the sea? I actually believe there is a very small and dying element on the right and also one on the left that is not committed to reconciliation, but I believe that it is the middle ground we have to build on, and there is a lot of goodwill there. I say that on the basis of the fact that I see a shift, a change. The workshops are not as tense. There is a recognition that we need to share and see to things together.

White people are slowly acknowledging this need. Once we got a lot of tension and anger and denial, but now people are far more willing to go along with one another. One of the things that makes people more aware is that we now live in a transparent society. It is also part of our problem as a nation in that people know about things that go wrong in government now that they did not know about before. The cost is there, but it is better that we do. I regret that the media, which is primarily white-controlled, especially financially, is still steeped in deficit thinking. The starting point is that with the government being predominantly black it cannot be as good as if it were white. This constantly feeds a negativity that is not contributing to reconciliation at all. The recent commission looking into the media will help. Racism is not just about being direct but about the things that you do not say, the positive things that do not get coverage, the things that are not mentioned. Omission as well as commission can reinforce differences and divide the society even further.

Whites are not making this shift because they feel guilty about what happened but more as a practical matter of getting on in this new society. In some workshops it comes out directly: "I was not there when this happened. Why do you want to remind us of these things that we were not part of?" They do not see that it is like sexism. I did not start sexism but, God, I benefited from it! And I have to own the fact that I benefited from it. It is not my fault. I do not have to blame myself. It is a fact and a truism that I was captive to it and a product of it, and I have to own up that I was a sexist. And when I own up to it I can become an ally in the process of struggle against sexism.

It is the same with white people. If they can only hear racism as a fact, a truism, and not as an accusation it will help. It is not their fault. They did not start it. But at the end of the day they can recognize that they have been socialized into it and that they benefited from it.

The ideology of white superiority, which is a global phenomenon, is more sharply obvious in South Africa because of our history. But because it is so sharp here we have more chances to recognize it and, therefore, a greater opportunity to deal with it. White people did benefit in terms of infrastructures, services and resources, wealth, beaches, whatever. White people need to own that. There are some who do and who have become allies in the struggle against racism.

There are more white people who are changing and shifting, but many are doing it for the wrong reasons. They are saying, "Well, this is where the country is going to, and in the new South Africa we have to go with it and get our equity plans together and employ black people now whether we like it or not." So many people are doing it for the wrong reasons. But we did warn five years ago that if you do not do these things voluntarily now for the right reasons then we are going to need legislation like crutches to help us move in the right direction. Most whites are moving because of legislation.

Yes, there are white people who have moved and even come to tears in workshops who say they are angry because they were lied to, because they did not know, and now they are deeply pained about what happened in their name. There are people who are deeply pained and own it in that way and have shifted and say, "Let us acknowledge it." But there are still many who are defensive and say, "It wasn't me, and you are accusing me of being a nasty person and I am not." We say, "You are not a nasty person. It is not your fault. It is a fact of being a product of a racist society, having been socialized." It is the owning up to those two things that make reconciliation possible.

So I say in workshops it is not my fault that I grew up in a "coloured" area and went to a "coloured" school—I use the term "coloured" here purposely, though I prefer calling myself a black person of mixed descent. It is not my fault that I went to a "coloured" church and to a "coloured" youth club. It is not my fault that I associated with "coloured" adults and played with "coloured" children. It is not my fault. I did not choose that. But because of it, I did develop a particular identity, a coloured identity. An identity which said you are not quite as good as the Spongs of this world, but you are not as bad as the Ngidis of this world either. You are somewhere in between, and if you do anything at all, try and get closer to whiteness.

That was not my fault that it happened to me, but I need to own the fact that it did and what it did to me as well as what it did to "coloured" people generally. "Coloured" people in the new South Africa practice racism toward black people and even now want to place themselves closer to white people. They have to own that and recognize that. And everybody in South Africa was affected one way or another. It is not enough for us to try to forget the legacy of apartheid. We must own that legacy and the benefits and then act on that ownership through positive actions.

If we do not do it in actions, then this home and the children in it can be socialized in the same way as I was. So I have to go out of my way to make sure that people of other racial groups naturally pass through here so that my children relate naturally to all. That is one action that each family in South Africa could do, but there are lots of people who will say you cannot force that kind of thing. They say, "I have nothing against them, but why should I have them in my home?" You say to them that it will be better for our children. Otherwise you are passing on the same prejudice of society, the same pattern of behavior. Reconciliation in the new South Africa will take us much longer if the homes do not change.

FROM WHAT I READ in the papers, the benefits of the Truth and Reconciliation Commission for black people were in terms of hearing the truth, in actually knowing what did happen, of actually being taken to the sites where loved ones died and to receive the dead back and to go through traditional ceremonies in order to properly mourn. To say goodbye and know that your loved ones rest in peace. That is a benefit. But beyond that, I do not know!

I AM NOT SURE about the inclusion of so many religious persons on the Commission. It depends. If you have someone on there who is religious with the right kind of contextual theology rather than the "cheap grace" theology, then it would be very helpful. Cheap grace theology says that so long as you say you are sorry I expect nothing more of you. That is more of a hindrance than a help. The general impression I got was that the people who were on the Commission were more into that: so long as you can get people to repent and confess, then success had been achieved. I think that for me that process was in some ways too narrow. I would have liked to have people who will tease out this whole concept of *metanoia*. What is reparation? What are you going to do to show the confession is real? And that is sad.

Craig Williamson walks away free. He vilified me in a disinformation pamphlet published in Botswana and distributed globally that put my life at risk. He can obtain amnesty by simply saying, "Yes, I did that." People who were involved in a raid that killed three of my friends in Gaborone can just say, "I am sorry" and it is all over. Where is the reparation, and where does it help those who earnestly *are* sorry? I think that if there were people who were sharper in the process even of how the hearings were held, it might have taken a different form and contributed more to the process of reconciliation. It aggravates me at times.

I feel hurt by the amnesty process but have to confess that, for myself, I have not been able to think of any other way we could have gone. It feels unsatisfactory to me, unpalatable. It is not about revenge; it is about the doing of I am sorry. Reconciliation from a religious perspective differs from the secular at that point. It is not enough to put everything out on the table and say this is it and that is acceptable: now we can go ahead as if nothing ever went wrong. As I say, the leftover feelings about what did go wrong are still there.

Some white people are still saying, "O my God, what do you want of me now in opening up all this stuff from the past?" and "Let us leave it and go on." And some black people are saying, "Well, I have an RDP home and it is better for me and I do have water which I didn't have before and certainly even if life is not better for my children surely my children's children will catch up."

THE CHALLENGE OF WHAT NEEDS TO BE DONE is not being heard, and I think, from my perspective, nobody is doing very much. People are talking about the need to do something but nothing has happened. And the talk is almost like flavor-of-the-month talk. This is the thing to talk about now, but what happens next is not action but merely some new phrase or catchword.

We talk about the TRC process not going far enough, but what do we do to face the issues in our denominations and our communities? How do we move beyond the church? How do we deepen an understanding of reconciliation? How do we get groups of white and black people together so that we can come to a common understanding of the prerequisites for this kind of reconciliation?

We need to get people together if only so that some people may better understand why some of the things that are happening in our society are happening now. How do we help people to understand why South Africa has been a crime-ridden country for thirty years or more? How do we help people to stop treating crime as a new phenomenon? This is especially important if that is what is causing so much of the division and lack of reconciliation.

When the Group Areas Act was passed I said to my church—I was only a student then—that instead of building in the new divided areas and instead of having overseas support for church extension programs to cope with the Group Areas Act, we should invest in buses so that we move people to where we want them to be together. That would ensure that this division, polarization, and indeed collusion with this act does not happen within the churches. I said it then. What are we doing now?

Bryanston Church remains Bryanston Church. It is a world very different from the Soweto United Church. There are two worlds of two sets of Christians, and it will remain as it is until we do something practical and not just talk about it. How do we get a meeting between those two congregations, for example, to a point where they understand what is happening in our society? There is need for this in our own churches, let alone the whole nation.

What is needed for us Christians to move toward reconciliation? The church is doing nothing. My own denomination produced a pastoral plan for transformation. What transformation? What was the pastoral element in this? What does it mean in congregations? What do we transform toward and what did we transform at all? Or does it stay another jargon word? It could have meant so much if approached contextually, but it seemed to be acontextual.

Churches seem to want to reach out to bring in more people in order to cope better with their financial needs, and that has nothing to do with transformation for me. It may have something to do with it at the end, but there is something far more fundamental than that needed. After the TRC finished I thought that there would be ecumenical attempts through the SACC or Institute for Contextual Theology to set in motion a process to do what the TRC was unable to do. We can at least make an attempt.

The churches need a new discovery of each other as black and white people in South Africa at the church level so that the people who go through such a process can be ambassadors for reconciliation as disciples in the wider South Africa. Nothing formalistic and facile and public, but something that has greater value at the ground level, at the grass roots. We must influence more and more people who will in turn influence more and more. It may be only to simply challenge and say, "Excuse me, but where did you get that idea? Is it true?" And pass on information such as, "Did you know, for instance, that in the last year of apartheid under the de Klerk government the national debt was increased by sixty billion, and in our last budget we paid 50 billion just on interest?" What could we do with that money if that had not happened? We complain about crime and services. What could this country have done with so much money?

Giving people the ammunition to deal with what has happened is part of helping them own what has happened. Black people need to own up to the fact that we have internalized the idea of white superiority—so much so that in the new South Africa we are not saying "Yah, Baas" anymore but we are saying it inside! And white people are no longer saying "Hey, boy!" but they are saying it inside their heads. It comes out in simple things like my questioning a white contribution even in the church. The attitude is, how dare you! Do you not know that the white way is the best way and the white contribution is the one that really helps? It is hard to get out of your role, in the same way that men treat women. They are not allowed to assert themselves and question us because then we accuse them of becoming aggressive and getting out of place, and they ought to know that they should not question men in that way. That is the ideology of male superiority.

It is through those behaviors and the change in those behaviors that reconciliation can take place. If it can be done ecumenically, fine. If it can only be done denominationally, also fine—or even just in one or more local churches and local areas.

I THINK THAT RECONCILIATION in the way I have mentioned it can only be at an individual level, and blanket amnesty can cover too many people. One has to ask, how many ills will it cover at the same time? I find the concept extremely difficult.

THE REV. DR. MAAKE MASANGO

Thursday, August 19, 1999

And something that is healing me is to see black and white children in the morning holding each other's hands as they go to school. I just raise my hand and say, Lord, you did it! We have been nurtured for forty years by hatred of others. And here are children holding on to each other as they cross at the traffic lights. Caring for one another, smiling. That is a blessing. That is the future. If these children can grow with a different nurturing, as they are, then healing will come.

MAAKE MASANGO is the black Presbyterian minister of a predominantly white church. He has been Moderator of his own church and is a Vice-President of the South African Council of Churches. The slight American twang to his voice gives away his place of study.

I THINK THAT FOR ME, dealing with healing ministry in terms of psychotherapy, reconciliation has been part of the scenery in bringing people to reconcile with each other, psychologically, emotionally, and spiritually. So I have been dealing with that in family therapy.

My understanding of reconciliation is first to recognize that something is not right. And if something is not right, as a psychotherapist the first thing I ask myself is, what is the red flag? And once I get to the problem I diagnose it. Then I can create healing structures and steps on how I am going to deal with it. Then therapy can begin. Healing is a two-way thing. It includes psychological problems as well as theological problems. And the theology is addressing the psychological problems, not the other way round. So theology says, these are the problems as we see them, for you are dealing with the image of God that has gone wrong.

And as you try to dialogue with that person, you try to heal that person by giving them strength where they are weak, and as they borrow strength from you reconciliation begins. It is a very serious understanding. If you move with them there does come a time when you have to say, "Wait a minute, where do you want to confess and repent before we go on to forgiveness?" This is because human forgiveness has to do with the damage that has happened. And if the damage is there, if it is not confessed, if it is not told out, there can never be the forgiveness, which leads to reconciliation.

The one who is injured needs to tell the one who has injured, to tell them how they felt when they were robbed of their dignity. In terms of the South African situation there are many who have gone through traumatic situations of humiliation because of the color of their skin.

I have had to face this myself. I was invited to do a program of reconciliation at the Top Security Company in Hamanskraal. As I walked in I saw that one of the guys there was the one who had tortured me when I was held in Pretoria. They had moved some blacks into the meeting, and there was a lot of tension between the whites and the blacks. So I immediately said, "Guys, I am coming to do reconciliation, but I have always had a lot of anger against you, Hendrick." And Hendrick said, "I don't know you." "I will help you," I said, and I told the story of how he tortured me in prison in Pretoria. My God, he was shocked. I then went on to say that before we could proceed with the whole thing he and I needed to reconcile.

The whole group was shocked. He wanted this to be our private thing. I said no, this thing is part of the community. I have come to help heal this community. You wounded me, and until you and I reconcile there is no way I can help heal the others. We need to be reconciled first. Then if you and I are healed the community process has already begun. That, for me, is the dynamic. The story must be told. When you speak about reconciliation you must know that there is the victim and the victimizer. And until the victim can claim and have enough strength to speak out his private story that has been silenced for so long, there is no way we can go for reconciliation. The other must receive it and, even though it is painful, he must deal with it. As they dialogue the process of reconciliation begins. It must include confession.

It begins with the victim who claims his story and tells it out. Perhaps the other will not know that he has offended, or may have an idea but would not know the depth of the hurt and how much he has wounded until it is shared. That is deep reconciliation.

The Bible is full of these things—Joseph facing his brothers, for example. But, for me, that is how reconciliation happens. It is more than dialogue, it is relationship. It is relating to one another through the problems that we face together, going toward a solution that will be helpful for us both.

So it starts with the shared history. And once that story is out it is no longer my story. It is our story. It is our story, and that's how reconciliation should be.

THERE IS A DIFFERENCE between religious and secular approaches to reconciliation. The religious approach holds the image of God as we move into reconciliation. The Christian holds the King of Kings, Jesus, who came to reconcile us from sin and who came to reconcile us with one another.

The great command is to love your neighbor as you love yourself. And you cannot give love if you have not reconciled with that person. So you must have good enough love in you that you would love yourself and be able to confront that which has tried to destroy you. As you pour love outside of yourself, it then brings the presence of Christ who is the reconciler and redeemer.

The secular would say, "We have got to work with each other. We have got to tolerate each other. We are in a factory together. Therefore, for the sake of the company and our jobs we got to put aside our differences here at work." But the religious way says you cannot just do that. Before the sun sets you have got to go and reconcile with your brother before you come to the Lord's Table. So it is a command of Christian living, a command about your lifestyle, about Christian values. It includes bringing the other who has fault, who has fallen short of the glory of God, into fellowship with you. So you have the command and the belief system that you believe. And if you believe in that system you have got to act it out in the way the Master has acted it out.

Secular may even go to the point of payment for being reconciled. Religion will go three or four miles without being paid, and that makes a difference.

WHAT IS NEEDED is that people take stock of themselves in the new situation. Let me personalize it with myself. I came back to South Africa after many years in the United States. People were already beginning to work toward the new South Africa. But I had not been part of that. I was still in the bondage of Egypt. For an example, I saw a black and a white holding each other and I got frightened. This guy is going to be arrested! I had not moved with the country and what was happening in preparation for the new way of living with one another. So there is need for a kind of self-diagnosis. It is important that each of us look into ourselves and try to discover where we are blind and what needs to change. So I am discovering my racism and when I see black and white I still say, waawoooh!! But I am being cleaned and that is what is needed.

The second step, as I see it, is that we must regain the place of spirituality. We spend a lot of time and energy on the political prophetic ministry in the church, and there is a deep need for spiritual ministry. It is in spirituality that we will be able to gel with each other in worship and our living together. If we worship having the hang-ups of our political problems, we will not be able to unite in spirit in the church. The church is going to have to face spiritual journeys. This creates a healing of the spirit, of the soul, so that the soul is freed. When the soul is freed color will not be a problem of politics, but it will be a problem of seeing the beauty of God in our different colors. That is a crucial part that the church has to play.

The church fought for liberation, and after that we were confused. We did not know what to do. The enemy was gone. We could not pinpoint the enemy. Then we realized that people were hungry for the Word of God. People were hungry, and the spiritual strength and morality were no longer with us. Hence we have rape, we have abuse and crime. People are empty in themselves, and many are trying to find power that will help them live real lives. That is another level in which the secular would not have the power to heal, but the church would have the power to heal.

The religious role is crucial in our country. I am talking not only about Christianity but also about Hindu and Muslim. For Christians there is this added difficulty, as we have to learn to receive the Muslim and the Hindu without overshadowing them. We come from a history where Christianity overshadowed these other religions. We need to ask ourselves about the gifts that these other faiths have for our nation. Mahatma Gandhi used to say that if the people of the Bible lived according to the Bible they would be changed. We need to hear what is said from people of other faiths.

THE TRUTH AND RECONCILIATION Commission was very helpful. One of the greatest experiences for me was to attend the opening session of the TRC as a representative of the church leaders. Then I subsequently went to several of the hearings. I even had the privilege of counseling from time to time when the going was tough.

Spiritual leaders have a great privilege. People entrust them with their own stories, with the hope that confidentiality will be held. They are able to pour out their soul to us. And as they pour out their soul, their story becomes our story. Now what I saw in the TRC was that people were heard. And as people were pouring out their stories it also opened up the wounds of those who were listening. The difficulty was that they did not know what to do with their own pain that was invoked by the pain of others. Much help was needed, and is still needed, there.

Secondly, it brought the truth out of the silent mute world into a communal world. Then we were confronted with either punishing or forgiving. Our TRC experience was beautiful. It helped us not to move for punishment but to seek the truth, and it is the truth that will set us free. That was the justice in it. People were no longer having nightmares. They began to understand what had happened to their children. The Nuremberg trials were painful. They were more for justice and punishment, but they did not reconcile the souls. Ours began with reconciling the souls and moving into forgiveness. This was to prepare the nation to tolerate and live with each other.

We could have had a blood path. It was by the grace of God that this machinery moved on. In part this is because when the political leaders were arrested the religious leaders took on the leadership and journeyed with the people. That was a blessing in itself.

And at the TRC the prayer and worshipful atmosphere meant a great deal. Desmond (Tutu) was in trouble with the people who said that he was making the TRC into a religious thing. "Do not pray," they said, "observe a moment of silence." On one occasion when they tried that he shouted out that something is wrong, let us pray! The atmosphere changed immediately. Then there were those times when the pain was excessive and people would begin to sing. They sang songs that were healing. That was another way in which the flavor of it uplifted the people to God more than to secular. The setting of it was the greatest, and I think it is a gift that we have and that we should give it to the Lord.

I am giving a paper at a meeting of the World Council of Churches on the weaknesses and the strengths of the TRC. In it I speak about how genuine it was, and I am telling the story of an old man in Alexandra who had waited so long for this moment to tell his story. I think the TRC was a gift. It is our gift to the world. Ireland says, tell us about it. Rwanda and the whole world say, talk to us. And we have to take it in a spiritual way of healing the soul, mind, and body. It is not just healing the soul or just the mind or body. There must be wholeness about it. Even though the past will not be forgotten, healing has taken place in the soul, in the body, and in the mind. This gives us the possibility of looking forward to the future.

It provided a much needed preparation. Now what is needed is for the church to take it seriously and lead the people on a spiritual journey of continuing to nourish the soul. In worship, in Bible study groups, and in various organizations we must begin to move the people to another level. Then they will move to a deeper level of spirituality which will bring back those Christian values of respect and humility.

WHEN I TALK about white people accepting any kind of responsibility for the past, I need to talk of a black ministry in a white church. This was a very conservative church. We now have about nine to ten percent black members, and if we take the congregation in Alexandra together with this we are almost forty-five to fifty-five percent.

How did I come here? I was working at the Presbytery Executive. I was able to visit the churches, and I did a lot of ministry with this church, St. Giles. I knew how conservative they were. When their minister left, the session met and decided that they must call a black minister to help them move into the future. They actually began to talk about that in 1994 so that when their minister told them at the end of 1995 that he was moving they had already begun to talk in that way. They turned to me.

They made some important decisions. One was to call a black minister. Two was to agree that if any of the members decided to move they would be called to the session to give account of their reasons. They would be given transfer certificates but fellow colleagues would be alerted. That was crucial for me, and when I saw what they had decided I thought I could now come to this church. It was a turning point. But I was still working in the Presbytery. There was an old lady who kept calling me to say, "We want you. We have done what you wanted." I was getting tired of her calls. Just to get away from her I said that if she could get the signatures of seventy percent of the church members I would come. She came with 84.2 percent. I had to come.

The difficulty that I experienced straightaway was that they lived in fear. We were reaping the elements of the old government propaganda that said the ANC and others were communists. So they had the idea that communism was taking over and religion was going to be destroyed. That was one major problem. The miracle of the election helped in a way, even though, as you know, the shops were cleaned out. They confessed to it later. They had cleaned out the goods in the shops out of fear.

The good part came when I was inducted. We had to have a service of farewell to those families that were going. I had to do it. Five families were going. There was one lady, the only one who said that she did not want a black minister and that is why she was going. That was the truth. The elders were hurt. But I was excited, because here was a Christian speaking the truth about why she was leaving. She was an elderly lady and she was leaving because a black minister was coming. The others hid behind things like saying there is a big distance to travel and things like that, which did hurt me. It hurt me much more than the old lady telling the truth. My session could not understand me. I was excited because she spoke the truth in love. I had a suggestion. We told those who were leaving that we would have this farewell service where they would receive their disjunction certificates. Just as we welcomed them in a worship service we would say farewell in a worship service.

There was an interesting part. Two kids were in my confirmation class. The parents wanted to pull them out. They refused. They said that they wanted to be confirmed. They made a compromise and said they would move after their confirmation. They stayed when their families had gone and then later made the move themselves. A colleague called to say that if they were running away from me because I am black he was not prepared to receive them. And I told him the story.

That is the process. It is the process of experiencing the pain, but not holding it to yourself—sharing it so that the pain is not yours alone. The community now shares it, and then the community can begin to deal with it.

I saw a young man who was abusing his wife. And as he was trying to hit the wife, men and women neighbors gathered round the house with their pots and pans, which they banged and banged. They did it to stop him. That is the dynamic that we must not lose.

I have learned a lot about the different ways we do things, especially in going through grief and death. When I heard about the first death that came I dropped telephone and drove to the home. When I got there they said that this was a family time. I said no, you are hurting and I am here. That is my Africanness. Where there is pain you do not wait to be invited. But I have also had to learn to respect their privacy as well.

These were new things for all of us. The question for me was whether I was I going to lose my Africanness and act as a white person. That would cheat them of the blessings that the African community can bring. Those were the difficult parts.

Then I said to them that Alexandra is very close but you have never been there. I began taking two or three with me to experience what it is like there. And now the Alexandra people close their service once a quarter and join us here to worship. They come and participate with us and at communion the people are served by both black and white. The people say that they did not know about Alexandra. And so next year my program is to treat them as one church. In that way we are moving on. And, for me, this is the continuing process of reconciliation.

WHITE PEOPLE generally have not accepted their responsibilities. That is obvious. I have invited the ministers around here in the ministers' fraternal to look at our model. It has to start with somebody. Somebody has to say this is a model that we have.

Some of the people are happy until they are hijacked or when crime invades their life. Then their anger shows, and they get back to "them and us" feeling again. But the ministry that the white church has to experience is the healing of feeling. There is a lot of fear which leads them into suspicion, which then makes them not to trust, which then contradicts the Christian being. How can you love the Lord and find it difficult to love your neighbor? It is a very challenging message that the church has to preach to help the people move into the area of sharing.

If we had bishops we could have them say that so-and-so will go to that church and so-and-so to that. We could make sure the churches have those ministers who share a different experience of life and faith. But we don't have that system. We have to work in a democratic way in which people are prepared for change and sharing. I think that it is help for those white people who have not moved to be told the stories and shown the models. For example, in our denomination we are using Lesley Morgan[1] who made a submission to the TRC as a white bystander. She moves around among the churches to share her story. That has helped as she tells her story in the context of worship, preparing the hearts of everyone.

AMONG THE BLACKS there is a lot of anger. Some are extremely angry that in spite of everything that has been done there are no reparations. They get angry when the government says they will have a ten percent increase and that they will spend millions on the President's House, but when it comes to reparations they say there is no money. Then we have to ask about the priorities. For us in the church we need to address the issue of priorities.

There has just been a big fire in Alexandra and many people are homeless. So we took some people and went there. We sent money to the Council of Churches to buy blankets, food, and other things that are needed. But it is not enough. We need to go and worship with them. We need to be there and share their pain with them.

And when we were there we experienced something that is frightening. We were there with the blankets, food, and all. Then along comes some guy who shoots in order for the people to run, and then he and his friends will take the things for themselves and sell them. And the minister turns round and says, "You will have to shoot us before you take one." There is the gospel in action. If only people could experience it and understand. They complain about crime without any idea of what crime is really like in the townships. It was there before it came to the suburbs. That is a ministry of its own.

We need creative liturgies, liturgies that really address the situation. Sometimes on a Sunday I will ask if anyone has been damaged that week. Once someone told us about a boy, a matric student, who had been shot. We prayed for that kid, and we wrote a letter and sent it to him and his family to let them know of our prayers. It is important. Then the following week we get news from Alexandra to say that someone has been shot there. People learn that it happens all around and that we need to take care of all the people. It should not be one-sided.

When you do that in the liturgy, in the worship and prayers, it makes it meaningful for the people. It touches their lives where it matters. I try and get people to tell their stories so that it is *our* worship and not a one-man band. Our liturgy has to reflect what is happening in our lives and that is what is happening.

Last year one of our members was leaving. He said it was my fault. I asked him to tell his story, and he told about being retrenched and how all the jobs are now being given to black people. He said he was going to England for at least two years to try and do something and hoped that if he came back then there might be a job for him here. The idea of sharing does not humiliate him. The idea is for people to hear and to share. I told him that I was very sad. We laid hands on him and told him we would continue to pray for him.

That is what I mean by liturgy. Share with people and get people to share. I think our worship on Sunday or our Bible study should be a place where healing takes place—healing of fear and of anger. We must allow people to share what the week has been like for them and only then pray. My idea is to share all I do with them, and then I ask them to share with other people. This is how the good news is spread. The good news does not have access to the media. The media is full of crime. Somehow the Christians have to sow the seeds of what God is doing.

YES, IT WAS A GOOD THING to have many religious persons on the TRC. It was in many ways a religious experience and needed those people to help it on its way.

WHEN WE LOOK at what the church has to do I think of our position here at St. Giles. We are in the midst of three synagogues. We are struggling to relate to the rabbis. One of the things we are struggling with is this Jews for Jesus movement. We invited Jews for Jesus to come and lead the Tenebrae celebration. We wanted to experience it in the Old Testament way. And the communion in the Old Testament is very powerful. But it frightened some of our colleagues and caused tension. We have to relate to our Jewish neighbors. Some people seemed to use the Jews for Jesus event for their own ulterior motives.

We have to relate to the Jewish community and also to the Muslim. We need to learn about the Hindus and experience their way of doing things. We may not agree with them, but an experience together will help us to come closer to one another. We have had Jewish young people come to experience our worship. It helps us to be sensitive to one another.

The black and white reconciliation situation has begun. It may be filled with tension and it may provide conflict, but it has begun. But we have not even thought about the Jews. We have not even begun to think about the Hindus. There is much we have to learn, especially for us here among such a predominantly Jewish population.

Reconciliation is a priority in the Presbyterian Church. We have our Justice and Social Responsibility division in which Lesley Morgan has a half-time position. She has really been stirring the church. We are saying this position is vital because it sharpens the ethics, the morals, and our Christian values and helps us see the social problems that we're facing.

But we still have to deal with some of the apartheid legacies in the church, the skeletons that still haunt us. When I came into the ministry I was paid R75,00 per month. My white colleague was getting R400,00. I had to pay R10.00 for the pension fund. He did not. These tensions from the past have to be faced, and we have created structures to do that. The church still has to look at its apartheid symbols. This is part of our plan for reconciliation.

I look forward to times when other white churches will call black ministers. It is easier for a white to minister to a black church than the other way round. People like me are very few. And when black ministers are called to white churches it is as assistant minister, not the senior position. We have to face that issue. Our church is one hundred years old. I was only the sixth black moderator. Ninety-four of them were white. These are our legacies that must be faced. It is not enough to say we have changed. We have to acknowledge that past as well.

I have a problem with the idea of a blanket amnesty. It makes people not to face reality as individuals. It is a corporate thing. It blankets everybody and it shares it as if we are a community. When you are in an African community and you have done something wrong, you are ostracized, you are isolated, and you are rejected until you confess. Then the corporate comes in. When you confess, the issue belongs to all of us and we are all concerned in creating the new way.

But individuals must accept their responsibilities before we have any blanket amnesty. That is the problem I have. It makes the person not to stand in front of the community, and confess his or her own sin.

ONE OF MY TIMES OF PRAYER at the moment is when I leave the house to come to this church. I turn off the car radio and I pray.

That's a spiritual zone for me. And something that is healing me is to see black and white children in the morning holding each other's hands as they go to school. I just raise my hand and say, Lord, you did it! We have been nurtured for forty years by hatred of others. And here are children holding on to each other as they cross at the traffic lights. Caring for one another, smiling. That is a blessing. That is the future. If these children can grow with a different nurturing, as they are, then healing will come.

NOTE

1. See the interview with Ms. Lesley Morgan in this volume.

BISHOP PATRICK MATALENGOE

Monday, August 23, 1999

And now the religious community has to be very, very aggressive. If we really mean it we have to be the first to reconcile among ourselves to show we do take it seriously.

PATRICK MATALENGOE is a bishop of the Church of the Province of Southern Africa. This Episcopal Church, in communion with all other Anglican churches throughout the world, is one of the largest Christian denominations in South Africa.

Bishop Patrick was one of the first people we interviewed. He is not in charge of a diocese but is the Coordinator of the Programme on Truth and Reconciliation for the South African Council of Churches. This seemed an appropriate place to start. He is diminutive in stature but huge in his concern over reconciliation. We met in his office in Khotso House, the "House of Peace."

WHEN WE TALK about reconciliation my first concept would be the Christian concept that Christ died upon the cross and by dying he reconciled man to God. But further along, having accepted that reconciliation with God, we do become the ambassadors of reconciliation. That should be the church's everyday task. If that task had been fulfilled in South

Africa the Truth and Reconciliation Commission would not have been required. The Commission became necessary because of the failure of the church—the whole church.

THERE CANNOT BE TOTAL RECONCILIATION without confession and forgiveness. My approach is always to believe that I have to forgive myself first before I can reach out to the other person. That presumes an acceptance of having done wrong—only when I accept that can I forgive myself and reach out. If I have not done this then even the attempt at reconciliation is going to be empty. And what do I do when the other person says, "No, I do not want to be reconciled to you"? Then I become angry and hurt. But if I know what forgiveness is for myself, I can reach out, and if the other refuses it is still okay for me. I am not damaged.

Where does the process begin? I think it can come either way. If we look at the Commission you discover that some people began the process for all concerned when they admitted fault. Let's take an example. One bishop I know got up without being pushed, and he talked about his own involvement and how he was so very sorry. Where the Commission was difficult was when it was so legal and people were told that on such and such a day you go and do this and say that. You could sense the anger when being asked questions by the lawyers or by the Commissioners themselves. The anger remained with both victims and perpetrators. It can come both ways as far as I am concerned.

THERE IS A DIFFERENCE between a secular and religious concept of reconciliation. I really agree with the person who said that the Commission was a civil commission that hijacked Christian terms. Those terms continue to be used in the debates about reconciliation. But I now divide that academic debate and discussion that has to go on at that level from the Christian task of helping the process of reconciliation itself. We, in the church, must be seen to be ministering to our people, to their pain and to their hurt. The discussion still goes on at a secular level with Christians taking part in it, but Christians must be seen ministering.

THE TRC HAS CONTRIBUTED to national reconciliation, I think, in that they have brought the truth to the fore, and strictly speaking, when we see why the Commission was set up they have done their work. But now we are at another level and need to aim for reconciliation.

The Commission could not do that. There were only some few and very small signs of actual reconciliation within the context of the Commission—a number of experiences of people saying sorry for what they did and others being ready to forgive.

But forgiveness is not cheap, and it is good that most of our people are saying, "I don't forgive you." That is good. Forgiveness is not cheap. Forgiveness must always be coupled with some kind of responsibility and reparation. So when someone says, I am sorry I killed your husband or your son, the question is about the cost to the victim and the need for something to be done about that cost. Perhaps the victims need to say, "Because of you I do not have a husband, my kids are not educated—and if I am going to forgive then I feel that perhaps you have to look after me for so many years. Then I will be prepared to forgive when I see you do something about it."

If the victim just says, "I forgive you," then you are both losers. Neither gains from that. It is cheap reconciliation not worth the name.

National reconciliation needs another step in which the perpetrators engage themselves in reparation. And the perpetrators include all who readily accepted the franchise. If you take the people who had the franchise you will find many who say, "I never voted" or "I did not support apartheid," but the thing is their children still had a gain because of the color of your skin. Because of that it is not only the actual perpetrator who needs to make reparation but also all the people who have gained from this inhumane system. I would be happy with a tax for everybody that is from that skin color and perhaps extra from the perpetrators.

I WOULD SAY there are a percentage of white people who have really acknowledged the wrongs of apartheid. Some have made their statements to the Commission. Others did not go to the Commission but have made their own moves to do something like share their skills with those who suffered. There is the example of one man who is an engineer who has trained black engineers and business people out of his own time and energy. But it is not enough. The percentage of this kind of person in the white population is about 5 percent—very few—a lot are in denial. They say, "Let's forget it ever happened and get on with our lives."

SURVIVORS HAVE BENEFITED by hearing the truth and now knowing the truth, sometimes coming face-to-face with the killer of their loved one. Some individuals have benefited by having their children or husband re-buried. Once I went to the border of Botswana for a service at a place where young people had died. Toward the close of the service the mothers of these comrades took up earth and talked to it: "I am taking you home." So it has helped in a way but not enough, and many people still want to know what happened to someone they loved. They will not rest until they bring their remains home.

PERSONALLY I SEE that there must be reparations of monuments and memorials. But more than that the victims must really be symbolically at least supported. To what extent I do not know. We must not make them get into a receiving mentality but a small amount would be of help both practically and symbolically.

I THINK THAT IT WAS HELPFUL for the credibility of the Commission to have a large number of church persons on the TRC; otherwise the TRC would have been seen as a very civil thing like all other commissions.

AND NOW THE RELIGIOUS COMMUNITY has to be very, very aggressive. If we really mean it we have to be the first to reconcile among ourselves to show we do take it seriously. There are churches where salaries are not equal and churches whose pastorates and manses are different. The manner of appointments has not changed. White-to-white churches and black-to-black continues. If the church really believes in reconciliation, that would be one of the first things to see to. Let us begin doing this.

Once that begins happening people will see for themselves that the church means it and is doing something within themselves for South Africa. But the church has failed people. For instance, when you go to the city churches here in Johannesburg it is all black membership—the cathedrals, Methodist City Mission, etc. If the white members who used to fill those churches are moving into other churches in the suburbs, why are they being received so easily and not being challenged to stay and carry out the ministry of reconciliation? I think we are squandering the opportunities that God is giving to the church.

I believe the church needs a vision of a reconciled community. Does the church have such a vision? Do bishops, church leaders? I do not know, really do not know. Sometimes I doubt it. There should be projects established by the churches to help people meet and engage one another. Instead of playing games with our people the church should begin teaching the truth about what happened and what continues to happen. We need to ask the whites, "Do you really know what this thing has done to our brothers and sisters? Do you know how they lived and live?" Why can't a congregation have people who will go and live in areas they do not know and live as normal as possible, like the people do there? Live in the small houses, travel the distances, take a taxi or use their car, if it is not stolen, and then they will have a real feel of the wrongs that have been done. I am sure that not all would turn their back but would have a great experience, which would leave an indelible mark and help them understand what was caused by apartheid. There is a great need on behalf of whites to learn what happened and continues to happen to black people.

WHAT IS THE TASK of the churches? We talk so much about reconciliation and renaissance in our country. The government can make all these pronouncements but unless the people at grassroots know and really practice the dream it will remain a dream. And I believe that in the whole of South Africa the best organization suited to this is the church. But we need to be visionaries. Bishops and moderators and other leaders need to be visionaries—but they are not because they are responsible for the programs and priorities of the church, and these have not changed. Why? I do not know.

The Roman Catholic Church at least started a language school so that priests could be helped to learn other languages. We have not learned from the Catholics. I mentioned the need for learning other languages at every Episcopal Synod I attended from 1976 to 1986 but nothing has happened. Teach the students one other African language—we have not done that. We need to speak the language of the people. Instead the church continues to reflect the society in which we live—still separated and still using the same excuses about language and culture.

THE SOUTH AFRICAN COUNCIL OF CHURCHES does put the resources we receive from outside the country into the hands of the churches for reconciliation programs, and they seem to be using the SACC. But we have to ask how serious the people really are because they do not match those amounts with their own church resources. Most would like to turn their backs on the reconciliation programs, especially church leadership. We had a meeting last week, and all local church leaders were invited to be present. Not a single one was there. The Anglican bishop sent a representative from his office, but otherwise right across the board there was no one there from among the church leadership around Johannesburg. The people who come are those who always come—the ecumaniacs who attend all SACC meetings—outside of that no one. It is the same with black and white churches.

Most churches are putting their energy at maintaining the status quo. We need to give them a vision, but if you say, here is a workshop, they do not turn up and if you send them a book they throw it in the wastepaper basket. Just small groups are interested. You have to ask, where is the church going to be in ten or fifteen years? No one seems to bother so long as they have their buildings and salaries and are able to do their day-to-day thing.

I would say that for me that is the church of yesterday, and it is not the church for tomorrow. The church needs to change its vision so that it can be seen as really ministering to the people and giving the people a reason for living. We are not doing that.

What is so difficult is that the vision during the days of apartheid was fixed on helping get rid of apartheid. Many closed their eyes and ears, but for the most part that is where the energy went. Now that big wall has fallen and we do not know what to do. It was so good to get rid of apartheid, but now we need a new vision and recognition of the new challenges. A new South Africa needs the church. There is no other sector of society that has the network and structure to help the people. The Jews, Hindus, and Muslims cannot do it. They are too few. The church has to do it. And where do we begin as churches? We cannot act without acknowledging our part in apartheid. Each church needs a truth commission of its own—to speak to one another and get at its own truth. We must *be* an alternate society to show it in action rather than in words judging others.

A ND BLANKET AMNESTY? It must not happen. It is a no-no. It would take away from the good work done by the Commission. It is not on.

MR. DAVID MATTHEWS

Monday, September 27, 1999

I am working very hard to try to get the children to respect one another; to try to negotiate when they have a conflict, not simply to hate each other; to try to listen and see and understand, or try to understand where the other person is heading and allow people to be different. I don't think reconciliation is abandoning one's values; it's maybe a tolerance of somebody else's.

౭

MR. MATTHEWS is the Head of the Tiger Kloof Institute near Vryburg in the Northern Cape. This missionary-based school has recently reopened after more than a thirty-year closure through apartheid legislation. Both he and his wife, Hilary, are striving to create a learning environment relevant to the new South Africa in which both academic and practical subjects are covered.

Although some distance from Vryburg itself, the confrontation between blacks and whites at the Vryburg High School, which has resulted in violent clashes involving parents as well as students, has demanded response from staff and students at the Institute. I have to admit a personal interest in the Tiger Kloof situation, as I was responsible, as a young missionary, for the final services held around the closure of the institution as an apartheid "black spot in a white area" in 1963.

IN RECONCILIATION I believe we are talking about a very tender, vulnerable, and deeply personal process. So our self-esteem, our self-confidence, our wish to achieve an uncertain goal, is all-important. As an educator I must try to prepare young people for life. Whether in Ireland, where I have been, or South Africa this must include a preparing of the soil of the mind for reconciliation. I am certain that reconciliation will not happen by chance. It will happen because those seeking reconciliation are not threatened by the risks involved, but are encouraged and driven through their awareness of the riches that lie within it.

Whether we are children, old people, or young adults, we are less threatened by differences in cultures if we are pleased to be the people we are. If we are open-minded and if we know who we are, by which I mean that we know about our culture, our weaknesses, and our strengths, we are able to respect others.

We can prepare the ground for reconciliation. We cannot make it happen. I think this is demonstrated again and again by the Truth and Reconciliation Commission. We cannot make it happen.

The fear of insecurity inhibits the generosity which is an essential ingredient to reconciliation. In South Africa very few are neutral. Most carry baggage that makes us insecure where reconciliation is concerned. The fear of losing one's identity, dare I say the fear of losing one's hatred, has to be overcome if reconciliation is to be won.

IN SOUTH AFRICA, as indeed in Ireland, confrontation is violent. We are people who seek confrontation almost as a solution, although it is no solution at all. One of the things that I feel that I have got to try to do as an educator is to introduce children to dealing with conflict differently. Conflicts invariably end up with a fight. This is the way they have always seen conflict resolved. We have got to start encouraging them to negotiate. We have got to start encouraging them to listen to what is actually at issue rather than simply fight. If we can start that in schools I think we are laying an important foundation that could alter behavior patterns and attitudes. It could affect how they set up their homes, how they solve their domestic problems, or how they solve the issues between one section of society and another. I think it is a hugely important role for schools because I am sure the solution and hope of this whole reconciliation process lies essentially with the young.

I am working very hard to try to get the children to respect one another; to try to negotiate when they have a conflict, not simply to hate each other; to try to listen and see and understand, or try to understand where the other person is heading and allow people to be different. I don't think reconciliation is abandoning one's values; it's maybe a tolerance of somebody else's.

I would be bold enough to say that we have the structures in our society for this reassessment of conflict. Conflict is essentially a stimulating and challenging thing. We mustn't regret conflict. We can say that conflict is an enriching process, a challenging process, not an undermining process. If that is the case then conflict resolution, conflict management, is further underlined as a very important part of education that possibly has been neglected.

A N INTEGRAL PART of the curriculum here at Tiger Kloof will be community service. I wish that could happen at all schools because the amount a child can actually learn in addressing issues within the community, especially its own community, is enormous. They learn, above all, that they are not powerless. So many issues do not require money. They require a helping hand. That is something they do have, and it could be an important step in reconciliation when you reach an understanding about someone who is even more vulnerable than you are. Whether it is working with the aged or with the very young, our children gain a great deal from community service.

W HAT IS THE ROLE of the church in this educational process? I think the structures are there, but I am worried at the moment as to the role being played by the church in this whole matter of conflict resolution. If I look at the churches here in Vryburg, I see an Anglican church in Vryburg that is mainly occupied by whites and coloureds, and I see an Anglican church in Huhudi that is occupied by blacks. I see a Methodist church in Coleridge, and I see a Methodist church in Huhudi. I don't see the church bringing what must be, or should be, like-minded people together. I know there are linguistic problems and all that sort of thing, but if, in practice, the different congregations within our individual churches are not being brought together on any circumstances or at any time in common worship, I believe we are entrenching and reinforcing our differences.

I am not even talking about meetings between one denomination and another. I am talking about the self-same church in the one town that has three to four different congregations who know nothing about each other. There seems to be very little common endeavor to reinforce what is common. Instead we continue to reinforce our differences. That is a great pity. There is a structure in place that is not being used.

I am very worried about what seems to be happening in schools. The church is playing no role in public schools. At least, if it is playing a role in public schools and public education I do not know about it. It's rather like the call I remember hearing so often in South Africa that we must keep religion out of politics. That leads to keeping religion out of schools, out of education. That is backside to the front. It has got to be entirely the other way. If religion has an impact on the way in which you behave and conduct your life, religion must be in politics and religion must be in schools. Religion must be part and parcel of our very lives. It is not something that we pack away on Sunday afternoon and then pursue whatever we want to do during the course of the week.

If we are going to change people's attitudes so that they don't bring the baggage of the past with them, the church has to take its role very seriously. It should be playing a role in education and not outside education. The church cannot say that this does not belong to it. It concerns the church in a very important way.

Apartheid gave the church a role. Many churches directed all their endeavors against apartheid. In this post-apartheid period the focus is less clear. And focus is hugely important in terms of your faith influencing your life and the way you behave. If the church does not encourage that to happen then we become insignificant. The church has got a huge role to play in education and the morality of the people.

IT WAS GOOD that there were a number of prominent religious persons on the Truth and Reconciliation Commission. If I had had any part in the selection of such a team I would have done the same. People of faith have given some thought to philosophy, and I would have thought, therefore, that they would be better prepared to encourage and foster reconciliation than a businessman would have. I did not feel that it was put together with the wrong set of people. I just thought the task was enormous. Reconciliation is not something you can make happen. It has to be encouraged.

IT IS HUGELY IMPORTANT that the children have a faith. I am not saying what that faith has got to be, but that we would respect and nurture that faith and try to help make that faith part and parcel of that person's life. This school is not exclusive to Christian children. It is entirely open to the community. We have just one Muslim child and we hope we will have more. Quite clearly our heritage is Christian, but it is not exclusively so and the school is open to all. This is an important aspect of the school in comparison to its time as a missionary endeavor of the mission society. It was debated very clearly and the decision made after a great deal of thought. South African society has to rid itself of exclusivity in any form. There will be no reconciliation without that.

As AN ENGLISH-SPEAKING SOUTH AFRICAN, if I've got to identify with a particular people, I am very sorry about the role the English played in the Anglo-Boer war. I really am very sorry. I think the English-speaking people could not have been more arrogant and self-enriching than they were. They had no regard for anybody and they trampled them underfoot. I think that contributes hugely to where the Afrikaner finds himself. It contributes to how the Afrikaner handed out similar treatment when he was in a position of governance. They had received dreadful treatment and they handed out dreadful treatment. They were not able to separate the two.

So I think that if you are going to review critically where you are and what you trying to do in terms of reconciliation, then repentance must happen. Otherwise I do not see how one is going to critically analyze and say, "Ouch! That is a huge mistake." And that does not mean throwing stones at each other. It means I am just trying to identify and be honest about my heritage.

I think the TRC was an essential ingredient in reconciliation in the nation because it made many people aware of a process they hadn't considered before. You can't just carry baggage and baggage forever.

Would you like to comment on the current Vryburg situation, which seems to indicate an impasse between whites and blacks?

In regard to the Vryburg situation I need to go back to where I believe some of the fundamental errors were made. That may help to untangle the knot. Vryburg High is over one hundred years old. Vryburg High, rightly or wrongly, is a bastion of Afrikanerdom. It was a center of security for farmers sending their children into boarding school. This was a school they had worked at; it had a heritage, and this school belonged to the Afrikaans-speaking people.

Then 1994 comes along, and one of the targets of the black leadership in Vryburg was Vryburg High because it is a bastion of Afrikanerdom. Now we have two groups of people. One is trying to preserve something and the other seeks to demolish it. I think you have got to bear that in mind as a precursor of where we are coming from. I think there were some errors made by the administration. There is nothing in the constitution that says Vryburg High cannot exist, or continue to exist, as an Afrikaans medium speaking school. But the education administration of the Province decided to make it not so. They said it has got to be a parallel medium school because it is now going to have some black pupils attending who want to study through the medium of English.

So, we now have Vryburg High School as a parallel medium school. The children of the Afrikaner farmers are in the Afrikaans set. The black girls and boys who attend are in the English set. It becomes a parallel medium school with one part populated by blacks and another populated by whites. This results in two schools in one. It is not a mix. It is not a healthy position.

We can still have a different solution. I hope very much that real effort is being made to address the real issue. I wonder whether they should say that we acknowledge that we have this parallel medium school, but we can re-think that in about three years' time, and Vryburg High will be an Afrikaans medium school only. It will be open to all people who wish to study through the medium of Afrikaans. Then it will have black, coloured, and white children attending on equal terms and going into the same courses. But to have two schools in one actually reinforces racial differences.

It provides the context for the sort of confrontation that we have seen where people accuse one another one hundred percent and do not accept any wrongdoing on their own side. Do not let us say that all the guilt is on one side. That is another point I feel very strongly about in terms of reconciliation. I don't think you get reconciliation if you see the whole blame on one side. If there is an innocent party and a guilty party, then reconciliation is very difficult. In fact both have got to admit to some guilt. It is a two-way traffic. If they both admitted to that guilt then there is a possibility of some reconciliation. But unless you have that two-way traffic I think it is very difficult to get reconciliation.

PROF. PIET MEIRING

Tuesday, August 31, 1999

A number of white people ended in very deep despair. Some emigrated outwardly and they left the country. Some emigrated inwardly. They just withdrew themselves from society. We find this in the church even now. The Afrikaans churches suffered from an identity crisis. They have withdrawn themselves.

PROF. MEIRING, a Dutch Reformed Church minister, is a professor in the Department of Religious Studies at the University of Pretoria, where he is known for his sharp theological intellect. He was a member of the Truth and Reconciliation Commission's Reparation and Rehabilitation Committee.[1]

I HAVE COME TO REALIZE that reconciliation is a very costly thing. It is easy to speak about it and it is wonderful if it does happen, and it did happen during the days of the TRC from time to time. There were beautiful instances of genuine reconciliation. But I think we have to rewrite Bonhoeffer for South Africa, not in terms of the cost in Nazism but in terms of the cost of reconciliation.

The prerequisites for reconciliation are that there should be truth, there should be justice, and there must be some sort of meaningful restitution.

In practical terms in South Africa, to really have justice after everything that has happened is, in a sense, impossible. The whole amnesty process takes the legal idea of justice away. But people must feel that justice, in terms of the process, remains important. Justice has to be recognized even if there is amnesty. The amnesty arises out of pure grace. In South Africa, not only in terms of the Truth Commission but also in terms of the future, people must be able to know what happened. There must be a feeling in the country that there is justice. If the amnesty process is seen as taking away justice, it must be balanced with proper reparation. One of the major problems we face is that it does not look as if that is going to happen.

Restitution is so important. Tutu often jokingly told the story of a man who stole a beautiful golden pen from somebody and then after many years came back and said, "I'm sorry. Please forgive me." And the man embraced him and said, "I forgive you, but can I have my pen back!"

I think that many people who profited from the past, especially white people but not exclusively, should be ready to give the pen back—to give something back to those who lost so much. Reconciliation has everything to do with restitution. I don't think that retribution is a necessary prerequisite but restitution is important.

ABOUT HALFWAY THROUGH THE LIFE of the Truth and Reconciliation Commission a long drawn out argument developed within the TRC on what reconciliation really is. It was one year into the life of the TRC that the Commissioners realized that they were doing a lot in terms of truth, but the concept of reconciliation was not being given enough attention. I remember long debates in the Pretoria office about this. What do we do? What should we do? What are the needs for reconciliation? The real point, which I did not realize at that stage, was that there was a huge discrepancy in the definition that people had for reconciliation. We differed on the definition.

On the one hand, you had the lawyers and politicians. They took a politico-judicial line. They said do not expect too much of reconciliation. If you can just arrive at the stage where people stop fighting one another, when the dust settles in the streets, when things are sorted out in a judicial sort of way, then be very grateful and thankful. That is reconciliation enough.

Then we had all sorts of variables on the continuum right up to the very far end where Archbishop Tutu and the other ministers and a number of Commissioners who were really committed Christians stood. They said that when you speak about reconciliation, the term is so loaded religiously, that you need to fill it with a religious content. Tutu often said, and others identified with him, that true reconciliation has everything to do with 2 Corinthians 5. Once you are reconciled to Christ, that gift from God to reconcile us with him, then there can be proper reconciliation. And Tutu unashamedly used that throughout the course of his work. He said, and I think correctly, that South Africa is a religious country and this is the wavelength people operate on. If you speak about justice and reconciliation and truth, these terms are so loaded that you can only really work with them when you see them as a religious process.

But there was a huge discussion. In the end I don't think it was clearly resolved. When you read the recommendations you find that some reflect the more political and judicial concept of reconciliation, while others, especially those addressed to the faith communities, speak of a really religious concept of reconciliation.

There is a rather amusing story about Desmond Tutu at the beginning of the Johannesburg hearings in April 1996. Some of the Commissioners were concerned that the proceedings were "too religious" especially in opening with prayer. He was asked not to pray at the start of the hearings but rather to have just a moment of silent meditation like they do in Parliament. The Archbishop said that if that was the way they wanted it he would do it that way. On that first morning we opened with silent meditation. We all closed our eyes and had a half-minute or so of silence. Then Desmond told us to sit down and we sat down to start the day's proceedings. It was clear that he was not happy. He pushed his papers all over the place onto this side and then that side and eventually said, "No, this won't work! We really cannot start like this. People, close your eyes, we are going to pray." And then he prayed properly and I think we even had a hymn. Then he smiled and said, "Now we can start!" The majority of people on the Truth Commission had high sympathy with that, but there were some who had problems with it. There was this difference.

O F COURSE IT WAS HELPFUL for there to be religious leaders on the Commission. The churches were so involved in getting the process going. The South African Council of Churches was so involved in thinking through the process and drafting some of the initial material. It was only natural for some church ministers to sit on the Commission.

It goes without saying that many of the people in the ecumenical movement in South Africa should have been there. The ecumenical contacts were so helpful. In the hearings we were totally dependent upon the local churches for briefers and for statement takers and to see that the whole local process went ahead in the best way possible. The church contacts were so necessary.

It was more than organization, though. In the eyes of the majority of South Africans there was a religious undercurrent to the whole process. So in the organization, providing a necessary dimension in the flow of the TRC, even in devising the report and in the ramifications of the committee itself, the religious participants did play a part. That is, of course, a very subjective viewpoint as I was one of them.

I experienced that the people on the Truth Commission were very warm toward me. They bent over backward to make it possible for this Afrikaanse Predikant, coming from the horrible examples of the past, to be part of the process. The first week or so I was a bit conscious that they were looking at me with a wooden eye. Who is this man? What will his role be? What does he want here? But very soon I was taken up and embraced day after day, literally and physically and spiritually.

W E GOT VERY MIXED SIGNALS from the white community. These came from the Afrikaans- and English-speakers. In the end they didn't differ that much. The Afrikaans-speakers were more in the limelight because they were the obvious supporters and sympathizers for the previous regime. They profited very much from apartheid and many of the perpetrators came from their ranks. The signals were mixed. On the one hand, a number of people, and churches and congregations, really wanted to go through the process of trying to understand. They were ready to listen and to ask themselves the difficult questions. On the other hand, there were many people who were not interested at all. They laughed at the Truth Commission or were angered by it. And they were not touched by its results and final report. That goes for perpetrators who did not want to go for amnesty. And it goes also for the rank and file.

For two and a half years, every Sunday I was invited to speak in churches, mostly in Afrikaans churches, and most of those were good experiences. People were critical from time to time. So when, for instance, I went to the Free State I knew what I was in for. But usually people were willing to listen and gave me time to answer the difficult questions about guilt and about what should be done, but unfortunately it is also true that many people chose to switch off the TV programs about the TRC at night. They did not want to be confronted with the truth.

There are different reasons for that, some because they feel guilty, others because they did not like the whole process. There were some that felt awkward with the process. My work, as the Afrikaans dominee, from time to time was to liaise with whites who needed to come as victims to the Truth Commission. Some of them came. Others wouldn't come. I remember there were a few families in the Louis Trichard/Messina district who we really wanted to appear at the Commission because they were victims of farm raids and of landmine explosions and they suffered a lot. They would not budge. Each of them said, "Do you want me to come and sit in front of the TV camera and cry before the whole of South Africa? That is not my style."

We used to try to explain the different reactions from the white community, especially, I suppose, because it went against our hopes. Maybe we were a bit starry-eyed in the beginning. Then someone who taught us about crisis therapy helped us by teaching us about existential crises. Somebody is in an existential crisis when they are in a process where nothing can stop it from happening—imminent death or terminal illness, divorce, or the death or illness of a child. Then they are in an existential crisis.

There are a few classical stages people go through, and the therapist must try and analyze or understand at what stage the person is before he can help that person. Those stages are very telling because it seems to me that those are the stages most white people found themselves going through. The first stage is that of disbelief, of denial. The second is that of anger, and the third stage is that of rationalization, bargaining. The fourth stage is of deep despair, and only then can we move to the sort of adult stage of acceptance, of having worked through the process. It seems to me that many of my friends, my own people, the church, and I felt it for myself; we are going from one stage to the other.

The first stage was really that of denial. In the newspapers and all over the place people said that surely this is just propaganda. Surely it is exaggerated. And then came the anger. I think of the politicians, like F. W. de Klerk and the others. Their reaction was that of anger. Then there was the bargaining. People say, okay, it is really sad that bad things have happened, but was it really that bad? Doesn't every country in the world have its dirty tricks department? Don't the CIA and others do similar things? And you must remember that communism was a real threat and a total onslaught was real. There was a lot of bargaining going on. It still goes on.

A number of white people ended in very deep despair. Some emigrated outwardly and they left the country. Some emigrated inwardly. They just withdrew themselves from society. We find this in the church even now. The Afrikaans churches suffered from an identity crisis. They have withdrawn themselves. They are not sure whether they should involve themselves in this community anymore. Fortunately there were also people who remained with the process of the TRC and who themselves were healed by that process.

I suppose the different groups would be about fifty/fifty. If I were gracious and generous I would say sixty/forty positive. I think the worst thing is not that people were really positive or were really negative. The largest group was the middle group of people who were not really part of it at all. That is a problem, and they can be swayed from one side to the other side very easily.

At first the NG Kerk (Dutch Reformed Church) was very positive toward the Commission. They were even at the point of proposing a few candidates, but when the first reports came out they withdrew. Then there were long discussions. Should we or shouldn't we? Do we have to go to the hearings on faith communities? Some wanted it and others not. There were difficult discussions. At the end, when Ds. Frik Swanepoel, the moderator, went to the TRC he went with the unanimous blessing of the whole church. And when he reported back last year to the General Synod on what he had said, there was high appreciation for what he did.

What are the Afrikaner attitudes toward former leaders P. W. Botha and F. W. de Klerk and their refusal to either appear at the TRC or admit to any wrongdoing? Generally, Afrikaans people laugh at P. W. Botha, *die groot krokodil* (the great crocodile). They find him amusing and also a little bit annoying. But F. W. de Klerk is fallen from grace. Not, maybe, because of the Truth Commission so much as what happened in his marriage. It is a pity that F. W. didn't retire in 1993 just prior to the election. He would have been held in high regard.

People laugh at the antics of *die groot krokodil.* They say, "Well, he is an old man and you can expect that from him." They are very disappointed with F. W. not only because of his marriage but I think it also has to do with his leadership since he became Vice-President. I speak for myself when I say that I hoped that in the spirit of things F. W. would play another role than he did. And to many thinking Afrikaaners his appearance before the TRC was not good. It was an angry appearance. It was not an appearance in the spirit of reconciliation.

The problem is that many Afrikaaners are having a difficult time at the moment in identifying with anybody. We saw this in the recent election. All my life every Afrikaaner was dead sure where he wanted to vote—up until now. And in this election, right up to the moment people dropped their papers in the ballot box, most of them, myself included, were not very sure where one should vote. We felt that we needed to vote to show our responsibility, but there was very little enthusiasm for any party. I think many would have voted for the ANC but they said, "No, the ANC is too strong. They already have nearly two-thirds majority. This is not good for any party." But the other parties were scattered. The more enlightened people wanted to vote for the Democratic Party, but the DP had quite another image in the months prior to the election when it became, in a sense, a very *verkrampte* (right-wing) reactionary party.

The reaction of the English churches was very much the same as the Afrikaans. I was invited to share with some of these, and they were also split in their response to the Commission. Lesley Morgan is a wonderful example of an English Christian who really took the process seriously. Hugh Lewsi, who was a member of the TRC's Human Rights Violations Committee, got very angry with the English-speaking people. Lesley Morgan is *not* typical, he would say. He said that the Afrikaaners were at least honest about it. If you like it you say so and if you don't like it you say so. But he was angry with the English people and their lack of involvement and response to the process.

THE PROPER ANSWER to the question about the benefits of the Truth Commission to the victims and survivors will only come in a few years time. Again, there are different views. If you ask the members of the Khulumani[2] groups, they were critical of the results. But if you speak with the ordinary people who came to the Commission from time to time to tell their story, it gave you a lump in the throat the way they really seemed to experience the Commission as something special.

It seems to me that the vast majority of people, more than 90 percent of the people, especially those who came to the public hearings, were grateful for the Commission. They felt the cathartic experience to be helpful. They said they were healed and the tears were tears of healing. But as time went by and discussions started on reparations and people's expectations grew, the numbers changed. People said that we have had the truth and it was wonderful to be able to tell our stories, but now let us see what there is in the process for us and for the country.

I am really very concerned about the government's seeming lack of enthusiasm to get along with reparation. The first criticism against the whole process was from people who said that amnesty was unfair to the survivors, to the widows and the orphans. And the answer time and time again was that it is necessary for a number of practical reasons and for idealistic reasons, but it will be balanced by proper reparation. The bread and butter will be put back in the mouths of the orphans and the widows. But it has not happened.

THERE IS SO MUCH for the religious communities, especially the churches, to do. In the NG Kerk we took the recommendations of the Truth Commission to our committee and used them as a basis for our discussions. At the end we were trying, maybe without explicitly saying this is what the Truth Commission asks, to propose similar things. It seems that on a national level the faith communities, the churches, all of them have a large role to play. It could be a symbolic role in the sense of bringing people together, of devising ceremonies and liturgies for reconciliation itself.

We know very well that what we want to propose and what we want to do can really only be taken up once we have discussed them with all the other churches. Many of the ideas are not the prerogative of one church, especially not the Dutch Reformed Church. Many years ago they said that the Dutch Reformed Church did not accept invitations, the Dutch Reformed

Church invites. We don't want that any more. We cannot be like that any more.

For instance, we are suggesting an annual day of reconciliation. We have held long discussions about whether it could be on Good Friday or at Passover or should it be on the Sunday nearest to December 16, which is officially a national Day of Reconciliation. We believe it will be helpful to have this special day to fix the thoughts of our people on reconciliation. It needs to be discussed with all other churches, for them to discuss and, hopefully, own it.

We tend to think that the real process of reconciliation needs to be at the local level. We want to involve local churches in mini Truth Commissions. We are exhorting them to have as many meetings as they can with other people, listening to their stories, telling their own stories, sharing with one another. It is necessary to try to network and to create bonds between people.

We also know that other things need to be done. The proposals of the Truth Commission on the things that the church owns are important. The church has land and structures. We do hope that we can sway our church to do some things and set up projects. We need to help our people in terms of a proactive way of doing something with land and doing something with church facilities that would help the whole community. During that process I hope that some of the land will be given back to the people.

IT WAS SUCH AN INTERESTING THING to me to realize that Christians do not have exclusive use of the process of reconciliation. We do not own the patent rights to reconciliation. It belongs also, going back to the deepest roots, to the Jewish community, the Muslim and Hindu faiths, and to traditional African beliefs.

There are a number of building stones that we can use from the different faith communities to build the wall of reconciliation. They really differ and complement one another. Chief Rabbi Cyril Harris, for instance, told us that Christians speak about reconciliation in terms of the love of Christ. The Jewish faith, he told us, speaks of reconciliation in terms of justice. There are different aspects of reconciliation we can hear from other faith groups. Everyone has a very special contribution to make.

BLANKET AMNESTY may be necessary at some stage but I would say not now. It would make a farce of the whole process and of the pain of those people who did apply for amnesty. But my main concern is that if they want blanket amnesty they can have it only when they have started the reparation process in a meaningful way. If the real victims feel that they are being taken care of and that they are being seen, then I think we can talk about blanket amnesty, but not until then. I really wish and hope that the President and his office and the others will start working on reparation.

NOTES

1. See Piet Meiring, *Chronicle of the Truth Commission* (Vanderbijlpark: Carpe Diem Books, 1999).

2. These were nongovernmental organization groups intended to help victims and survivors deal with their trauma.

MS. LESLEY MORGAN

Monday, September 20, 1999

I go to lots of conferences where we talk about reconciliation and everyone says, "Yes! The faith communities must do it," as though the faith communities are okay. And the faith communities are not okay. There is entrenched racism and all sorts of difficulties within different denominations and groups. This is right across the board, Christian, Muslim, Jew, or whatever. There are huge difficulties and I'm very aware of them.

LESLEY MORGAN is a member of the Uniting Presbyterian Church of Southern Africa. Describing herself as a white "middle aged, middle class, South African housewife," she made a personal submission to the Truth and Reconciliation Commission.

RECONCILIATION IS IMPOSSIBLE! But, I am a Christian so I believe that through God all things are possible. Reconciliation means very different things to all of us, being different people. Initially, when I started working in this area about two and a half years ago, my concept of reconciliation was tied to a simplistic black-and-white issue. Blacks and whites had to be reconciled to one another. But the more I've worked with it, I realize it's not only about these issues but also about gender and sexual orientation and so many varied prejudices that we all carry. All of us that have grown up in this country are tainted by the apartheid system where everyone was put into neat little boxes. It's hard for us to break out of those boxes. I always thought reconciliation to be most difficult for perpetrators and bystanders. We are the ones who have to acknowledge doing wrong and repent and that's difficult for us. But I've also come to understand that it's very, very difficult for victims and survivors. The cost of forgiveness is so great.

I myself wrote a submission to the TRC in June 1997. Since then so many black people have come to me and said, "You moved me," or "I was touched," or "You challenged me." It has not always been supportive. I've been challenged. Some people have said, "How convenient that you are sorry now, but where were you in the last forty-eight years?" I accept that. But the majority have come up to me and said "You moved me" or "I was touched by it" or "It challenged me" or "It really made me think," and then have said, "I so nearly came up to you while you were speaking to embrace you and say I forgive you." And my question is, "What stopped you?" Even as we are speaking there's a hesitation.

I attend many conferences and workshops. Many black people ask, "Where are our white brothers and sisters?" which is a huge problem because white people are not coming forward. I attended a conference that the South African Council of Churches organized. I was the only white person there and the response was the same. I said to them, "Here I am. Are you ready to listen to my repentance? Are you ready to deal with my shame?" I think often when you've been deeply hurt you think if someone comes along and says they're sorry it'll be okay but in fact it's not. Reconciliation has got to take place deep inside you. You've got to let go of the anger and the bitterness. That is hard.

And I have come to understand that, because I was abused as a child, sexually abused by a member of our congregation over a period of three years. And I know that I've got to forgive that man because I know that until I do so I am less than whole myself. But it's very hard to give up that hurt because it's very familiar to me. So I can understand some of the difficulty that people who have been traumatized through apartheid have to go through, especially how difficult it is to let go of it. So that's where I am now in understanding reconciliation.

There is the need of acknowledgment of wrong and that is a big part of it, but it is not the only part. There is the need for forgiveness and the creation of a new spirit. Reconciliation is not only about economic issues and adequate health and housing and equal opportunities, although those things have to be addressed. But it is about repentant hearts and forgiving hearts. I can repent away to my heart's content, but unless someone forgives me there is no reconciliation. So it is very costly for all. It is very costly for all.

There cannot be reconciliation outside of faith. A secular form of reconciliation is not possible. I really believe that religious organizations and the faith communities have to take ownership of this reconciliation issue.

And there is a difficulty there, of course. I go to lots of conferences where we talk about reconciliation and everyone says, "Yes! The faith communities must do it," as though the faith communities are okay. And the faith communities are not okay. There is entrenched racism and all sorts of difficulties within different denominations and groups. This is right across the board, Christian, Muslim, Jew, or whatever. There are huge difficulties and I'm very aware of them.

At our Presbyterian Church of Southern Africa[1] Assembly last year our Justice and Social Responsibilities Division proposed that the first reconciliation initiatives must take place between the ministers, and then, as a follow-up, reconciliation initiatives should be within and between congregations. That proposal was not accepted. The ministers said that they had retreats and everything is okay. And I know we're not okay. A lot of black people hold enormous anger and misunderstanding. And among white people there is enormous anger and misunderstanding. It has got to be dealt with.

Will the union between the two Presbyterian churches help?

I think it is going to act as a catalyst for something. It changes the racial balance within the church. I am all for it, yes! But having said that, you have to be aware that there are tensions between the black ministers of the Presbyterian Church of Southern Africa and the Reformed Presbyterian Church.

The PCSA, like many churches, has a Black Forum. I do not have a big problem with the idea. I think black people do need to have an area where they can talk on their own. The problem I have with the Forum, and I am not speaking out of turn because I have spoken to many of the members, is that it has existed for fifteen years and there seems to be little empowerment for our black people so that they can take leadership roles. I see the same ten black names on every committee within the denomination. This means that they are spread too thinly and they cannot do the job properly. So some whites say, "Look at black people. You know they can't do the job we need doing." On the other hand, black people say to me that if they do not accept the positions then whites say, "You see, black people do not want to take office." So they are on the horns of a dilemma. There is very little discussion about it. We are still very polarized.

I THINK THE TRC did contribute to reconciliation. I am very supportive of the TRC and the whole process. I think the problem is that there were many difficulties with the Act, especially in the actual function of the TRC. My understanding also is that nobody expected the overwhelming number of people who wanted to tell their stories as victims and to apply for amnesty. There was a belief that maybe a thousand or so would come as victims, maybe a few hundred for the amnesty. But there were thousands for both. Over seven thousand amnesty applications are a lot. They were not geared for it. They just did not have the resources for it in any area.

I realize that there had to be a finite time for the TRC, but my feeling is that it stopped a bit short. And, of course, the big problem now is that there is no follow-up for the victims. I am hearing that it was excellent, a wonderful process for people to go and tell their story. It did help enormously at that time. But nothing else has happened. It has been a year since the report came out. Government has not said anything about reparation. There is a big difficulty there.

A lot of the victims feel that they have been let down by the TRC, notwithstanding that the Commission made it clear to say that reparation was not for them to decide, only to make recommendations. Victims are feeling very disempowered as a result of this. They had to give up their right to civil or criminal prosecution. They felt all along that the Commission was very perpetrator-friendly, and now there is nothing coming out of it in the way of reparation.

I need to get back to what I was saying about forgiveness. It concerns me, and I've voiced this concern at meetings, that the expectation seems to be that if victims get some money it will all be okay. And it's not! It is about more than that. There are spiritual and psychological elements that must be taken into account.

What if they do not get any money? And what if in some township this group of people is declared victims and that group is not? There is already a divisive element coming into it. And what if I get emergency reparation and you don't? And how do you decide on how much money to give? What is it worth for the fact that my whole family was incinerated in a shack or my husband was shot dead? I do see the difficulties, but I still believe the TRC helped the process of reconciliation. I know of many instances where there was a lot of anger and resentment, and very powerful things happened to bring healing and peace.

VERY FEW WHITES have accepted any social or personal responsibility for what happened. Very few! And I understand that. It's enormously shaming to accept such responsibility. I watched the TRC hearing on television and it just appalled me. I did not think it could be possible. There is a strong denial in all of us. It is not that we do not believe what has happened. It is just impossible to think that this has happened so close to us. How did we not see this? But these awful things did happen. And we have to admit the problem of the religious communities' part in all this. Some gave open support to the apartheid structures and others gave tacit support. We are left with all of that to deal with. And even now we have things like a huge disparity in stipends. It still exists.

There is a huge element of shame in the white community. And that's very difficult to deal with. And so often our black colleagues do not help. I went to a conference on racism within the churches, and I have to tell you that I left that conference so battered and bruised and tearful. I cried for two days and eventually went for help to try and work through the experience. There was a lot of anger, a lot of anger. I felt that my voice could never be heard except through the walls of apartheid. Is everything I say going to be always transmitted through that experience? Will you never hear what I'm saying and not what you perceive me to be saying? I was helped to get through the experience, but it is hard.

One of our ministers who happened to be at that conference said that when he is with white people he is made to feel inferior. I told him that when I am with black people I am wary because there is a perception about me because of my race before we have even had any conversation.

But white people are very tardy about acknowledging this. And I keep on saying that it is such a liberating experience. Do not be afraid, I say, just work through the fears. But there is a lot of shame and a great need to acknowledge it.

Most white people want equality. They want black people to be uplifted and have access to all the things we have, but not at any personal cost. There is no personal sacrifice involved in this. Yes, I want people to come out of the townships and have a decent education and be able to go to the best hospitals and clinics, but not if I have to give up my house with its three bedrooms and a swimming pool. There is no sacrificial element. This is why we've got to get back to a spiritual understanding of reconciliation. We must accept that there is a cost to reconciliation. That cost is not only spiritual and psychological, but there has to be some kind of financial cost as well. And it cannot just be a one-off tax amount but a continuing payment to help bring about equality.

I try to do something myself. I help facilitate healing of memory workshops where we try and get people to start that reconciliation process. I work with groups. I try to put something back into society, but I am well aware that it is still not really challenging. It is still within the range of what I am able to give. There is no real sacrifice involved in it. We don't want to give up our home down at the coast and our annual holidays in the Game Park. We don't want to give that up.

I had a paper sent to me from the United States about white privilege and male privilege. The woman who wrote it works at a women's university. She deals with gender issues. She says that even the most liberated male, while acknowledging that there is oppression and disadvantage, will not acknowledge that men are over-privileged and over-advantaged as a result of their gender.

It is quite interesting—this invisible knapsack of privilege that we carry around by virtue of our skin color. There are things that we take for granted, buying houses wherever we want to, for instance, and being free to take something or leave something. Or when we do something we do not represent our race. If we eat with our mouth open or we don't answer a letter people do not say, "Oh, you know, all white people are like that." But they do say such things about black people.

There is a lot of work that needs to go on individually. Reconciliation really does start here. It is a question so often of what am I prepared to let go. Too many of us in religious communities simply say that God is over us all. But which God? I listened to Paul Smith, a black American Presbyterian minister who was very active in the civil rights movement in the sixties with Martin Luther King. He said that he really had to recreate God in his own image. He understood God at first to be a white male and as such he had absolutely no relevance in his life at all. We need to talk individually about our God.

WHEN THE TRC WAS IN PROGRESS I think a lot of victims benefited enormously. It was very painful and difficult but it was cathartic. It was helpful. But that process has slowed down, and they are just left with having told their story, and they are still living in poverty. They continue to have physical and emotional wounds.

I am trying to get both ministers and lay people some traumatic counseling training. This is essential. There is a desire to try and help victims and survivors, but ministers particularly, possibly because they have some skills in counseling, are very wary because they know that they are not skilled in trauma counseling. You do need to have some basics in that. It just takes a long time. I have been trying for more than a year now. I need a place for the training and people willing to train them. I think that churches should be involved in trauma counseling. They have the facilities and they have people. We need space and time and training for willing people.

But I am sure that victims are certainly feeling quite let down now, quite let down. This whole process of applying for victim status is so slow. They have to fill in long forms and wait for a reply and then, possibly, fill in another form. It is so slow, and during this time their circumstances have not changed. They still live in informal settlements. They remain poor.

And there are many that still do not know what happened to their relatives. For those who found out the truth about what happened, the TRC was helpful. But there are a lot of people who made submissions to the TRC, and they still do not know what happened. I would have liked some sort of investigative team or committee to continue to work on the statements. But the TRC did not have the resources in two years to try and investigate as many as twenty-three thousand statements. It was impossible.

IT WAS IMPORTANT that there were a number of religious leaders sitting on the TRC. We are a deeply religious country. We may have been misguided, but this is a very religious country and there is a lot of support for the role of religion.

In the recent elections we were looking for observers and monitors for areas that were considered trouble spots or hot spots. It was hard to find an election officer because there was a lot of polarization in the community. Again and again, the one person the communities would agree on was the church minister. The church still has credibility in society. We should be utilizing that.

There's still hope. Maybe we got it wrong before, but God is on our side and there is still hope. So, yes, I do think it was helpful to have religious figures on the Commission. Otherwise it would have been very dry and analytical. Religious people brought spirituality and compassion and understanding. They brought the spiritual attributes that we actually need. If it had just been a secular thing it may very well have just deteriorated into a legal process.

I think it's quite difficult for us as South Africans to understand the full impact of the TRC. We are at the coalface, so to speak. A lot of foreigners think that the TRC is fantastic. These are people from countries in South America who have had their own truth commissions. They say to us that we do not know how lucky we are to have such an open record of the country's history. That record may be biased, according to some people, or not the whole truth. But it is a record. I was speaking to a young woman from El Salvador. She said that a whole period of her country's history has disappeared. There are no records of it. Gone! There is nothing written down about it, however biased or skewed it might be. There is nothing. We have these records and they are so important.

But to get back to the question of religious participation in the TRC, yes, I am a Christian, a religious person, and of course I would support their being on the Commission. Religious people do have a higher aim and purpose to look to and that is an important element.

In fact, the Truth and Reconciliation Commission process in South Africa is very much a religious process and we have to recognize that. This is one of the reasons that it cannot simply be exported to other countries because it depends so much on the whole religious vibe of the country.

I just wish the church would recognize that and seize the opportunities. Some of the groups I go to are of desperate victims and survivors that have got together. They are not there from any religious groups, but they start every meeting with a hymn and a prayer and they close every meeting with a hymn and a prayer. That, to me, is something very special.

THERE ARE INITIATIVES to foster reconciliation at grassroots level. I am aware of them. A group of us meet once a month with the very long-winded title, "The Gauteng churches' response to the TRC and the reconciliation process." Last year we organized a forum on reconcilia-

tion because people were asking what the churches are doing. We were actually overwhelmed by the response. It really was very well supported and very
broad-based. People are interested and want help and information.

In our denomination there is a township congregation and a suburban
congregation that meet once a month and have a meal together and talk to
each other. I know there are other initiatives. I have been asked to go to
Catholic, Protestant, and Dutch Reformed churches, for instance, to talk
about what I understand about reconciliation. I work with Anglicans and
Catholics and Lutherans and Methodists. Yes, there are initiatives and things
are happening.

But I do think that there is need for the higher structures of the churches to take ownership of what happens. Lots of our religious leaders sit
around and say that we must do something about reconciliation. But that is
where it stops.

They need to initiate things within their own denomination. Sending
out statements is not enough. We must all be active. We have suggested in
Gauteng that religious organizations, faith-based communities, should be
taking ownership of our public holidays. There are huge political rallies, but
why aren't we having huge church rallies? The Day of Reconciliation is a
God-given opportunity. Who does reconciliation if not churches and other
religious organizations? The religious communities really should be taking
ownership of our holidays and doing something with our people to bring
them together.

My own denomination does not put much into supporting this activity.
I work for Justice and Social Responsibilities, which has always been a Cin-
derella division of the denomination. We do have financial constraints. I get
a lot of verbal support, which is great, but I do not get a lot of physical and
material support.

The major task of the church is to help its members talk to one another
and to listen. We must listen to one another carefully. I think so many of us,
especially in religious communities, say, "We're Christians so there's no
anger and no confrontation. There's no conflict and we are all nice with one
another." And in fact there is anger, and when confrontation and conflict
come along it is very difficult to deal with because we think that because we
are Christians we should be loving one another. But conflict, managed
properly, can be very helpful, and we need honesty and the skill to deal with
the confrontation and conflict.

I DO NOT AGREE with the idea of a blanket amnesty at all. I just think it's too easy. A lot of perpetrators got a shock when they saw the TRC process, and a lot of them did scramble to apply for amnesty. But a lot have realized that in actual fact not much is going to happen. Somebody living in an informal settlement is not going to have the financial resources or any other sort of resources to prosecute.

I think people must be accountable. People are saying that you've got to have an end to the process at some point. I accept that, I suppose. But I would have a problem with blanket amnesty. I think too much will get swept under the rug.

What has been your own experience in working within the church and community groups on the issue of reconciliation?

I have found my work in the church very challenging and it has helped me grow enormously. I have always found it difficult to be objective or dispassionate about myself. But this task has given me such a better understanding of me and my faith and of other people's faith. It has made me far more tolerant.

One of the first issues raised was about the lack of white people going to the hearings, and I started thinking about that. I remembered that when the TV camera panned over the audience it would be just black people. I started wondering why I wasn't going to them, and I realized that it was just because I knew that it would be too painful and too difficult to just sit there and listen to all this pain. It was hard enough to watch it on TV, but to actually be there, where you can see the whites of their eyes, so to speak, was infinitely more difficult. I was afraid of what it would start in me.

So after a great deal of agonizing I made my submission as a bystander to the Johannesburg Central post-hearing public follow-up workshop in June that year. I spoke about my submission to the TRC at our Congress in 1997 where the Rev. Bongani Finca[2] came and did a wrap-up every day. I had quite a powerful experience there.

They had arranged for the Leeukop male prison choir to come and sing. I was fearful of what this would be like. Well, these guys arrived and I looked and they were actually everything I fear most. Here were murderers, rapists, black men, drug dealers, and car hijackers. Most of them are in prison for life. And then they started to sing! Ah! Their voices are amazing. They looked exactly what they are, hardened criminals. And I sat and I listened to them as they ministered to me and just for a second it was really quite a strange experience. God put me where they were standing, these broken people, and I looked out at the church and I saw myself and thought, what are you doing about who is your neighbor? I could hear it: "Who is your neighbor? Here is your neighbor," and I actually had to leave. I was really quite overpowered.

I was so overwhelmed thinking about reconciliation and the whole question of who is my neighbor. I now realized that my neighbor is just everybody. It is not just a black-and-white thing. It is about me as a law-abiding citizen and these lifers here who ministered to me. Here I am, the Christian, the church elder, the goody-two-shoes, and these guys sang so powerfully to me. They ministered to me.

And now? It makes people uncomfortable when I speak. I say that I am going to make myself vulnerable to you and that is difficult to listen to. If you're really going to hear me you have to make yourself vulnerable to me. And we all have our defense mechanisms and protection, and it's very hard, not only for us to break it down for someone else but also for someone else to let their guard down. It is difficult for people to do that.

There are always going to be huge difficulties that we can't get over, but we must be able to listen to one other and respect each other's opinions. And the church must claim its leading role in the whole reconciliation process.

NOTES

1. This interview was held just prior to the September 1999 Uniting Assembly between the predominantly white Presbyterian Church of Southern Africa (PCSA) and the all-black Reformed Presbyterian Church (RPC).

2. Bongani Finca is a minister in the then Reformed Presbyterian Church and served as a Commissioner of the Truth and Reconciliation Commission.

BISHOP M. PHASWANA

Tuesday, May 16, 2000

I discovered that people are very fond of revenge. If you hurt me I must hurt you in return. But where do we end this circle? It is a circle of destruction and it is a circle that must be broken. The TRC has given us an opportunity to break that circle of revenge and destruction.

♪⁓

THE SMILE IS WHAT I REMEMBER MOST. Bishop Phaswana is Bishop of the Central Diocese of the Evangelical Lutheran Church of Southern Africa. His office is in what is known as "Deep Soweto" and that placing suits him well, for he talks out of a deep concern for people, a deep experience of his part in the struggle against apartheid, and a deep sense of African culture and its part in reconciliation. There are still two Lutheran churches in South Africa. They work very closely together at denominational and personal levels, but the essential difference of "white" and "black" remains.

M Y UNDERSTANDING of the concept of reconciliation, religious as it is, is informed not only by Christian religion but also culturally. To give a very simple example: when our people realize there is something wrong in the family—it may be a dispute or a sickness like ordinary flu or even cancer—they quickly say, what have we done that has wronged the ancestors? Then they will think of slaughtering an animal which will appease the ancestors and that to them is reconciliation. So Christianity comes, as far as I understand it, to build upon that, to say over and above this slaughtering that you do, Christ has done reconciliation already. Christ has brought reconciliation between God and us and between us as human beings. We are also reconciled and Christ is the one who is slaughtered on our behalf.

W HEN YOU LOOK at Paul's letter to the Romans it says that reconciliation is not between Christians and non-Christians or confined to human beings: it is also creation as a whole. The whole creation is yearning for reconciliation. So for me reconciliation is holistic. It touches the issues of ecology, nature as a whole. In traditional western theology ecology was removed from the concept of reconciliation, but for me it is all-inclusive.

So the issue of religious and secular does not enter into our thinking, our African thinking. From an African perspective I am not a different person when I am at church and when I am at work. I am one person from Monday to Monday. Every aspect of life as we live it is lived in our totality—not as secular or as sacred but as a whole. Life is a whole, permeated by

God's grace at all times—when I jump, when I sit, when I sleep, and when I think God's grace permeates all of these and engulfs all of my being.

THE TRUTH AND RECONCILIATION Commission has sensitized people—let me say, even lawyers who are supposed to know and understand so much. For example, the lawyer who took my statement in 1996, she did not have any idea of what was going on behind those four walls of the prison. And when I related my story to her and I showed her my scars, which are still visible on my wrists even today, her first reaction was to ask how I could relate this story smiling and even joking about it. "What do you want the state to do to the people who tortured you?" she asked me. Then I said, "Nothing." She could not understand why. She was completely lost.

I discovered that people are very fond of revenge. If you hurt me I must hurt you in return. But where do we end this circle? It is a circle of destruction and it is a circle that must be broken. The TRC has given us an opportunity to break that circle of revenge and destruction.

When the TRC sessions started to broadcast live the testimonies of the victims, some white people realized that their neighbors, relatives, and friends did not tell us all because now we hear new things over the radio and we even see it on the TV. Some people began to say that what happened was wrong, and we cannot continue to be perpetrators and victims in the same society and hope to cherish our new democracy.

But there are still problems because many still see it like that. The world, for them, is divided still into black and white.

Some whites who had hardened their attitudes have now started to believe, especially when they heard the perpetrators confessing. When we spoke about the torture behind those high walls they could not believe it. It is so brutal that they said, "No, we belong to the white community. We could not stoop so low to treat people as barbarians; it cannot be done by us." And now when they see one of their own confessing they start to realize it is true. For some, that has brought to them a sense of being human—we are human beings capable of being used by either the devil or the Lord.

So now they are saying that they were taken for a ride. They realize that the government, which taught them and nurtured them through the apartheid state, has misled them. "This is our country of South Africa and we have nowhere else to go," they say. "It is better to come to terms with it, admit we have done something wrong, and own up to that and then see how we can move forward from here." I think there are a number of white people who are of that opinion. I have met them through the Lutheran Church.

It is interesting that since my inauguration as bishop there are some whites who have told me that they have come to realize that there is no point in remaining separate as white Lutherans and black Lutherans. Some white pastors visited me here in my office, and we made a very simple suggestion that it will be better to start with ministers fraternals where black Lutheran ministers and white Lutheran ministers come together to discuss appropriate issues. This is a very simple start to bringing us together as one.

The idea is also that as time goes on we should take some of our congregants along as well. We want the congregants there as well, because we have realized that the pastors, especially those younger ones who trained together, black and white, at the University of Natal, have a bond of being together. The wall of separation in this layer of the church is not that strong. But the white congregants are still thinking that they cannot be at one with those black people. This is because of the education they received through the years. I am thinking especially of those who are fifty years of age or more. Only a few of them have come to understand that we belong to the same Christ, say the same Lord's Prayer, and are fellow Christians.

THE VICTIMS feel that they have been doubly taken for a ride—victimized by the apartheid system and now by the government they have elected because the government through the TRC raised expectations of restitution. These expectations have not been fulfilled.

People were promised R3000 just as a start. There are a few who got it. Some of them are the ones who were tortured with me but I have not received a single cent. But I am thinking more of those who do not have any regular income at all. They were banking on that amount so that they could at least take their children to school and be able to buy food. When that money does not come they become extremely frustrated. They say, "What is the use of this TRC? We exposed ourselves. We told our story to the public and to the whole world and we have gained nothing except further pain and at times even a sense of shame. Why did I expose myself to the people and now there is nothing forthcoming, and yet the state spends billions to buy weapons?" It blows your top. Where is the priority of the state now? To its people or to appease the multinational companies who get employment at their homes through our buying of their weapons?

IT WAS EXTREMELY HELPFUL for me that not only were there religious people on the Commission itself but that religious organizations like the South African Council of Churches stepped forward to present themselves to the TRC. They shared the sufferings and the hopes that people have in the religious organizations. There was a sense of humility in the whole presentation. They presented recognition that we are feeble human beings even in an organization like the SACC, which was at the forefront of the struggle against apartheid. This sent a very strong message to the nation that we either reconcile to live together as brothers and sisters or we remain in our own separate cocoons and perish together like fools.

There are people who chose to see the TRC as a religious exercise, but the fact that there were legal people as well made it for me a well-balanced team. Together they created an aura of dignity and seriousness. When I made my own presentation as a victim Thom Manthatha was there and he was sandwiched by legal people. It gave me a sense of a body that is objective, a body that will let me tell my story in my own way without being judged a liar.

I appeared on October 4, 1996, to tell my story. Later I went to listen to my perpetrators asking for amnesty. I must be honest. I felt extremely angry because those who were presenting their applications for indemnity were not truthful. I felt even angrier because I had driven so far to hear my perpetrators opening up and being remorseful and repentant, and I did not get that at all. I was so angry. Later on there were others who testified and I felt they were really truthful. Three out of the five of the policemen who asked for amnesty were refused because they did not disclose the truth. Two did get amnesty and I felt vindicated, as I was supportive of them getting the amnesty.

I think the three who did not get amnesty should be brought before the courts. I am not so worried about myself but about the one, Mr. T. I. Muefhe, who died in detention. They were so quiet and did not even mention his name; they were so quiet about it, as if we did not know what happened. Yet when they tortured us they were boasting that if we didn't sing their song we would follow the one who died in detention.

IN SOUTH AFRICA we need religious organizations and bodies to be true to themselves while accepting the rights of others and cooperating with others. In South Africa we are so divided even along denominational boundaries. If I am to look at the Christian community in South Africa, which according to the latest census forms plus or minus seventy-seven percent, we are so divided, and yet when we go to our different denominations we all pray the Lord's Prayer. To me, that is a contradiction. When we pray "Our Father" we do it in our own denominations in our own small kingdoms, and we elevate those kingdoms, and they become the big thing in such a way so that if you are not a member of my denomination I do not look upon you as a full-fledged Christian. You must belong to my denomination.

And even when we belong to the same denomination we have scales. If you are a male or a female there is a negative division not acknowledging that when I am male and she is female we are God's creation. So we seem to divide ourselves. And then within our denominations we look to our tribal affiliation—not in a positive sense but in a negative sense, so that if you are a member of the Lutheran Church but you are Tswana-speaking and I am Zulu-speaking we keep apart, we keep distance. So there are a lot of challenges that we need to face as churches and as religious organizations to bring us together. Look at John 17 and the priestly prayer where Christ prayed that "they may be one." This togetherness does not mean that we cannot maintain our differences, but our differences should not be made to build walls around us. They should be a recognition, an acknowledgment, to magnify the name of God, that in spite of the different languages we speak, despite tribes that we belong to, we are one in Christ. Our differences should be used as complementary, like different colors of bricks used to build a beautiful, magnificent, and very strong building.

We must talk together. When you write something, as you are doing now about reconciliation, I hope that when we read it we will begin to realize that this point or that is valuable to us all. Through that and through the resuscitation of bodies like ministers fraternals, pastors of different denominations set aside time just to sit and talk together even about this very same issue of reconciliation—talking about different items that they can identify in their community and talking about pulpit exchange. One thing I like about Genesis is that the world was created through the word of mouth. God said and it happened, so if we say right things it will strike a chord in the minds of our communities and the minds of our people. They need to realize that if you are white you are white but it does not mean that you are superior, and if I am black I am black but it does not mean that I am inferior. We are all created in the image of God.

And such ecumenical cooperation will foster reconciliation not only within the churches but also within the community as a whole. We must be active in the community.

Once the churches started to operate in their own isolation we began to miss the boat. We must work and operate within our denominations for the sake of growing strength and vision to go out into the community. We must not operate in our denominations merely for the sake of keeping them alive as institutions. Institutions do not bring praise to God. People do that. You remember the story of the Samaritan woman? She met Jesus at the well. After meeting Jesus there and after discovering who he is she became the first female missionary. She went to the village and called the people to come. Denominations must meet on their own not for their own sake but for the sake of gaining strength and sharpening the vision to go out and share with others.

I also think that religious organizations, such as the South African Council of Churches, should come up with different types of interdenominational community worship. We did this in Petersburg for the taxi violence. We went to the taxi rank and we had a cleansing service. It was packed with people. We need similar services in places that have bad memories for many of us. And we invite everyone. For example, we organize and go to John Vorster Square to cleanse it from the past. We can go to Parliament or hold a service on the grounds at the Union buildings. Television crews can help the nation see that we are cleansing South Africa of the differences that nearly destroyed us. And we can build ourselves then as a new nation with the differences shown in our rainbow nation to build us up to be a strong nation. We must take note of the past to cleanse us from it in religious rites and symbols. So we can move forward.

A mistake we made is to say we must not look at the past because when we look at the past we are so frightened that we wonder how we lived through it. But we cannot ignore it, for if we ignore it we run the risk of repeating it. Perhaps even after thirty or forty years our grandchildren may repeat it. But we need to acknowledge it and say these are the mistakes of the past, we have done wrong, we have wronged our country, we have defiled our country, and now we want to cleanse ourselves and go forward.

I have a very strong belief in rites and ceremonies. In western culture it seems that it is more of a legal approach. If it is taken to the courts, what have we to do? The magistrate and the judges and the prosecutors will do it on our behalf. But bringing the community together to perform a rite together is our cultural practice, and we need to do this here and there and everywhere.

In the Evangelical Lutheran Church we are talking about a program on reconciliation but do not have one in progress at the moment. But whenever we meet as pastors the issue comes up time and again. We need to set up a mechanism where the mistakes of the past can have a platform to be aired and forgiveness is asked for and absolution is pronounced. That is being asked for especially for me here in this diocese. That message is verbalized at meetings for church workers that I have arranged. It is up to the church leadership to design the program and the services. We will be doing within the church what I mentioned as needed for the public.

A BLANKET AMNESTY would be a cardinal blunder that the government would make if they succumb to the cries of the foot soldiers and generals that there must be a blanket amnesty to all the perpetrators. If I get amnesty so easily it does not make me feel responsible for the mistakes of the past. It makes me feel that what I did was okay so if the opportunity avails itself again I will do the exact same thing. Blanket amnesty will send a wrong message to the perpetrators, and it will be abandoning the victims of apartheid.

The victims would be hurt for the third time. First they were hurt by apartheid and then by receiving no restitution. To see the perpetrators go free would be a third hurt.

And for the perpetrators there remains the need to say what they did. This is not for us to exact punishment but because it is also a liberating experience to the person who is relating the story. Once they have related what they have done they will never be the same and will never ever think of repeating it again. But if they get a blanket amnesty they will think it is okay, like the Afrikaans idiom that says, "*Stil water, Diepe grond / Onder draai die duiwel rond.*" They will say that the pool is so deep that I can sneak under it and do what I used to do. That will not be good for us or for them.

RHEMA BIBLE CHURCH

Tuesday, August 24, 1999

We realize that in Christ we are all one. That is what we are striving for. We do it through every activity in the church. I am not saying it is a one hundred percent because we are dealing with people with attitudes, but we are moving toward it. Probably some of the best fruit, obviously, is in the young people because they do not have all the baggage and the guilt and the shame and the anger. Older people have that. In fact, my personal belief is that we will only get rid of racism when all that whole era of people dies out. Just like the people that had to die off in the wilderness and the young generation came in and took the Promised Land. I believe very much that it can apply to South Africa.

⟡

RHEMA BIBLE CHURCH is a major partner in a growing Pentecostal movement in South Africa. I met, at their large office building in northern Johannesburg, with the Rev. Ron Steele, Media Officer for Rhema, and a pastor, the Rev. Dick Khoza. In this transcription of our time together I felt it important to identify the speaker with an *R* or a *D*.

R: BECAUSE WE ARE CHRISTIANS we will start from the position that reconciliation, true reconciliation, has to be between man and God first. This gives us a better possibility of then reconciling people together. That does not deny the good work that is done without God, but there is always the greater possibility of the failure of that reconciliation to be really genuine. So I think that is the reason why there should be the spiritual dynamic. It does not mean that it is always going to be successful, but I think that it is why the church should be playing such a big role now in genuine reconciliation between all South Africans.

D: I agree that what God is not involved in is very shallow. I think it is not in man to reconcile with another man unless God really has become personalized in one's life. Reconciliation between people can work to some degree, but to be true it needs the spiritual dimension and biblical approach. My understanding of reconciliation is that the problem between man and God was the sin that was between us, and Jesus removed sin. But what happens between man and man will only sometimes remove that stumbling block, so we talk over each other's heads.

R: I think a classic example of this is in Ireland. You have got religious people involved. But a lot of the neglect in Ireland has been the reconciliation with God first. It is said to be a religious war all the time. That is what it has become—a war of religions without any meaningful Christianity that produces the fruits of faith. It was Jesus who said you will know them by their fruits. The Bible teaches us that there should be peace and goodness and kindness. And so one has to judge it on that basis without being too judgmental. But the point is that any reconciliation without God is going to be fragile. You can produce it for a while, but it is going to crack again, and that I think is the great danger for South Africa. We must not be fooled into thinking that reconciliation is a one-off thing. It is not. It is a continual process.

There is a spiritual dimension to true reconciliation. That is where the church now has to be practical in terms of "show me your faith and I will show you my works." That is important now for the church.

D: I have realized that in South Africa we, blacks and whites, coloureds and Indians, are not talking to one another. We talk among ourselves here. I, as a black person, and Ron, as a white person, we can talk heart to heart because we share our faith. The cry among many blacks is that they feel that they have done a lot to try and reconcile but they do not seem to find the other side willing. They say they are willing but do not show that in reality.

R: That is the point. I did not want to say it, but we have to admit that white South Africans, white South African Christians, have got to show in no uncertain terms the fruits of reconciliation. They have got to be more practical. They really have got to show it. Let us not fool ourselves; there is an awful lot of racism left in white South Africans. We would be really foolish if we did not accept this and deal with it as the church. The church is best equipped to be able to handle it.

R: The Truth and Reconciliation Commission has not contributed to reconciliation. We made a mistake; it should have just been called a Truth Commission. Reconciliation can only come afterward. It should be a fruit of the truth. Once you have exposed everything then people are going to make decisions about whether they want to be reconciled. So I think we were wrong to expect the Commission to be the reconciler. No, it was not. It exposed the wrong, and now the real job of reconciliation is left to us.

D: There are many questions that still need to be answered, like the issue of justice. We have seen a lot of white people saying that I did this and that and then they are given amnesty. But we read about the Nazis who are still being hunted today. In our country they are not hunted but given amnesty.

R: But who is hunting the Nazis? It is the Jews. The Jews work on the basis of an eye for an eye, while we work on the basis of grace and mercy. It is important to recognize the Christian heritage of so many South Africans. There is a willingness to forgive. I agree that we must never think that the Truth Commission will bring justice. It exposed wrong. We have got to know some of the truth about our past. But justice, I am afraid, is not what it was about.

D: There is some confusion about the Truth Commission in the black community. There is still a feeling that when it comes to a black life it really is cheap. We recently had the issue of some elephants that were badly treated and everyone made an outcry. At the same time on the news they tell us about a black man who was painted by silver paint. It was on the news but that was all. People want to bring back hanging but they do not want to say P. W. Botha must go to jail, in spite of all that happened when he was in charge. There are many contradictions within the whole thing.

R: From my point of view as a white, I am disappointed at the few whites who have actually accepted responsibility in any way for what happened in the past. To be brutally honest and frank, there are a lot of words said but there is little experience of the fruit. I am looking for the fruits of reconciliation, especially from the white community. I am not saying there are not any. That would be unfair. I would not like to generalize too much, but I am personally disappointed that there is not more openness, more acceptance, and more genuine reconciliation happening from the white side. Whites are actually tending to isolate themselves. That is my perception. I hope I am totally wrong, but it is my perception that whites are withdrawing. They are saying, "Leave me alone. I am not a racist. I just want to get on with my life." And so outwardly there is no racism but inside there is still something that needs to be dealt with. And again I come back to my belief that a spiritual dynamic is needed all the time.

In some ways we have been very fortunate in Rhema that we integrated on a natural basis. Our white members have been exposed to a whole broad spectrum of black people. We are beginning, and I emphasize that we are only beginning, to see something of a new culture and understanding. We have gone out of our way to take white people into Soweto to spend week-ends there and to be exposed to what life is really about in the townships. We have cultural evenings where the black and white cultures are discussed and also exposed to one another.

Sadly, you have got to admit that apartheid was highly successful in keeping the cultures apart. We do not understand one another. There is a lot of misunderstanding. At the same time, speaking about this one congregation, there is a lot of good will here and we are beginning to meet one another on a social basis. This is not to say that there are no people who still have to battle with racism within our congregation. It would be wrong to say that.

D: Pastor Ray [McCauley] has done much to change attitudes. He was very quick to identify the issue, and he is still even vocal now to the congregation. Looking back at what we have gone through, it seems that the people have trusted him, especially the white people. Good racial relations are coming. But we do still have to do more.

You get two types of black people. There are those who were born again during the era of apartheid when politics was not right to talk about. Then you have blacks who were in the black consciousness movement, the Rev. Frank Chikane and people of that sort. They would say that Rhema is becoming opportunistic about the issue of race. But now they are beginning to say that they think we are right. There is a growing trust on both sides. When Rhema was to be taken out of broadcasting by the South African Broadcasting Corporation it was the black people who complained. They want Rhema. We have been accepted fairly in the black community. We still have a long way to go but we are accepted. We have many black personalities and even top politicians who come to Rhema. They may not agree with us on certain issues, but we are united in the message, the spiritual part is real.

From what I have heard I do not think that the survivors have gained much from the Truth Commission. They have heard the people say about how they killed their husbands and sons, but after that there seems to be nothing. There are those who have received the remains of their loved ones and that must help, but beyond that it does not seem as if they benefited.

R: In my experience there are very few black people who feel satisfied with the Truth and Reconciliation Commission. The other night I was lecturing in our Bible school and I opened a little bit of a debate about truth and reconciliation. The reaction from black people there was to say that there really is no satisfaction deep down. Yes, there has been some exposure of the truth, but only some of the truth. That is what I hear. There is a belief that many other things remain hidden. I do not know what they are and I do not know what more anyone can expect. Generally, black communities are not one hundred percent satisfied. White communities, on the other hand, are happy to say that we have had enough and we need to close it up. They do not want to hear anymore. It is too torturous to their ears and to their hearts. And we have to ask about how much longer we can keep on opening up the wounds.

R: WHEN IT COMES to religious leaders playing a prominent role in the Truth Commission, I am obviously biased and believe it was a good thing. The protesting church in South Africa played a key role in bringing about the transformation in our country. No one should underestimate how powerful that influence really was. Therefore, it was only just that they should be part of the Commission. At the end of the day we have to see that the route we have come through in the struggle and through the negotiations leading up to the election is marked by the Spirit of God. All God-fearing people will correctly give thanks to God for the great miracle of transformation. It is a good thing that church people are involved in all sectors of our society all the time. There is a spiritual dynamic that is working in our society. Whether people want to admit it or not, it is a very powerful influence.

D: It did help for religious leaders to be on the Truth Commission and for all religious leaders to go to the Commission to admit their wrongs. We who started attending Rhema in the eighties remember that they used to pray for the soldiers to go into the army. That was a contradiction to us because we knew what was really going on and how those soldiers were seen by the black community. By going to the Commission and admitting that ignorance, it has helped people to accept Rhema. I have met a lot of black people who are saying that it was good that Ray went public on TV and admitted the wrongs. We can now forget and go on.

R: All the confessions and stories of hurt were understood much better by the Commissioners because of their religious and Christian background, whereas, if the TRC was only made up of advocates and lawyers, it would have been a very clinical and cold experience. It was necessary for the TRC to allow the emotion, to allow the expression of the tears and of the anger. As Christians we understand that these are a part of the whole healing process.

D: The media played an important role during the apartheid era. It protected white people from the truth. So though we normally say that all white people are guilty we have to accept that many of them were deliberately made not to see what was happening. The media played an important role in blinding people to the truth. They did not know what was really happening right under their noses. That is why some of the revelations that came to light through the TRC have come as a shock to some white people. They cannot believe it. They cannot believe that they have been party to a country that was doing such dreadful things. Some of them are ashamed, but what makes them feel even worse is that they did not realize it was happening like that. There are some who knew, but for many it is a deep shock.

R: It was very much the same in Germany. The average German person would have said that they did not know there were concentration camps such as Belsen and Auschwitz. They did not know of the horror that was going on in there. When it was eventually exposed they felt let down. You feel the same here. You actually feel that this government that you supported (if you voted Nationalist) has totally let you down and you feel guilty. There is shame. There is guilt. You do not want to admit it, and so sometimes you simply keep glossing over it.

D: Yes, we are all learning things. The majority of black people used to believe that all white people are rich. And now when we meet a poor white we cannot believe it. I think it is a same reaction.

R: This is just an aside, but if you want to watch apartheid operate, go to the street corner and watch the beggars there. See what color gives to what color. Apartheid works one hundred percent for the beggar, though I must say that more black people would give to a white than a white would give to a black nowadays.

R: Rhema does not have specific programs geared to reconciliation and what has come out of the TRC. The TRC has challenged us to become more and more practical. We have increased our commitment to the upliftment of the poor. Many of the poor would have been the victims of apartheid. Our social programs have already expanded dramatically. We are involved with hospitals, with hospice, with programs for HIV/AIDS people, and with street children. We are negotiating to get another hospital so that we can take in HIV babies.

The TRC spurred us to greater social involvement in the communities. I will never say that this is a reconciliation program as such. It is part of our attempt to see the fruit of faith. If I am genuinely sorry about what happened in the past, corporately sorry as a white person, then I must show my sorrow by doing something. There must be some form of reparation. And there are all-powerful Christian themes of restitution. Therefore, what we are trying to say to our white people is that you have got a great responsibility to do something to uplift the poor. That is the message. We are not saying that this comes out of the TRC, maybe because this upsets some white people and causes uneasiness. They are uncomfortable with the TRC. It would be unwise for us to say that this is our TRC program, but what we are doing is in fact very much spurred on from what came out of it.

D: I would like us to go back to when Rhema began. Reconciliation is not starting in Rhema now. It started right from the start. Maybe we were not aware of it, but it was there. In the eighties when we came to Rhema it was, if I remember well, the only church that would accept blacks to attend the same Bible school with whites. Other churches would not, even though they were born again. I would say that the seed of reconciliation started when this church started because for the first time, even though the environment was still hostile, we would come here and mix. We would have to separate when we left the church, but we started a long time ago. We are in a process.

It depends how you interpret reconciliation. Jesus said that the greatest commandment is to love God. This church strives to teach people God's principles on how to live in a way that would help us all to reconcile. I believe strongly that it is when you grow in God that you can love your neighbor as you love yourself. I cannot love myself until I know how God loves me. These are the things that we as black people should work on because of our low self-esteem. Even if white people try to help us, that low self-esteem makes it difficult. We need to love ourselves. So, I would say, take the TRC out of the process and accept that we are dealing with reconciliation as Christians. We are doing it but we are not there yet.

R: Maybe we have been doing the right thing but not just realizing that we were. We have tried to the best of our ability to be true to the word of God. So, even in our stupidity but in wanting to obey the word of God, we find ourselves doing the right things in our attitude toward other people, toward the poor, and in our attitude to racism.

The word of God is our final authority. We tend to emphasize that in our particular flow here. The proof of the power of the word of God is that, without even saying, yes, we must start doing this and that, we find we are actually right.

We are spurred on because the needs of the country are so much greater. We cannot expect the African National Congress to govern for forty million people with the resources the previous government used only for five million people. That is unfair. But many white people do not seem to realize that. They just criticize the government because things are not like they used to be. That is terribly unfair. Of course that goes back to the racism that still exists within the white community. We know that services are poor, but there is a very big difference from giving the crumbs to the 30 million people and really looking after 5 million.

R: I am now speaking purely as a Pentecostal. That is my position. In 1979, which is now twenty years ago, a black American preacher by the name of Price made prophecy. Part of that prophecy was about South Africa. One thing, which came out very clearly, was that there will be no reconciliation until all the people become one in spirit. Then there will no longer be black and white. For twenty years that prophecy has actually hung over this church and we have seen it fulfilled slowly. It is something which God, we believe, is doing in a Divine sovereign way. Maybe that is why we do things right without realizing it.

It is sovereign. It is just something wonderful about God's grace. There is probably a conscious and an unconscious striving for reconciliation all the time. We realize that in Christ we are all one. That is what we are striving for. We do it through every activity in the church. I am not saying it is a one hundred percent because we are dealing with people with attitudes, but we are moving toward it. Probably some of the best fruit, obviously, is in the young people because they do not have all the baggage and the guilt and the shame and the anger. Older people have that. In fact, my personal belief is that we will only get rid of racism when all that whole era of people dies out. Just like the people that had to die off in the wilderness and the young generation came in and took the Promised Land. I believe very much that it can apply to South Africa.

I realize that an Afrikaner in the middle of the rural area will find it very hard to change. He is not exposed to the greater mass of the urbanized and sophisticated black people. I hear about this from our pastors in those areas because there is that hardness of heart in those areas. It is tougher for a pastor in the rural areas to see that reconciliation is worked out. In many ways we are fortunate in the cities because we are all thrown together and we bump against one another. We are like the stones; we all start to rub one another and we all become smoother in our characters and personalities.

D: God has been doing things here which we are not aware of. We do not preach reconciliation in terms of blacks and whites, but we believe that the word that comes every Sunday is contributing toward such reconciliation. We have never had to deal with the traditions of the Baptists, for instance, where they are still struggling just to merge as one church. We did not start in the same way. We do not have this baggage to deal with.

We have to deal with cultural differences. The new government has given us a new constitution and a new sense of justice. We must learn to live together, and so we are trying to address our cultural differences. We can look at the cultural differences and learn to accept one another.

R: We have got to realize that many things that divide us are not necessarily black and white issues but matters of difference in cultures. We need to accept all the good things in our cultures that line up with the word of God and are not contrary to the word of God. We will then begin to find reconciliation much easier.

We have got to challenge those who are racist. We must not allow that spirit of racism to stay alive in South Africa. We listen to some American preachers who come here and learn that despite civil rights and new legislation there are still tensions in America. We must not let it happen here. Racism is a challenge. The danger of it is that so often it operates in the name of God. It exists in the hearts of many white people and in the unforgiving nature of some black people as well. When a person never forgives he becomes very bitter and angry and will only be satisfied with vengeance, and that applies whether he is white or black.

D: But a black man cannot be a racist. If I do not get along with a Zulu or a Shangaan some people will say that I am a racist. But I am *not* saying they are inferior. I still see him as a human being and that is the difference.

The biggest problem we are facing with white people is that they still feel they are superior. White people look at others, such as Greeks or Italians, and see them as a different race but not as inferior. But when it comes to black people, there is an assumption that the black person is inferior.

R: What could help us as whites is for more and more black people to be seen in positions of power and authority in a positive way. That will begin to eradicate that sense of superiority. We have to be honest and recognize that whites, especially those brought up in South Africa, do have an in-built feeling of superiority. It is a British-type of class thing, which obviously expresses itself in South Africa on a pure black-and-white basis. Like the upper, middle, and lower classes in Britain, you stick within your boundaries, which still exist and will exist.

D: I have never been a member of the black consciousness movement but I subscribe to the concept. Most of my life I have tried, God is my witness, to be me. I have never allowed myself to be assimilated. Some black people will perceive me as a token. I have never given up my conviction as a black person to try to be accepted as I am. I have seen that it is normal for black people in a white institution to automatically succumb. I belong to the Shangaan tribe, which suffered within the black tribes because we were undermined. We grew up speaking Zulu so that we would not be seen as Shangaan. It was a big problem for me in the seventies. But black consciousness says you are beautiful as you are and you do not have to be like somebody else. So when I became Christian that helped me, especially with the Bible saying I have been created in the image of God. It makes me to be me, not because I am always right but because I can enter discussions without trying to please everyone else. I can be me. That helps and it does work for me.

The process of reconciliation must continue. Maybe we do not know in-depth what the word *reconciliation* means, but we must just do what we know and continue on that way and trust God to help us. God is in the process of reconciliation.

From a black standpoint a general amnesty is difficult. The majority of black people wanted white people to say that they were wrong and ask for forgiveness. Then we could forget together and move on. As Archbishop Tutu used to say, all we need is white people to say they were wrong and we can work things out together.

R: Some white people will leave the country. And those who cannot afford to do that will go into a laager of their own making. This can be a problem as they can always be the seed that sits there and it can take root again. That is my real concern.

D: It will be unfortunate if that happens. Black people were beginning to suggest that our former President was good, but he was bending too much to accommodate the whites. Black people are saying that white people cannot appreciate what has happened. They did not lose their houses or their jobs and nothing changed for them after 1994. The crime that is happening is happening everywhere. It happens to blacks even more than whites. Yet white people still act in a racist manner. Those perceptions do make black people to conclude that white people by nature do not like blacks. That can make things difficult in future if it continues that way.

R: Much as we rejoice with what we have come through, there are a lot of red lights flashing still and we must be aware of them—not afraid of them, but aware of them. God has something good in store for this country.

It is a blessed nation. It has got tremendous resources, and there is an incredible reservoir of good will among the people of South Africa.

ॐ ॐ ॐ

THE REV. SELAOTSWE TSINGTSING

Thursday, March 2, 2000

If we are to come through the transition and make our country really democratic, we need to reconcile. A change of government and the embracing of human rights in our constitution are one thing, but we definitely need to look at those things that hurt people in the past and at the way they affect our relationships now. We have to do that so that we can honestly look at one another as equals.

ॐ

REV. TSINGTSING is one of a group of ministers at the St. Mungo's United Church (Presbyterian and Congregational) in the affluent Johannesburg suburb of Bryanston.

M Y CONCEPT OF RECONCILIATION is based on my understanding of creation, that we are created in the image of God and that the love of God is unconditional. I think, therefore, that there is a difference between secular and religious understandings of reconciliation. As a religious person I will look at reconciliation out of my relationship with God and my understanding of who God is. God is love. That is a crucial factor in religious reconciliation. I do not think that the secular society is looking at that. It is looking at coming together for the benefit of working and social relationships. It is concerned with working at a situation for the needs of all. Religious reconciliation is deeper.

If we are to come through the transition and make our country really democratic, we need to reconcile. A change of government and the embracing of human rights in our constitution are one thing, but we definitely need to look at those things that hurt people in the past and at the way they affect our relationships now. We have to do that so that we can honestly look at one another as equals. I think for me it is in that process, when we look at one another as equals without any preconceived ideas, that society will be completely reconciled. It is a great task that still lies ahead of us, the people of this country.

THE TRC DID HELP open, in an amazing way, those truths that the white people in this country did not want to know. As we listened to interviews and sessions on the media, there was no way we could hide ourselves from the things that have happened in this country—that helped people to start talking and look afresh at our society. Not just to put them behind us, but to say these are the terrible things that have happened. We need to acknowledge, recognize them for what they are, and then we can begin to talk at that place. For me at St. Mungo's, in a very small way, we have started to do that. Whites have said we never knew it was so bad, and from that point we can talk together about what we need to do to move forward as a nation.

MY EXPERIENCE OF WORKING in a predominantly white church leads me to say that it is just a small section of the white community that has accepted any responsibility, either individually or collectively. I have raised some issues of reconciliation, issues on social action where we have to be doing things as a church. There are some people who have said to me that they feel terribly sorry about things that have happened in our country and that they see how they became part of it, whether they voted or not. They acknowledge that they enjoyed the privileges and have benefited. They received a good education, got good jobs, and their children are well-off in life. They say, "I see what I have done and I am sorry for that." Others say, "Phew, I did not know things were that bad. Sorry that it was so bad, but do know that I had nothing to do with it." So I think there are a minority who acknowledge and a majority who do not see themselves as part of anything in the past that was responsible for the deep divisions in society.

My personal presence in that church community has helped the process. That was part of the reasoning at St. Mungo's when they extended a call to me. I need to be present to help the church in shifting from where it has been, to have them see the changes in society and help them deal with them. From the outset they were very clear about what they would expect from me. I was fortunate to have a predecessor who was the first shock absorber to help in the ill feelings that might have been there. I am able to build on that, and there is an acceptance that my role is to help the community move—not just to work among the black people who now attend or come for help, but to help the whole community move. We begin to transform the church community so that we begin to reflect where the nation is and in what we believe God is calling us to be and society to be.

A S FOR THE SURVIVORS, you watched the way people spoke, the tears and the memories. I believe the Truth Commission helped by allowing the people an opportunity to talk about their pain and their suffering. That was an important part. But the other important part, about what material benefit they have received, I still battle with it.

I HAVE A SLIGHT PROBLEM with the composition of the Commission, but the inclusion of religious leaders excited me. I want to think that religious people understand more what we mean by reconciliation and that it is based really in our understanding about God. They are the people who could begin to interpret this real understanding of reconciliation to the people who came to the Commission. The people came from diverse sections of the society. To have religious leaders there to guide them and help them see that we have moved from there to there and we can now start to look to a new future was an exciting part of the Commission.

W E MUST ATTEMPT to foster reconciliation on the ground in the local community. At St. Mungo's we have started with contact between the church and the community in Diepsluit. We are looking at ways to help us understand one another and allow interaction so that people meet one another. And we are hoping that through the TRC process we can get groups from each community to talk about their history and what we can do for reconciliation. Hopefully, we can then take that further into the communities and expand the process a step at a time.

We are, for instance, planning a trip of members from St. Mungos to visit black areas, stay there, eat there, and begin to know each other for the sake of reconciliation.

I HAVE MIXED feelings about blanket amnesty. Perpetrators need to do something to give something back to show they are sorry. There is no provision for it and that is sad. We have to call for it. It is urgently needed. But then I have to balance that call with my idea of God and total forgiveness.

There are so many people who have benefited through apartheid. The government had the opportunity to see how they could help the many others who have been disadvantaged. Somehow we have to share the wealth of the country.

THE REV. DR. DESMOND VAN DER WATER

Thursday, March 2, 2000

We set in motion a political process of reconciliation, which is essentially socio-political. But we then used, to a large extent, a group of people who by their very nature tend to impose a certain perspective, a religious perspective, on reconciliation. That is partly why you cannot talk too much now about reparation. It is the disclosure only and unconditional acceptance that was emphasized. They have actually functioned with the religious premise, but the people expected more in regard to material reparation and that for me has been the problem with the process.

DESMOND VAN DER WATER is the General Secretary of the United Congregational Church of Southern Africa. This church is a union, brought together in 1968, of mission activity of the United Church of Christ, the Christian Church (Disciples), the London Missionary Society of Great Britain, and a locally established Congregational Union of Churches. It is a church well known for its emphasis on ecumenical activity and issues of justice for all. We met in the church's head office in Johannesburg. In the former South Africa, Desmond van der Water would be designated as "coloured."

MY POINT OF DEPARTURE would be that when you talk about reconciliation it presumes alienation of some sort. There has to be an acknowledgment that something has gone wrong. There has been a fracture or break in relationship. So reconciliation, on a purely secular level, would be an attempt to get together where individuals, groups, or communities have, for some reason, become estranged from one another. There are these two ingredients, recognition of alienation and a desire to be reconciled. That starts the process of reconciliation because at the end of the day it is a process.

IT IS DIFFICULT to see much difference between religious and secular reconciliation. In the end I would have to say, yes, from a Christian perspective reconciliation happened between God and human beings on the basis of God's unconditional love. When it comes to secular reconciliation, there are definite conditions that come into play in a much greater way. The short answer therefore is, yes, there is a difference but it is a nuanced difference and not very clear-cut.

The reason I say nuanced is that if, for example, you take the story of Zacchaeus in the gospels, reconciliation and redemption go together. There was a real component of reparation and restitution, so it was not just an unconditional coming to Christ. It was on the basis of him giving back materially that reconciliation and, of course, redemption happened. The secular implications are the same and come into play as well.

There is a need for reconciliation for the simple reason that we are a nation divided within itself. We have a history of being separated, of being alienated at various levels—racial, class, social status, denominational. So we are a nation that needs to be reconciled within itself and among itself. Yes, there is a need.

IT HAS BEEN SAID that the TRC has been a process of much truth without significant reconciliation. In some ways that is true, but in order to achieve reconciliation of any significance the truth has to emerge about our history. In that sense the TRC process has unearthed things of our history, which many people would not want to hear, or simply wanted to ignore. The TRC process has created the space for us as a nation to come to terms with our history. With all the criticisms, some of which are valid, it has nevertheless set us on a path from which there is no return. I think we still have a long way to go, but we at least have a consciousness now about our shared history and the TRC has opened up that space for us.

IT IS DIFFICULT for us to speak for white people, but my dominant sense is that it is only a minority that has come to a point of acknowledgment of their culpability in apartheid. The majority either does not want, or are unable, to understand that they have been part of the apartheid process. I have to be honest and say I do not see a greater shift on the part of most white people. The apartheid process was so good in shielding whites from the reality that it is very difficult for them now to enter into the past history and see what really happened. Therefore I would have to say that the degree to which whites have accepted responsibility for apartheid and for its excesses is very limited.

The survivors were helped in being listened to. In a significant way this restores dignity, and so they benefited emotionally through being listened to. In some ways it did not help that it was staged, but they did get to tell their stories, or some of them did, and that must have been beneficial. But the downside is that having spilled your guts out, having said what the consequence has been for you, you do not have any recourse to any material help. That must be an anticlimax to many having come to the TRC to tell their stories. Unless society addresses that one, the whole process will not have achieved what it set out to achieve. There must be some form of reparations, and it is very sad that it was not mentioned in the budget.

I WOULD HAVE TO SAY that having so many religious people on the TRC confused the issue of reconciliation in the country, especially having an Archbishop as Chairperson. Not that they themselves did not do a good job, but it confused the intention of the process. I guess that one would need to give it a bit more time to see if the process was helped. Religious people have a way of imposing their ethos on a process, and that did confuse issues at times. Having so many religious people was in my opinion a mistake. It should have had more of a balance. I can say this on reflection after the event. I did not think it at the time.

I would have drawn from all major sectors, ensuring that there was representation of all the major groupings. The sectors would be business, labor, possibly more from the protagonists of apartheid to get them to own the process rather than stand aloof. It has been seen as an ANC initiative and that, as the ANC was near to the ecumenical churches, it was obvious that they would go for the Tutus and so on. The TRC has been discounted by some because of the predominant role of like-minded church people. Some denominations such as Rhema and other religions were not well represented. That is partly why the whole process has been confusing to many.

We set in motion a political process of reconciliation, which is essentially socio-political. But we then used, to a large extent, a group of people who by their very nature tend to impose a certain perspective, a religious perspective, on reconciliation. That is partly why you cannot talk too much now about reparation. It is the disclosure only and unconditional acceptance that was emphasized. They have actually functioned with the religious premise, but the people expected more in regard to material reparation and that for me has been the problem with the process.

Have you any comments on the seeming lack of coloured participation in the TRC process?

A fact of the process has been lack of coloured participation. We cannot ignore this. It is symbolic of the way in which in the current environment coloured people seem to struggle with their identity and their place in the new society. It is a relevant issue. Many coloured people see the site of struggle and the issues that are being played out in terms of black and white in South Africa. They believe that the coloured community, as in the past, has been caught somewhere in between. They say, "Under apartheid we were not white enough and now we are not black enough." There is a grain of truth in that, but it is also part of the apartheid classification where coloureds were third down in the tier of classification. Currently many coloured people struggle with where they ought to place themselves politically and socially. Unless we recognize that as a nation and start to address that issue, reconciliation will be also half-baked. The coloured community is not an insignificant section of our community.

I THINK IN SOUTH AFRICA the religious communities are well in touch with each other so that the religious communities among themselves are not alienated. There is a rapport, such as in the Moral Summit process. There is a working arrangement for coexisting and for collaboration. It is a remarkable relationship given apartheid, but maybe it exists because of apartheid.

The business of reconciliation, bringing people together and building relationships, is the business of the religious community. In that sense it is the stuff of being of faith to reconcile people to one another and with God. The question is, of course, in what ways are we doing it or not doing it.

The United Congregational Church has its own problems. We are a church of so many different groupings, language and international, and not always in touch with one another. We need an ongoing consultative forum process to check with one another where we are in terms of the process of reconciliation, or we could very well face a racial split. There is a problem in that the current leadership, by and large, comes from one particular grouping.

As a church we have touched on reconciliation in ad hoc ways, but there is no concentrated project, no focus on it. This is mainly because we have been struggling in recent years just to keep ourselves together. We have come through that crisis, and we can begin to do preemptive work and not reactive work. It is strange, however, that the new dispensation, contrary to our expectations, has emphasized our group identities.

The churches have formed themselves into some kind of a forum in response to the TRC. I do not see much coming out of that to date. Perhaps where it will count is where you bring people together in small ways to encounter one another, working together, breaking down the stereotypes and cultural barriers. The church is very well placed to facilitate that kind of coming together as it is a safe environment to do it. We have a big and exciting task at that level to foster reconciliation between alienated race groups. Churches need to apply themselves to it with a bit more passion and vigor.

Reconciliation must happen at the local level to be significant. It has to happen in those churches where people of different races and different experiences are now able to be together. We can do what we like at the denominational level, but that is where the rubber hits the road.

We gave blanket amnesty some thought in the UCCSA when some thought was given to the idea that all the ministers who had been alienated, for whatever reason, during the past years should be invited to come back without conditions—a kind of blanket amnesty—but the idea did not get very far.

As far as South Africa is concerned, my gut level response is to say, let's go with it, let's allow it, and maybe it gives us a real chance. But, on the other hand, isn't there some form of tangible restoration to be done by those people who have perpetrated gross violations? The victims of human rights violations have needs that are not being met by anyone. Just a small amount of tax allowance would have meant so much. It would make such a difference to the families who need it. The government has lost such an opportunity to express its support for these people.

FR. DALE WHITE

Thursday, October 28, 1999

In South Africa the politics of forgiveness and the personal aspects of forgiveness have been addressed, but the economic aspects of forgiveness are blocking true reconciliation.

❧

This Anglican (Episcopal) priest and former Director of the ecumenically-founded Wilgespruit Fellowship Centre is well known for his expertise in personal and organizational development. The Wilgespruit Centre was well known for its development programs and as a host to many multiracial and radical style conferences during the apartheid years. He still lives at the Centre, once nestling in quiet countryside and now captured among the expanding suburbs of greater Johannesburg.

IT HAS ALWAYS STRUCK ME that the innovation of Christianity among all religions that we have had is that it has as its centerpiece forgiveness, a willingness to forgive prior to the other person even asking or demanding forgiveness. So forgiveness is a key element of the Christian approach to reconciliation. The challenge is to make oneself vulnerable enough to approach the person who has done wrong to you, to say to them "I, in some way, was involved in the wrong that you perpetrated and please forgive me and let's find a way to forgive each other."

So that is like the cornerstone that I have found in interpersonal relationships, in social relationships, and particularly in the barge-pole sort of relationship I had to handle between the state and myself. I had to keep them at a safe distance so they didn't crush me, and yet I realized that they were driven by a view and a vision that had a moral worth for them. Although I was in the totally opposite position, their humanity was at stake and my humanity was at stake, and unless we could hold an attitude of forgiveness toward each other we couldn't go forward.

My wife comes from the Afrikaner background and I come from the English South African background. The Boer war was a reality for her family because her mother's sister perished in the concentration camps. It seems to me that the Afrikaner people have been so bruised and hurt by the imperialism of the British that they came to feel that there was no benchmark against which they could be found guilty because they had been treated so deeply shabbily. So they couldn't get a perspective on their own cruelty in what was underlying apartheid.

So we had to look for alternatives to apartheid and pursue them without blaming the perpetrator. I think that taught me, whether it was through labor unions or civic associations or hawkers associations or invasion of squatters, that you have to do what you're bound to do morally. You have to take the consequences and not feel that you are necessarily going to change the other person, but it is certainly going to change you and those who benefit from you later.

I found in my twenty-two years of ministry in St. Paul's Church in Soweto during the period prior to 1976 and after that ultimately reconciliation between people is dependent on reconciliation to God. Unless you find that and cling to it you are the wounded victim of your own circumstance, and you can't come round to forgiving other people. God has at least in Christ set us forward on the path of forgiveness.

Forgiveness is also a political tool. It is important that we realize that the politics of forgiveness means that British people have to forgive the German people and the Jews have to forgive the German people. In South Africa we have to forgive vicariously the Afrikaner people and the British people who had put South Africa into this situation. So there's a politics to forgiveness, not just a personal feeling.

I believe that all religions have a sense in which you have to open yourself to change and not take from generation to generation so that the children have to eat the sour grapes that the parents have sown.

It's a sense that I had when I was in Germany in 1963. I was meeting a complete silence about the fact that the Nazis had perpetrated such heinous crimes. The older generation who were closest to the events were saying, "We have to forget the past for our children sake, we have to start afresh." And I was saying, "That means you're just postponing to the next generations the need to forgive and face forgiveness, for it is a burden we need to carry. If we just close our minds and we bury it, it will come back to haunt us."

MY DEEPEST PAIN and insight was when I was working in Soweto, mainly among blacks. I had to preach the gospel of forgiveness in the consistent face of the cruelty of apartheid grinding people down into the dust. I realized that we often become complicit by applying apartheid in the daily life we live. We may be forced to do that, but is there no alternative? Can't we make choices that open up the pathway forward? So forgiveness is a sort of a grinding of two upper and lower stones.

It's not a one-way process. It is for both perpetrator and victim. This deepens what forgiveness is about. If I look at the cross I see a suffering process. It is not a process that is without having to give a great deal of oneself and receive a great deal of pain from the other person. It's a two-way process.

In South Africa the politics of forgiveness and the personal aspects of forgiveness have been addressed, but the economic aspects of forgiveness are blocking true reconciliation.

When I was involved in industrial mission I found that the executives knew what they were doing by committing persons to single-sex mining compounds, grinding their families to the extremes of both poverty and hopelessness. It is a cruel system that management rationalized as akin to going to boarding school. How can you compare an adult in the situation of the mining hostels with a boarding school?

We had students working on the mines as a project. The head of Anglo-American made a statement to say that the notes the students were writing could go uncensored onto his desk. Suddenly he was aware of what was happening. One woman from Lesotho said "I wet my pillow with tears of hopelessness, because my husband is in the mines and I have to be both husband and father and yet keep a place for him in my home."

He bought and distributed more copies of the report "Another Blanket" than the churches ever did. He suddenly saw the full catastrophe of what the economic system was doing to human beings.

The affluent people are wearing a blanket that protects them from seeing what is happening to the poor. If you put a Lesotho blanket over your face, your eyes just peer through and you see here and there a little bit. I think the affluent white population and the nouveau riche blacks are wearing that blanket. They are unaware of the systems that are grinding the people into poverty.

Forgiveness, as I understood it, is the forgiveness of the unjust steward, the forgiveness that reaches the poverty that they were imposing on others and has it removed. It's another stage about forgiveness. That is why the idea of reconstruction and development is so important—that, together with the renaissance of the soul, changing the inner self.

THE MAJOR VALUE of the Truth and Reconciliation Commission was to delineate the differences between the western approach and the African approach toward reconciliation. There is the restorative approach to justice that is part of the African way of handling life, and there is the western approach that is legalistic.

The restorative approach means that people can see that hearing the truth, knowing what has happened, restores one's human dignity that was shredded by the terrible system of apartheid. The TRC restored the public dignity of humanity to those persons who came forward and spoke. You could see them and the community restoring that image of how their sacrifice had brought liberation, and how they should now be honored.

You get those instances where a boy gets a girl pregnant and isn't married to her and doesn't intend to get married to her. You have the concept of damages. Tradition says that the two families have to meet and restore each other to public faith. And this is for the sake of the child, to ensure respect upon the offspring that comes of that union. The meeting restores the future. That's what I mean about restorative justice.

On the other hand, you have the Afrikaners who so believed in the law that there were seventy-seven statutes on the statute book to justify what they were doing. It is a system that goes for what is right in terms of the law and what is wrong.

I can understand the differences between Archbishop Desmond Tutu and former State President F. W. de Klerk. Mr. de Klerk is a lawyer, and he's saying that in terms of the legal rights and applications he has met his obligations. He's not entering into this restorative justice frame at all. It's alien to him. It seems that Archbishop Tutu cannot understand that. It's two worlds clashing.

The TRC brought to the forefront the concepts of restorative justice that involves forgiveness and brings forward the humanity of people as against the systemic pattern of the legal process in which you find people guilty and then punish them. So always there's the specter for the Afrikaner of "are we going to be punished? Are we going to be legally fried for what we have done?" That is the eye for an eye form of justice which is really so different from the restorative process and what Christianity introduced.

MY OWN IMPRESSION is that the revealing of how horrendous the apartheid system had been shook the comfort zone of most whites. They believed that they were doing their honorable duty. And then they find that under the blanket there was this dishonorable cruelty that was meted out with such disdain for humanity. The braaivleis and boerewors sort of stuff while you are killing a fellow human being. (In the TRC Amnesty Hearings some members of the Security Force revealed they barbecued (braaivleis and boerwors) while killing dissidents.)

I think it did shock. It is not acknowledged because it is not comfortable to acknowledge. There was so much compliance from whites with the apartheid system because they were benefiting from it. And then to see publicly on the television and other media that their benefits were based on the destruction of other people in such a barbaric manner was a great shock.

Apartheid was a vicious system that made this huge division between black and white. I had to go through some interrogations, but I was always treated as a white. There was a kind of natural courtesy just because of my skin color. They had the same attitude toward what I was doing as they had toward the black communist, but they gave me a different sort of treatment. The treatment against blacks reached even across deep-seated taboos that are in humanity, such as that you do not kill children and you do not rape women in prison or put them among the rapists so they can be raped. And you do not kill and maim and enjoy the cruel process of doing that.

South African whites saw that displayed in the open. They saw what had been done in their name and for their privilege. I think many retreated from it. But they could at least react to something they were not aware of.

FOR BLACKS it was first of all an understanding, perhaps for the first time, of what they had to go through in order to endure, a realization of the sacrifices that had been made. And then the second part of it was the seeming unfeeling of whites. So I think it didn't really create the dialogue that was hoped for. It created awareness. It went only as far as creating that awareness.

IT IS GOOD THAT FOR THE FIRST TIME representatives of other faiths—that had been subjugated by Christianity—were given a role in the Reconciliation Commission. I believe that all the religious ministers and persons on the Commission had earned their credibility during the years of the struggle. So in a sense it wasn't saying we need a religious TRC, so much as saying these are the best people to set it up. It was not a matter of secular versus religious fervor. It was a case of credibility.

The Commission required people of all kinds of experience. Reconcilia-

tion comes out of struggles, and the struggles were both profound and profane. So it was in the mix of those you see in the people who were working
on the TRC having to deal with the profound and the profane aspects of
reconciliation.

When Desmond [Tutu] was questioning Winnie [Madikizela-Mandela]
I can still recall that instance when he pleaded—not to forgive sins or that
sort of thing—but to recognize that she had allowed things to go considerably wrong. And so she had accountability. It wasn't punishment, it wasn't
reprehensible, it was just "Do you realize you were not accountable in the
way we anticipated that you should act as a leader and the mother of the nation?" I knew how the state system had broken her down and infiltrated her
life with all sorts of slimy deals in the hope of denigrating Nelson Mandela
and herself, and the leadership. Desmond in a very sensitive way found a
route for her to be able to maintain her dignity, to soften her antagonism,
and yet get through to acknowledging that it had gone horribly wrong. It is
a profound spiritual experience.

Religious communities adopted the necessity of a just rebellion. We
gave consent as religious leaders to the ANC and the young people to conduct an armed resistance. No matter that we remained ourselves inviolate in
not using arms and we retained our nonviolent commitments to peace,
which I think we did as Christian leaders. Church leaders gave a needed
consent and consensual pattern to justify revolution. Armed rebellion!

I appreciated that the ANC had remained a peace organization and created Umkhontu wa Sizwe (their armed wing) as a separate organization and
could then call off the dogs of war and continue to strengthen their role
around peace. That, for me, was a crucial ingredient. And in a strange way
the Dutch Reformed Afrikaner desire for peace was able to cut it free from
the "bitter enders" who persisted right up until the election and say "We are
not 'bitter enders,' we want peace." The desire for peace was enthralled in the
process, and I think it created the opportunity for the churches to return to
their true role. You remember Desmond Tutu said that we must step out of
the national leadership and make way for the political leaders? Then the
churches got completely discombobulated for a period of time.

Here at Wilgespruit we were lost for a period of time. Desmond [Tutu]
said we were the first victim of the victory! Apartheid had gone, so we had
lost our meaning, and purpose, and focus, and source of funds. We had to
regain our balance and return to the issues of nonviolence for the new society. We began to examine how labor unions struggled against the inroads of

capitalism and further poverty. We looked to supporting civic associations in reasserting the civic nature of society, where street and block and civic association committees are necessary for the participation of people. We saw that hawkers mustn't be swept off the clean pavements of white South African pristine-user cities, but that people are cities and they must be back on the streets.

I learned, in the work I have recently been doing in Tokoza, that the young people have shifted from being the protectors to wanting to become the providers for their families. There has been a shift. And we have to ask if the church has been present in the shift that has been happening? Is it once more regretting its loss of role or assuming its mantle? This is where we must be creators of peace because if we do not create peace we will vanish as a species, never mind as just South Africans.

The churches in their just war and just revolution character helped create infrastructures that support war and killing. We have very little input in creating similar infrastructures for peace. We need a ministry of creating structures for peace that promotes peace and therefore brings about reconciliation with justice. And, therefore, we have to shift our emphasis from political freedom into the economic area of activity. I think we'll find our role if we go that route.

I think it is important for South Africa and the churches that we come back to understanding our roots of nonviolence, forgiveness, and reconciliation. There are signs of this. We have hope, and as the Japanese Professor Taganaki once said, "Hope is the bird that sings in the dark as the day approaches."

Part of the conflict resolution and peacemaking process that we have to develop applies in our courts—not simply a legal punishment process but a victim-offender negotiation process. It's important for us to get the victim-offender processes into our courts of law that are not restoring law and justice but are simply punishing the offenders. I think that the churches can play a role and learn how to counsel victims. At the moment we just leave the victims nowhere, but we haven't got a purposeful way for counseling them either.

This victim-offender process might help. It is linked back to the idea of the TRC as the perpetrator-victim-survivor process. Somehow the churches have to find their way into these sorts of issues. The churches have to get involved in sustainable work and wealth creation to the point where they unveil the enormous talents of people so they can begin to put their talents to use in their communities for their own purpose of survival and income generation.

I think we can't have durable peace without sustainable jobs and the creation of ecologically sound environments. So the way the churches are using land is important. I can't believe that we can't turn to examine and do something about our ecological environment and the use of stewardship.

That would help us look at the conservation of rain, for example. It falls on us all but we don't conserve it. We just let it race down the gutters and away into the sea. We don't have a concern for water. And unless we conserve water we can't then cultivate the small pieces of land we have. Our church roofs collect so much rainfall! Just think of the liters of water that we could be saving on behalf of the community if we put a tank next to each of our church roofs. We've just got no imagination in our use of God's gift of rain. We simply put up our umbrellas and then say, "Thank God that the storm has gone."

And then you know we can start putting in new styles of gardens that grow food rather than just look pretty with flowers and grass. Who can eat them? We have acres of lawns that take so much water, and for what purpose? Ecologically, church grounds could become an edible landscape. They could be giving food to people who are hungry and starving. We're just not interested.

We haven't arrived in terms of our present societal needs. The church has got these kinds of resources but we do not use them. We look around and discuss our role in the new South Africa but do not open our eyes to the obvious right there in front of us. And whether we're in cities or in rural areas or in semirural areas, we just close the God Box around us.

Here at Wilgespruit we're only just beginning to explore what we should do with our resources, looking at gardens and solar heating, solar energy, water irrigation. And unless we—the church—get to that kind of sustainable stewardship, we're lost. That's what I'm saying. And somehow we have to wake up!

The church has an important role to play in discovering and illustrating the use of our natural resources. Instead we say that cleanliness is next to Godliness and encourage people to have three baths a day and have swimming pools, all of which wastes water.

And the church says you must beautify and have flowers on the altar and that allows people to surround themselves with gardens that are consuming water and growing flowers while many of our people starve.

So let's wake up, that's what I say.

ROMAN CATHOLICS

❧ ❧ ❧

The Roman Catholic Church is one of the largest mainline churches in South Africa. While maintaining its own theological and organizational form, it worked in close cooperation with other Protestant denominations in the churches' struggle against apartheid. This relationship is now cemented with its membership in the South African Council of Churches.

BISHOP KEVIN DOWLING

Monday, March 27, 2000

But in the end real reconciliation, I believe, in our country is only going to happen when people experience economic transformation, economic justice. The radical redistribution of the resources of the country so that the degrading poverty and misery in which so many of our people lived and so many still live is going to change.

❧

IRISH-BORN KEVIN DOWLING is the Bishop of Rustenburg and Chair of the Justice and Peace Department of the Southern African Catholic Bishops' Conference. Words flowed from Bishop Dowling's mouth as freely and fluently as the water pouring down the hillside opposite us as we sat together at a retreat center overlooking the beauty of the countryside around Hartebeesport Dam. This provided an incredibly contrasting setting to talk about the cruelty of our nation's past.

MY CONCEPT OF RECONCILIATION is that there must be a profound coming together of two people or groups in mutual respect to be able to listen, to really discern the truth of each other's experience. The basis must be the openness, especially on the part of the party that really seeks forgiveness, to recognize the truth and accept it as the other perceives it, especially in terms of their basic experience.

That brings in attitudes that could be secular in the sense of a person's ability to listen, to recognize the other as a unique person or group that has their story which has to be heard without prejudice and judgment. I do not believe there can really be reconciliation without that as a first basic step. A secular approach could achieve that.

What I would see as the difference might simply be the individual or group's faith dimension as a motivation. It might mean they come to it with spirituality, which is central to their own journey, and so coming with a God-dimension motivating them, moving them to go far beyond what they could humanly cope with in terms of seeking forgiveness. It is the power within which motivates the person, putting a nuance on the reaching out and reconciling spirit of the exercise.

In our situation I would see a huge gap that needs to be bridged between white perpetrators and black victims. White people have not truly experienced the trauma, the suffering, and ongoing personal diminishment, and that means a profound journey in awareness awaits them. Unless that is done there cannot be reconciliation.

I THINK THE CHALLENGE of reconciliation in South Africa is enormous. We have only just begun to deal with the past in that sense. The general public has come to deal with some of the truths that have emerged through the TRC process, some of the horrendous human rights violations that presumably they didn't know about before. But that emergence of some of the truth has not brought about a change of heart or transformation. People have said that it is terrible without it actually producing a change in the way people look at other groups.

I would say we have only really begun the journey. In different ways and on both sides a healing process is required. For the white community this means finding ways to address their fears and enabling them to be open and recognize that they have been part of the process of the trauma, even through inactivity or lack of awareness and ignorance. The reconciliation process is a long journey that calls for honesty in looking at self and an examination of personal attitudes. It looks at the need to change from within. We have to recognize the stereotyping and to recognize how we have lived with an untruth for so long. That is a profoundly spiritual journey for those who belong to the faith community. And it is not easy at all.

A healing process is required in the black community, and not just those who suffered obvious and more extreme forms of human rights violations that require that their story is not heard only once but in an ongoing way which requires counseling and empathy from civil society, but also the vast majority who live in endemic poverty and systemic injustice and all that has been done to their psyche, their personhood, and their identity. I sense in our black people an enormous personal capacity, perhaps from the sense of community that has been preserved in the midst of everything, a capacity to survive which is enormous and a capacity to move on and rebuild lives again, to build from where they are and from what has happened. There is a capacity to forgive and allow the recognition that white people might have been ignorant, an enormous capacity to reach out and hope that it could be mutual, it could be a new relationship beginning to grow.

But I think that reconciliation really has to do with justice. Part of reconciliation is liberation of our people who were deprived and discriminated against and the elections that have brought our infant democracy into being. But in the end real reconciliation, I believe, in our country is only going to happen when people experience economic transformation, economic justice. The radical redistribution of the resources of the country so that the degrading poverty and misery in which so many of our people lived and so many still live is going to change. When people perceive and experience that, and not only have to believe in promises, it is only then, when people have the basic necessities of life, that they can participate in true reconciliation. It is when that impacts on the quality of the lives of the poor. Only then can we start to experience that we can come together as a reconciled people.

THE MANDATE FOR THE TRC was the outcome of political compromise in the negotiation process. Therefore to that extent it would limp in terms of trying to hold all the values together in creative tension. In terms of what actually happened, its great achievement was to allow the little ones who suffered to tell their stories and be heard with deep respect. I was struck here in Rustenburg where the hearings were quite late on that the Commissioners, who must have gone through this so often, still en-

tered into that day as they did with many of the earlier ones with a real capacity to listen and to hear the people and to accompany them in the telling
of the story. That was very important for the people, to sense that they were
respected.

The objective was to uncover as much of the truth as possible. It probably achieved a lot in that sense, with the truth being the basis for reconciliation. But my own perception, after sitting with others and telling my own
story in the Rustenburg hearings, is that the uncovering of the truth
through that investigative process linked to the amnesty hearings brought
about a dichotomy in the sense that the amnesty hearings, because they followed a different set of criteria and objectives, surfaced the issue of justice,
retributive justice, a justice that demanded a response, demanded the recognition of wrong. That surfaced strongly.

For victims whose lives were shattered in a dreadful way and those who
lost loved ones and did not have bodies to bury, what did it do to their spirit and psyche? They were present at amnesty hearings where the objective
was to hear disclosures about the truth, at least what appeared to be some of
the truth or perhaps nearly all of it. And then through that process they
watched the perpetrators literally walk away free, not subject any more to
criminal or civil litigation and without any possibility of the family bringing
a case against them—to see that person go free when they were not even required to say "sorry" or reach out and seek forgiveness or reconciliation.
They did not even have to offer something symbolic or even try to restore
some kind of relationship. To see them given amnesty for horrendous acts
when they, the victims, have received absolutely nothing was a profoundly
difficult burden to lay on people.

I think that dynamic between telling the story and trying to discover
what happened through being present at the amnesty hearings and watching the perpetrator go free created a profound awareness that this is unjust,
most unjust, and nothing could be done about it because of the agreement.
That brings anger. That for me is a difficulty with the process. In some instances—very rare instances—reaching out and asking for forgiveness did
happen.

And now on top of that the reparations committee, suggesting at least
symbolic reparations and some help to those declared victims, appears to
have been ignored. This is again a pain that these people have to carry. They
have been promised so much and received so little. This is unjust.

GIVEN ITS CONSTRAINTS, and these were substantial, the Commission achieved certain objectives well. It began the process of dissemination of the truth; hopefully it will in time help create a culture of human rights where this kind of thing must never happen again. But at the heart of it, for myself, is this real problem whereby the objective of the truth being revealed as a means to reconciliation was not attained. There was very little in that way and justice has been sacrificed. I expect that if the amnesty process were not there we would never have got the perpetrators there in the first place to tell at least part of the story. But that is where it was hamstrung and there are no easy answers. So it achieved much that was positive, but we have a long way to go in healing the violence that was done to people. It has to be taken seriously if the TRC is not to finish as volumes of words that actually lead us nowhere.

I LIVE PREDOMINANTLY among black people, so it is difficult for me to say the effect on whites. The only experience I've had is the occasional meeting with white people in and around Rustenburg. Many of them are expatriates who came in for the mining industry that tended to be influenced by the right wing and the political agenda of the area, which was AWB (Afrikaner Weerstands beweging) in many instances. (The ABW is a very right wing white supremacy group.) I found in those last four years or so of the struggle in Bophutatswana that there was a great deal of defensiveness, and aggression even, on the part of white people. Church people, people of faith, were no different. It was particularly painful that people were coming out of fear, out of ignorance, and out of what seemed to me to be an inability to face the truth from the perspective of the gospel. An inability on the part of people to apply in practical terms those values they have heard week after week in the church, social and cultural realities that were crying out to be heard and crying out to be changed. And it showed me in a very real way that people—good ordinary people—can be so blinded and so unaware simply because they had been cut off and had no real experience of black people.

I question whether it is changing. It is in the sense that most recognize this is the way it is going to be: we have a black government and that is not going to change. They have come to the pragmatic decision that this is the way it is going to be and we have got to live with it. But I would hesitate to say that conversion has taken place. There is a gradual growth in recognizing the need to listen in those people who do get some experience of interaction between the races through school boards and faith communities. There are some signs of change. But people are still battling with so much baggage from the past that they are still imprisoned, still bound, and prejudices are still dominant.

I BELIEVE THAT THE PROCESS of healing has begun and will, hopefully, continue for those victims who were accompanied and supported in the telling of their stories and are now part of ongoing support groups. My fear is that with so much that is demanding in our socio-political context today—the struggle to survive, the whole aspect of unemployment—that people are still carrying so much pain and are still forced into the struggle for survival just to keep going. As I say, reconciliation will really take place when economic transformation has taken place and there is real change on the ground.

We see some things happening, water projects and electrification, but for the vast millions of our people they are still waiting for significant change in their situation. So in terms of the TRC promoting real transformation, we still have a long way to go. I sometimes wonder about the expectations that were created at the start of the TRC. Many thought it would really make a difference on the ground. They are now asking, is life is really going to change for us? It is a question many are asking. There has been no real difference as yet. I cannot help but wonder that many would say that the TRC has done very little of substance.

RELIGIOUS PARTICIPATION in the TRC is a good question. At one level, some of those religious personages would have been coming out of a profound experience of oppression themselves, and so their heart and spirit would have been very much affected in terms of their awareness and knowing what the brutality did to people. I would say that in itself it would have a value in terms of their ability to hear. They brought not only a faith-grounded perspective but also one rooted in the reality of the suffering. Their presence was not a limitation, as they came not just as religious but also people with an experience of the times.

The limitation was not in the people but in the structure and required timetable. I would have liked a much greater dialogue and sharing. I missed a sense of challenge and questioning that seeks for truth without being legalistic. But I also recognize that there were the restrictions of time.

Perhaps if there could have been a greater presence of people who had been traumatized and who were not religious leaders but from other walks of life it would have been more balanced, but on the whole from what I saw there was a genuineness in what they tried to do. I see the limitations, but they did the best they could in that.

You were one of those to present the submission of the Catholic Church to the TRC faith hearings. What are your observations on those hearings?

After reflection it seemed to me that instead of an in-depth entry into developing an awareness of what that particular church group did, we had three sets of questions and an amount of allocated time and that was that. There could have been a much more fruitful way. I found that the questions imposed a limit. When you are asked how your church suffered, you think that the headquarters were bombed and this school closed and so on, and you make a list of facts and that was a lack. Perhaps the Church Leaders Forum or Religious Leaders Forum needs to take things further.

We could not look as deeply as we should into how the vast majority of our people experienced us as church leaders, for example. To use that dialogue in an open way as a means of promoting reconciliation within your own community would have much more meaning for the people and the leaders, and perhaps we have not looked at that enough. We said, for instance, that in fact we had a black church and a white church; we acknowledged that and that needed to be unpacked. We said it but we have not examined what that still means for us. We are only beginning in our church to grapple with such issues. It all points to the fact that we have a long way to go.

Our Justice and Peace Department is looking at the critical issue of economic justice and transformation. The departments have got to hold those sorts of issues before the church leadership and community and be involved in empowering initiatives on the ground. They also have to network with other churches, other faith groups and nongovernmental organizations if we are to deal with this tremendous need to transform the economics of the nation so that things actually change. That is where the church must be and be seen to be involved. We must empower people, for instance, to develop the skills to relate to local government structures, how to hold them accountable—human rights education, advocacy programs, democracy education in helping people who have been divorced from that process to grow in their knowledge of what the constitution is all about, what kind of a country we are creating. The church must be there because the church is the community on the ground and not just the leadership. The leadership needs to promote all of that, but the actual work is on the ground. We recognize that it is the programs on the ground, right there in an individual village where your own community needs to be empowered.

On the level of reconciliation it seems to me that we need to be doing a lot more in terms of the ongoing accompaniment of the people who have been hurt and traumatized. There need to be some symbolic means of holding the memories with great respect, perhaps planting a forest or a garden of remembrance, whatever is culturally meaningful.

We must help to keep alive the need for truth and justice. This means designing liturgies of healing, para-liturgies we call them: services of healing, storytelling, reconciliation events that are going to bring people together and, hopefully, in that faith context deepen and promote the ongoing journey of reconciliation. All that we need to do. Manuals are being designed to help all of this happen. But then your leadership needs to be motivated to take this on seriously and with commitment to training people to use the manuals.

Then there is the whole issue of development initiatives, community development and projects, in terms of really hitting the whole unemployment reality. People need to be brought into processes that will give them skills, ongoing skills development that will help them in management, for instance, financial management and marketing so that the small, medium, and micro enterprise system can take root in communities. I believe that is the only way we are going to make a dent in this. It is not going to come from big business, and it is not going to come from government. They can promote their programs, but in the end it is the communities themselves that need to be empowered with the idea that as a community we have within us the possibilities of making a difference if we can acquire the skills. And starting capital is needed for the projects that can involve individuals, small groups, and cooperatives. Those are the kinds of things we must be seen to be involved in.

Then there is the whole AIDS endemic, which is going to undo and cripple so many initiatives unless we get involved in creative response programs, not only in terms of AIDS information dissemination but the whole aspect of creating enlightened and caring communities. Pastors and communities need to lead the effort to break this culture of silence and destroy the stigma that is attached to AIDS that makes people feel so rejected and afraid to simply be who they are. We have to change the whole mentality of communities in regard to AIDS. I believe the churches have a unique opportunity there in terms of the value base that they are coming from to do something very constructive to change the culture of silence and create enlightened and caring communities—enlightened so that people know this is a sickness like any other and that it has particular ramifications which demand that we create a home-based care system and a counseling system which is going to accompany people, and whole families, who are dying with HIV/AIDS.

This has to be achieved in a medium and longer term because it is going to be difficult to create in the short term. This has to be established in all our communities if we are really going to turn around this endemic in terms of what it is doing to society at the moment.

Again, it is on the ground that the church presence can facilitate so much that is vital, and unless we do that, then again our aims of creating a reconciled nation are going to be crippled. It is a means of that happening. So those are some of the areas we can be involved in certainly.

॰ ॰ ॰

MR. ASHLEY GREEN-THOMPSON

Wednesday, May 10, 2000

You have got to have a genuine transformation of relations in order for there to be reconciliation.

॰

The name and the person do not fit! The name conjures up pictures of English, conservative, upper middle class, and the person is black and radical. We met at my large kitchen table, and I kept getting the feeling it would be better if we were walking somewhere so that there was more space for Ashley's restless emotional energy to express itself. Ashley is the Director of the Peace and Justice Department of the Southern Africa Catholic Bishops' Conference.

F OR ME RECONCILIATION conjures up images of justice and equality. It is a question of righting the wrongs. You are talking about the coming together of forces that were in conflict with one another. Usually conflict arises out of a desire for resources of wealth, minerals, and superior positions in society. So if you want to have reconciliation in a society, for me an essential part has to be the creation of equity, the coming together of people as equals. Without that you cannot have reconciliation.

THE TRUTH COMMISSION had a political and legal framework in which it had to operate. We may talk of nation-building and the rainbow nation, and it is all very feel-good stuff, but a secular understanding of reconciliation, if one understands it correctly, would include elements of a legal and political framework that must be in place in order for there to be processes that lead to a coming together of sorts. So, for example, your amnesty provisions are very technical. It was an issue that was grappled with at length and is probably the most legalistic aspect of the TRC legislation. How do you judge whether a person has made full disclosure? And that can be one of the criticisms that many church people can make: in the run up to the Truth Commission it was given to lawyers to create the structure. But it was a necessary aspect. People have very real concerns about being sent to jail and that sort of thing. That would be my aspect of the secular notion of reconciliation.

With the religious approach, the danger is that it can easily go that feel-good route. We must not fight, and we must hold hands and be nice to each other. That is a limited understanding, and I think a lot of white South Africans take that approach. You have got to have a genuine transformation of relations in order for there to be reconciliation. That is my experience of the approach taken by the people I work with. Certainly all those bishops of a more discerning mind would say that you cannot have reconciliation unless you actually transform the nature of that relationship between the protagonists, and that is the foundation of my religious approach to reconciliation. Certainly in the Catholic position there is also the question of forgiveness and repentance. One of the criticisms of the TRC was the lack of any requirement for repentance. You just had to fulfill the legal requirements, and there was not any need for you to make that step outside your own personal interest. That is a fundamentally flawed understanding of reconciliation, certainly from the Catholic tradition.

For me it is problematic that F. W. de Klerk and P. W. Botha could get away with it. They and so many other top leaders of the old apartheid regime continue to live a good life. There have been some perpetrators who have actually made the effort to try to understand and to express their remorse and show they wish to make amends. But it has not been a requirement. It has been left to people's personal choice.

So my understanding of the secular approach to reconciliation is that it tries to make sure all the legal aspects are covered, and we can then move forward and coexist within a legal framework that is acceptable to all. A religious approach, or what it should be, is a much deeper transformation of relationships with a demand for justice. There is definitely a demand for justice. That was probably the most glaring flaw in the whole Truth Commission. Again, it was a necessary evil at the time.

I disagreed with the whole concept of the Truth Commission and the provision of amnesty at the beginning. I felt that it was asking too much of people to sacrifice their recourse to justice. But victims and survivors at the time, through organizations like my own, were prepared to accept that they would have a chance to talk and that was agreeable.

SOUTH AFRICA needs a huge paradigm shift in the minds of so many different people. I am generalizing completely here, based very much on my personal experience in the work I do at the level of a national program. I think black South Africans, especially those who do not have the financial resources to make many choices, the ordinary people who live hand-to-mouth from month to month and week to week, have accepted the need for some sacrifices and some compromises in the pursuit of a stable and unified country. That has been a most profound thing that so many other people do not seem to appreciate.

The white community, by and large, has not understood what the system did for them, how it benefited them. Sure, it also victimized them in many ways but, by and large, you lived a good life as a white South African. And it wasn't by chance. There is a refusal to acknowledge that and it is sad. This morning on a radio phone-in program there was a chap who said that instead of going on strike the unions should take a leaf out of the white settlers and work hard to advance themselves. And that is a real phenomenon among the white community. There is a reaction against an ANC majority government, there is a reaction against the unions, and there is a reaction against affirmative action and against the equity bill. Anything that seeks to equalize relations by addressing the inequalities of the past is attacked. And without that paradigm shift it is going to be very difficult for there to be reconciliation.

Black South Africans are saying, "Look, we understand. We do not want to take your dog and your house and nationalize everything, but we do want you to give something back and we will be prepared to wait until you come to that point." I do not think white South Africa is hearing that. There needs to be a nationwide commitment to some of the brilliant legislation that is coming out of Parliament at the moment seeking to address the inequalities of the past. Once you can address that and you give people hope, people who have never had hope before, then I think you go a long way to effecting reconciliation.

I HAVE JUST RESPONDED to a lady from Ireland with a question-naire asking about the TRC. One question asked if the TRC did pro-mote reconciliation, yes or no? And there is a small box to tick, one or the other! It doesn't work that way. There are a number of very good things and a number of things that have been very bad. I think some continue to be bad.

There were some good things. There is now, for instance, a story that nobody can deny. It is there. It is on public record. They have had their chance, those who felt it was all a lie, to come and say, no, it didn't happen. It reminds me of the Jews. The Jews are very good at keeping the Holocaust in the public eye, and when people dispute the fact that it happened they are labeled immediately as lunatics and not to be taken seriously. A similar thing will happen here. We will not forget what happened here, not because we want to harbor any bad feelings but because it is our history. We have this very objective version right there, and that is most likely one of the most significant things that the TRC did. That is important for national rec-onciliation. In the competing political world that we are going to face in the future, where we are going to have different interest groups who will call on history to justify their position, we have an objective story to refer to. And for me that is important.

I think it has also contributed by allowing victims to tell their stories. There is nothing better than being allowed to talk about yourself. Even the shyest person, if they are in pain, they want to talk about it and I think that has been very important. And to get the acknowledgment that victims and survivors got is very important too. I think that has added to dealing with some of the pain. It is not the whole story by any stretch of the imagination, but it has helped greatly.

The disclosures by some of the perpetrators have been good. I do not work with perpetrators, but I am sure if you have done something bad it is good to purge yourself of it. It is also good that people know what happened.

The Commission placed the issue of reconciliation fairly and squarely on the national and international agenda. It raised the question of truth and how you use the truth to promote constructive interaction and community-building rather than suppressing it or misusing it to further your own aims. I think these are all things that have helped reconciliation in the country.

Reparations are the big concern just now. I think it is dreadful that the government has not acted on the recommendations of the Truth Commission. It is disingenuous. I just cannot find the words to express the anger that I feel about this matter. The Constitutional Court said that the provision of reparation compensates for the loss of the right to a civil action against perpetrators. Victims came forward and said, "We are prepared to accept the loss of our right to civil action as long as we get the truth and receive reparations." Once the truth came out the perpetrator process was over but the victims had nothing. They had the truth and only the truth. What do you do with the truth? You know now that your family was brutalized and dehumanized in the worst possible way, but what is the next step?

The Reparations and Rehabilitation Committee was about that. It was supposed to deal with the peoples' pain. And it is not just about the money, it is also about acknowledging and helping people get out of the hole that the pain has dug for them and put them in. It has not happened. It is the single biggest flaw and biggest betrayal if nothing happens. There is still time, but I think that the lack of reparations has raised the stakes in terms of reconciliation. You see people from poor communities who came forward voluntarily and accepted the whole process. They are now coming forward and saying, "We need you to meet your promise." And if our government does not do that and if big business and the white community does not acknowledge and do something as well, you are going to find that anger swell. That is something we were trying not to have.

It is as if the Commission opened the wound and allowed it to breathe and heal and get fresh air. But then this lack of delivery on reparations is an ill wind blowing off the rubbish dump and infecting it all over again. And when the eruption comes it is going to be something. I am not going to say it will be like in Zimbabwe, but I still believe that it can be dangerous.

I THINK THERE HAS BEEN some acknowledgment of the violations of human rights by a significant number of whites. There are not enough to constitute a social category, but certainly a significant number of people who, in my experience, have accepted that what happened should not have happened and they are responsible partly in that they did not stand against it.

But I think the institutions that reflect that kind of old privileged white class with their methodologies and their ways of interacting with the under classes have not changed. And for me the best expression of that comes in business and labor relations. Captains of industry know it is not healthy to have weak trade unions, even for their own profit margins, but there is still this constant demonizing of trade unions. I am not a great trade unionist myself, but they are important agents for social change in the workplace, in getting people to have decent paying jobs and to have better conditions of work to enhance their human dignity. And yet you have the captains of industry who say these unions are not prepared to be flexible and that is why we are losing jobs and that is why so many are poor. Yet we are generating more and more money in this country, our economy is growing every year, and they still flog the old horse that it is labor's rigidity that does not allow for a transformation in our society. For me that is the social issue that captures that inability of the haves to accept responsibility for the poor and the transformation of society. So yes, I think there are those who have made a change and they are working with us and they are good South Africans and they understand that it is tough now and not as easy as it was because of the need to address the legacy. But there are many who sit and bitch and moan and blame the blacks, blame progressive legislation, blame progressive measures, and have a victim and persecution complex.

I think it is fair to say that many whites have just ignored everything and retreated into their own laagers with TV and watching cricket and hoping we win at rugby. The inability to take responsibility for transformation is manifest in this escapist mentality that is saying, "I won't have anything to do with the great-unwashed masses." That kind of approach is widespread.

I have a drink now and then in a bar down the road from my home. I have been there often for about two years. I know the barman and some of the locals and these are lovely fellows. The other night I was in there and they were not there but the owner was, and she was complaining about the banks. I said, "Yes, I agree with you that banks can be dreadful." She said, "I hate banks and they treat you like dirt. The other day I was standing in the queue and as soon as I got to the front she put the closed sign up. I could kill her!" And I said, "Absolutely. You should take your business out of there."

And then she turned and said, "And you know what? They were all blacks!" My heart sank. I wanted to ask, where are you living, girl? Which continent, which planet are you on? I am looking for an alternative local now. So many of the people there have foreign British accents, and many of the patrons carry on almost like the world out there does not exist. I think that is a manifestation of the refusal to take responsibility and the refusal to accept that things are changing. They will accept someone like me who is black because I can speak their language, I dress like they do and I talk like them and I am culturally a westernized person. But the minute you start making challenges to them then they kick you out like a dog.

Perhaps that is another thing about the Truth Commission. While it was there, while it was on TV it was in your face and not even they could get away from it. But they chose to disregard it. That is why I still maintain we should have had the wealth tax. It would have been geared to the amount of money you have and it would have been okay. It might have jolted them because their personal comfort would have been affected. You do not change, it seems, unless you have to. You stay the same unless you are made uncomfortable. It is sad. It is the curse of our middle class living.

Having said that, let me tell you about a fellow I know and what he said. He is a white progressive and he made an interesting comment. Some of those white progressives of the struggle are now voting for the Democratic Party or the African Christian Democratic Party. That kills me! They were great in the struggle but now seem unable to understand the revolution and the transformation that we are all part of and it hurts. Anyway, this guy suggested that it's a frustration for people who realized the position of benefit that they occupy and have no qualms about committing their all and have done so in the past to help change the system. Now they have come into a new environment and understand and accept the need for Africanization and for the whole transformation process, but they really feel that they don't have a place in the new South Africa. So he was expressing a feeling from what we might call the white left. That was an interesting phenomenon and it is a worrying one. I wonder how we get around it because we need those people.

In my work I am relatively young, thirty-one years old, and I have to deal with people who are far more experienced than I am. I do not want to assume to know everything and I consult people that I trust from the old days. Many of them are white, and I have no problems with that and have even been accused of being anti-black—a bit strange, considering I am black myself—but for me it is not a contradiction. But it does seem to be a problem and I don't know what we do about it.

FOR THE VICTIMS the TRC offered the opportunity of sharing their stories. Apart from that not much, not much at all.

I AM INCLINED TO SAY THAT YES, it was good that there were a considerable number of religious representatives on the TRC. I am inclined to say that because I am convinced legal processes can only go so far. They are very important because they provide a framework in which interaction can happen in society. So much of our work, religious work, is attitudinal. It is about values and it is about committing yourself to something that is not often easily definable.

Justice is not about laws. Our criminal justice system is there because we have conflict in society, and we have to have some kind of system to govern us and to regulate our behavior. Justice is a far deeper thing than the courts or the laws. It is about the values that define our interaction as people. That does not come from lawyers; it comes from people who do what they do out of a value-based judgment. So I am inclined to say that it has been a good thing.

The crying by the Chairperson in front of everybody I felt could have been perceived as a bit contrived. I know it wasn't because he is not a contriving sort of man. But I am not sure if that is what we want white South Africans to do, to cry. We do not want those who have benefited to cry. We want them to say that they acknowledge the pain they caused and that they now want to change things out of a deep dislike and hatred for the suffering that has been caused.

I THINK THE TASK of the religious community is about, as our President says, rebuilding the moral fabric of society. I agree with him except that I do not think he is taking it as seriously as I would. His policies do not always reflect that commitment toward morality. It is a question of getting people back to basics. We often talk about African values, and that is very much a community-based coexistence, the extended family and *ubuntu*. Those are based on caring for the next person. I think that is probably the most significant thing that we have to do, and we have to try and get back to that.

I admit that we are fighting a losing battle. Globalization is based pure-ly on greed and self-promotion and profit. It is based on the total disregard of human beings. So you are fighting that, and you are fighting the develop-ment of a laager mentality where you retreat into your own small group. In the church this is expressed in gathering all the faithful and going into a cor-ner to pray because of the heathen liberal constitution and human rights that allow for all sorts of things. There is a reaction to the progressive law making.

In my church especially the reaction to the abortion issue, for example, sometimes clouds the issue so that you end up throwing the baby out with the bathwater as it were. You are not seeing the positive things because of one or two particular issues. You retreat into your closeted traditional Sun-day church, which prevents you from engaging with the agents of change within society and with other forces because you mistrust them. So on one level it is a government not giving expression to its commitment toward morality—GEAR[1] is an immoral system and against morality—and on an-other level you have the church increasingly saying that if you guys are go-ing to let all these things like abortion happen we are not going to talk to you because we don't trust you. We have to get past that and find new rela-tionships.

There are areas where we can cooperate strongly and promote change because this is about the best government we can have at this time. At the same time, we must maintain our critical voice and go to the President and say, "You are messing up on reparations" and not have him turn around and dismiss us, saying "Those b. . . y churches." We have to make decision-mak-ers and policy-makers uncomfortable sometimes.

At the same time, we have a pastoral duty to people in and through our churches. How many of our priests—I speak as a Catholic—are trained in trauma counseling? How many of our priests can understand the pain of one of the survivors who has lost a loved one? I do not think many, and we need, at the very least, to have programs that prepare people, particularly pastors, to actually minister to people where they are in their homes and communities.

I think symbolically we have a role as well. We need to constantly be holding memorial services in which we come together and let the Spirit in. Memorials are very important so that the memory never dies. I like the word *memory*—not to wallow in our suffering of the past but to remember. My eleven-month-old child jams his finger in the cupboard door and cries.

I pick him up and soothe him and as soon as I put him down he goes straight back to the cupboard door again. He does not have a memory of the pain and so he does the same thing again. We have to help him remember. It does not mean he will never open another cupboard, but that he will do it more carefully next time. So our memorials will act for us in the same way. I think the churches can play a role here.

Our Catholic hierarchy seems to be aware of the need for pastoral care and the need for memorials and symbolic gestures in special services. Our leadership is very concerned about reparations. So there is a lot of support from the hierarchy. I have not really explored to what extent they would agree with my analysis of the problems preventing us from doing more.

But what I say is based on the teachings of the church and that, in turn, is based on justice. It is about equity and justice. I think the Catholic Church has taken a pretty firm stand on the issues of poverty and the inequalities that exist in this country. Way back in 1992, when we were rejoicing in the new environment, they were saying, "This is fine. This is great. But unless you address the economic problems besetting this country it means nothing." So they have been visionary. I think the bishops have been supportive, but I am not sure if it reaches into the clergy at the local level and communities and parishes.

We still have the old divisions of white, black, and coloured churches. Because people are moving and local demographics are changing, you do find that the churches reflect that as well. But I think you still have these huge gaps. We have a movement of black Catholic priests who feel that not much has changed. I am not going to say that I disagree, because they obviously have a greater experience as black priests themselves of some of the differences between traditionally white parishes and township parishes, and they are most probably at the cutting edge of the skewed distribution of the resources. I disagree with some of what they say, but I think that what they say has a lot of merit as well.

The hierarchy is very white. But I think most have accepted that there will not be another white bishop in this country for a long time. That is only fair. In the next five years you have five or six dioceses that will be coming available. They are going to be black appointments. And there is some hope when you look at someone like Archbishop Buti Thlagale, who is the most outstanding advocate for human rights and social justice.

I CANNOT SEE THE GOVERNMENT granting blanket amnesty, although the ANC worries me sometimes. They fly kites, like they have with the reparations by saying that you cannot put a monetary value on suffering. When the churches challenge them on that, they say that the matter is in hand and that our comments will be taken seriously. But where are we now? So they do play a political game and, who knows, they might fly the kite of blanket amnesty. I hope they do not.

IN THE END RECONCILIATION in South Africa comes down to an economic question, unfortunately. We are fighting a rear guard battle, in a world that is so materialistic, to try and keep values intact. But until such a time as economic decisions in our country are made on the basis of giving poor people hope, it is going to be very difficult to obtain reconciliation. So if you want real reconciliation it has to be a revolution of thinking on social and economic relations between people.

People must make a personal choice. We have to target all the individuals we can and tell them that they must make the choices that benefit their community. If everyone who is listed as Christian in the last census would do that things would change.

Sometimes I feel hopeless and at other times I get full of hope. I try and pray but it doesn't seem to help much. I do not know. Where is the hope for any real change? Those of you who are older and went through all the struggle years must help us find hope once again.

NOTE

1. Growth, Employment And Redistribution (GEAR) is the name given to the development policy of the South African government. It is trade- and capital-based, in contrast to the original community-based Reconstruction and Development Programme (RDP) initiated immediately following the 1994 election and later disbanded in favor of GEAR.

MR. THOM MANTHATHA

May 23, 2000

Reconciliation is about education, it is about recognizing one another's worth, and it is about listening, really listening.

જી

THOM MANTHATHA, a former member of the staff of the South African Council of Churches and a leading figure in the internal struggle against apartheid, is a committed member of the Roman Catholic Church. He is a former committee member of the Truth and Reconciliation Commission and now serves as a commissioner of the Human Rights Commission assigned to the Eastern Province and to deal with issues concerning older persons.

I SEE RECONCILIATION FIRST in our ability to recognize, to offer, the dignity and integrity of an individual person, whoever that person is and wherever that person comes from. This goes together, of course, with having created such structures that can lead to the recognition and enhancement of this dignity. We need structures that will have a place for these very individuals where they will find recognition for themselves and are able to make decisions about themselves.

This is my biggest problem in South Africa today. There is a huge rift in our society. You will find the people in the rural areas, the people who have not had education and who have not worked at all, being suspicious about their kin, their own relatives, who are occupying the kind of positions they are in today. You will find a great deal of dissatisfaction that some are placed where they will tell them what they are and even seeming to say, we can do things for you, we can live your lives for you. So to me reconciliation means breaking through that and giving everybody a place.

There are young ones who are taken up by the affluence of their kin on the one hand and their own poverty on the other hand. It works against things like them attending school and getting education, which to me is cardinal in this whole process. And, of course, what makes it worse is this phenomenon where there is no education in the townships or in the rural areas. And this is even sharper when you compare that scenario with those children who are at independent schools, or even the model C schools, who are taught to understand what is happening and know what opportunities are available for them to grasp.

There are these two camps that support the division throughout the society where the poor have no resources and the independent schools have many resources. And it is not so much the lack of resources, as has been proved by those poor schools that obtain good results; it is much more a lack of confidence. Teachers even in the poorly resourced schools do not seem to acknowledge that according to the legislation all children are eligible for education without even having to bother their parents about school fees and uniforms and so on. People must understand that education is not tied to fees and uniforms. It does not mean all that.

I remember that I personally began to put on a long pair of trousers and shoes after having passed Junior Certificate. Before that I was in shorts and barefoot but that did not matter. It was the education that mattered. And I was not the only one. There were people far older than I who were in that fashion. But today we find a situation that teachers have not begun to understand or to be part of the poor community. There is a race to exit from the poor communities by the teachers and even by the religious leaders. I still say that nobody can interpret education and what it is for better than the church leaders. But the church leaders seem to be part of that exiting community that does not understand that the teachers and they themselves have to minister to the poor. There have to be schools for the poor. If the ministers were part and parcel of that understanding they would literally campaign for the poor children who are seen strutting on the streets because of their lack of school fees and uniforms.

I said reconciliation is finding a place for everybody, and for me education is the key in both receiving it and giving it. Not just education for the children to receive, or for their parents, but even for the teachers who can be empathetic. And the same applies to the minister and the church person who can be so empathetic that they can begin to say that we all form a community of poor people, and we must be seen to be pulling together. This is the time when one begins to see reconciliation.

If that takes off it can present a kind of a thrust to the people outside their communities that can in turn draw them in. So we become one community to talk together about the issues involved in reconciliation on the basis of man to man. It begins in creating these communities of equality.

I always find that when you talk about human rights the older person seems to have no place because we never address him on his experiences.

Many an older person can tell you, if you will listen, about his experiences, perhaps as a leader and expert in the circumcision school or as one who was expert in looking after cattle. But that is never referred to. The only time we come to recognize this person is when he can talk our language or when he can see human rights in a sense that is more western than representative of his own way, and in the process we fail to discover his worth. We fail to recognize his dignity because with older people their dignity is in the past. This man has spent his whole life at the cattle post, and he would rear so many cattle and become an expert in ear marking and branding and in driving them to other places when the wells dry. But that part of it does not feature in our contacts, and as a result, what is it that you can discuss with this person? You are lofty up there and he must do the listening. And the listening does not even come out with anything other than that he keeps quiet and expects you to come out with a grant or with old clothes or a loaf of bread. And once he gets that he walks away, and the only time he will be coming to you is when he has consumed that. There is no real meeting.

Reconciliation is about education, it is about recognizing one another's worth, and it is about listening, really listening.

THE TRUTH AND RECONCILIATION Commission made reconciliation an issue. Even in its process, regardless of limitations in time and manpower, the TRC did effect reconciliation between a number of individuals and groups. The only remaining area, which has to be followed up very strongly, is the one between white people and black people. Presently reconciliation between the African National Congress and the Inkatha Freedom Party, which became unavoidable after the political striving of the early nineties, at least shows that reconciliation is possible. Inkatha distanced itself as an organization from the TRC, and at the same time it encouraged its people to go there. So the TRC in that area created the awareness of reconciliation and helped it to happen.

But from the white communities there was a greater distancing, first from the liberal section, who felt that they had not abused anybody's rights—they were not in government structures, they were not the policeman, and they were not in the army and so on—and by so doing they quite literally isolated themselves from the process.

The Afrikaners asked, understandably so, why should we go into the process of reconciliation? Why don't we just forget, and then if reconciliation comes in it will be on the basis of our new shared experience? Some of them, when I went into the Lowveld with Prof. Piet Meiring, used to cite Mugabe. They said that Mugabe did not go into any Truth and Reconciliation Commission; he just let bygones be bygones. And today these are the same people who are coming back to say it seems there was substance in the TRC and therefore in conscious reconciliation and efforts to create reconciliation. They now want meetings to look at the farm situations with owners and workers. And the people we spoke to often about the TRC were the Dutch Reformed Church dominees whom we took pains to visit so that they would bring their people into the whole operation. But we were by and large alone, and they never came or encouraged their people to attend TRC hearings.

But you find that kind of scenario. Even those who were against the TRC have something to refer to. The TRC presents a point of reference, no matter what you thought about it or its purpose. There was this and we did not see it at that time. So that to me is what the TRC achieved among the people.

So the liberals did not come, and others saw it as a place where they were going to crucify the Afrikaans-speaking people. That, of course, was even worse, with the disclosures that came from the war generals and so on. They just felt those stories ought not to be told. We are white; we could not do that. Taking into account that most of these people will always say that they are religious people more than political people, one wonders why their churches haven't taken that whole element further.

WHITE PEOPLE will mostly hide behind ignorance—that they never knew what was taking place. I think most of them were humane, but they feared to be ostracized even by their own congregations and communities. And the whole apartheid system, in terms of group areas and job reservation, created this huge distance between the people. Take provinces like the Western Cape, where I think many of these liberals are coming from. They are still stuck to the idea that Cape Town is a preferential area for them. It is an area for whites and coloureds. Look to the coloured leaders, like Allan Hendrikse: it seems that they could never see that throughout the Eastern Cape the coloureds and Africans could have been one community. And, of course, it is further shocking that the liberals, who are mainly English-speaking people in provinces where they are predominant, allowed areas like Pietermaritzburg, East London, and Port Elizabeth to be some of the worst apartheid places where maybe the people would see the practice and rather withdraw into their houses and shut the doors.

I think now that what is happening in Zimbabwe is making some white people aware of the issues once more. Many of these English-speaking people are kith and kin with those in Zimbabwe. Most of those people who moved to South Africa from the north moved deeper into the country, whether it be East London, Port Elizabeth, Cape Town, and so on, and those areas were screened from the black hordes. We deplore what is happening in Zimbabwe. But we also deplore the way some politicians try to exploit the situation. Perhaps another generation beyond Tony Leon can succeed, but this present one, even when people are dissatisfied with the ANC, will say it is a better evil because when these others had a chance, when they were among the rulers, they did nothing.

ONE DOES NOT KNOW whether one aspect so overshadowed the other that you can say that the victims benefited nothing. But most of them benefited from giving testimony, public testimony on the violations. To them it was a burden eased. During that time they were saying that they are not giving the testimony for the money that might be lying behind, in terms of reparation. They were just too grateful to lighten the burden in their bosoms. But the promise of reparation and the failure of reparation, more especially seeming to come from the government, has been a very sad thing.

This once more ties up with the Zimbabwean thing, that if our present-day government does not offer reparations now then perhaps we will have the ANC leadership, in five or ten years to come, saying in order to get back people's votes, let us now talk about reparation. Who is likely to resist that? And it will be at that time that we are going to realize the depth of frustration that the people have arising from the failure to receive reparation. It is dreadful, more so, rightly or wrongly one is not trying to judge, that the government came up with the special pension largely for the people who had been in exile and people who were prominent in the struggle even if they might have been inside the country. But when you take into account how many people suffered in the process, you cannot be surprised when they say later, you benefited from special pension and we got nothing. And all these things can be very divisive and militate against all efforts toward reconciliation.

MUCH AS WE HAD people from religious sectors on the Truth Commission, we nonetheless had a great number of legal minds also. I remember at some stage some of them would be against prayers and some of them would be indifferent as to whether you pray or not. These were not clashes. I think the two kinds complemented one another and made for a balanced Commission.

TO ME THE CHURCHES in the white community and churches in the black community must work together. They have this common denominator of seeing themselves as the children of God and with almost the same perception of what is good and what is evil. They have a great responsibility toward effecting reconciliation.

Religious groups need to regroup to find their place in civil society. It seemed to me they failed when they could not debate the issue of receiving donations from their brothers and sisters overseas and when it seemed they agreed to let all the donations be channeled through the state for the Reconstruction and Development Program (RDP). They did not even appreciate that the person who was to administrate the RDP at the time was an agnostic who would have found it difficult to understand the churches. The churches simply handed over. So you talk to any minister or priest today about what should be done, and they tell you there is no money and we must go to the government.

Yet they jumped when there was money for the elections from the Independent Electoral Commission. As soon as funds are available the churches are able to act. The churches do have an important place and an important role to play, but they have abdicated responsibility to the government and let the government make decisions about the use of monies from abroad.

I believe the churches should engage in education, which the former and the present Presidents would so love to see. They could go to the government with a coherent plan and say, let us receive money from the donors specifically for this education program. We can also come up with a coherent work plan on reconciliation. And can we not just go out and ask for money overseas?

I attended a workshop in Norway at the end of April where the donor agencies were asking how they could enable the countries that have just come out of political wars to be assisted in democratization and development. They had called the Human Rights Commission to contribute with its South African experiences of the TRC toward reconciliation. So if reconciliation is an issue outside South Africa, where people believe it would be ideal for the creation of democracy and sustainable democracy, why can't the churches inside here make it such an issue? Why should they keep looking to the government and still abdicate everything to the government? Democracy means that there must be no single player in the society. At the workshop in Norway they wanted to know the existence and strength of the civil society. Now if there is no civil society they are all of one mind that democracy will not survive. And the churches are ideal for that kind of strong, sustainable civil society.

There is nothing new for the church in education. Churches have been involved in education for a long time. The denominations need to adopt schools and parishes need to adopt local schools. Some people are worried that it will lead to widespread proselytization, but the fact this time is that they will come into education in partnership with the state. The state will guard against discrimination on a religious level or discrimination on a denominational level. With that strong element I cannot see why they cannot work it out.

The element we are talking about is the element Verwoerd fought so strongly against because he did not want the churches in education. He could not legislate against the Muslims and their children and the Jews and their children, but when it came to the Africans he made certain that churches have no role. Why do we want to accept that as a *fait accompli* and we cannot do anything more about it? And unfortunately, it is the state that is asking the churches to go into partnership with it, and it is more of an affront to the state by the churches.

Would you agree with many of those interviewed so far that reconciliation must begin at the grassroots?

My biggest problem is this constant talk of grassroots. The grassroots are the poor who are vulnerable. It haunts me, because it is more a battle of the middle class for the grassroots or the domination of the grassroots without necessarily the grassroots itself fighting that struggle. I find it literally damning. I do not know what can be done. I will be so repetitive. Go and teach the grassroots for heaven's sake, take the schools to the grassroots— this is how to cater for the grassroots. It is not what the Council of South African Trade Unions is doing when it says that it is fighting for jobs and the unemployed are saying, but you are frightening away the investors who can give us jobs. What are those people doing to the grassroots? What are they talking about and who is doing the talking? Some of them become givers of welfare. I do not say that this is not what the grassroots want but that this is the sort of thing that the humanity and the integrity of a person does not want. Let us go back to teach the people.

We talk about African renaissance. Who is talking about that? When we talk in my field about caring for the older persons, a rich person—no matter how old and senile he is—is not counted old. He is not an older person, simply because to be old is to be poor. The same thing happens with the intellectuals and politicians. No matter how old he may be, seventy or eighty, he does not see himself in the mainstream of the older persons. The old are the poor pensioners who not only queue up for their pensions, but when they come out of there they will be maintaining their children and grandchildren.

Sin tax? Who will do it? If it can be done without creating bad blood then let it be done, but not by the churches when they are so grateful for whatever can be thrown at them. The churches can never face the rich up there. They cannot challenge the rich.

Part of my problem is that I still see the churches as able to do this if they can get their act together and begin to present their case in both education and reconciliation. If it can be done together let it be together, but if it can be done denominationally so be it. We are not expecting all denominations to respond alike, but we do hope that some will respond positively.

I COME FROM THE TRC and I cannot see blanket amnesty because you are saying people must remain in a situation where they cannot be helped, they cannot be understood, they cannot be sympathized with and cannot be enhanced. That would be my problem. To a person who suffered so gravely before I do not think it works. If the people were for the one-off tax, and let it be known that they were, then I would say let there be blanket amnesty. The people who receive the amnesty need to be serious.

I would just like to see a program on reconciliation and then we discuss that or see it in implementation. I would dearly love to see it from the religious sectors where there is no political face-saving.

FR. SEAN O'LEARY

Thursday, April 20, 2000

Those who think it [the TRC] was a waste of time are those people who are in denial. They are the ones who do not want to believe what happened and who feel that the process was to do with other people and not with themselves.

$\mathcal{M}$

FR. O'LEARY is the acting Director of LUMKO, an educational institute of the Catholic Church. His love of life is evident in his whole manner, and the rapid delivery of his views only serves to underline his deep desire for quick transformation of both church and society.

I THINK THAT PEOPLE very often confuse the word "reconciliation" and the word "forgiveness." Let's take a practical example. We get into a heated argument about politics in South Africa and we get overheated and insult each other. There is wrong on your side and there is wrong on my side. We need to reconcile. But what if I simply say to you that because you are a South African you are a lousy so-and-so? You have done nothing to me. I am the one who has instigated the action, and in this case it does not call for reconciliation; it calls for me to say I am sorry and for you to forgive me.

That is very important. Reconciliation is one of the most misunderstood words in our vocabulary today. If you take the Truth Commission, a number of very different and contrasting definitions came out.

The first was to forgive and forget, as if you could wipe out the collective memory of a nation. This approach would have negated and sabotaged the whole task of the Truth Commission, which was to acknowledge and record the past in such a way it would form the foundation for building a unified society.

The second was building bridges across the divisions in society, without seriously wanting to change the structures that maintained these divides.

A third was justice, equating reconciliation with the quest for reclaiming the rule of law. But clearly from the very beginning the TRC did not take the justice path. Given that individual justice was not a component of the Truth Commission's mandate, it was very difficult to use this working definition of reconciliation.

A religious understanding called for confession, remorse, forgiveness, and restitution. While good in itself, it did not seem to be suitable for use in the South African context to build a reconciled nation. The fact that those seeking amnesty did not have to show remorse or ask for forgiveness seriously blocked the application of the religious process for real reconciliation. It may work in individual cases, but has little chance for collective application.

Then there was the idea of economic and social reparation as a definition of reconciliation. This is a very challenging approach. For the majority of South Africans who saw little change in their situation, this was music to their ears. For those who continued to profit from the unequal distribution of wealth and opportunity, this definition was like a red rag to a bull. That said, this definition of social and economic reconstruction could not be taken as the definitive South African understanding for national reconciliation. In the final analysis, the lack of a common national understanding of reconciliation remains one of the greatest obstacles in seeking this reconciliation. This is the challenge facing the nation: first to agree on a definition of reconciliation.

Reconciliation means that there is wrong on both sides. That is what I am saying. When there is wrong only on one side, we are looking at the need for confession of guilt and the onus on the other to forgive. Who is the catalyst? In forgiveness it is the person who has been hurt. Who is the catalyst in reconciliation? It is both parties.

I THINK THERE IS A DIFFERENCE between the secular and religious approach to reconciliation, and that was often shown in the tensions at the Truth Commission. The tension rose between those who saw it as a secular event and those, like the Chairperson, who saw it as a spiritual process. The difference is that the religious accommodates the concepts of forgiveness and reconciliation but the secular society does not. Secular society chooses the rule of law as the way of dealing with deviances in society. So when a person is found guilty and condemned, there is little or no process of rehabilitation in the sense of restoring the dignity of the person. There is a very big difference, and from the religious point of view you see that people come to churches, to ministers, when they feel they want to reconcile and be forgiven. They do not go to judges or doctors. There is a huge difference.

IN SOUTH AFRICA the TRC process is the foundation stone upon which a process for reconciliation can be built. It was an important moment but it was only a beginning. It is, very clearly for me, the area of reparation and restoration and the issue of symbolism that is of importance now.

We call December 16 the Day of Reconciliation, and that is a golden opportunity to put in motion gestures of reconciliation. A clear example was the way the Catholic Diocese in Durban hired the Kingsmead Stadium and invited all those people from all over that diocese through KwaZulu Natal to come together for a service of reconciliation. I think that is quite powerful. There is the Vietnam War memorial in Washington, D.C. in the United States. Fifty-two thousand one hundred names are recorded on that wall, and it is a place where a whole country can come to mourn some horror that took place thousands of miles away. It is a rallying point for healing and reconciliation. We need something like that, and we need to do it in an African way. We need somewhere where the memory of the past can be kept alive, where the people can come and find healing and restoration. I think symbolism is very important for our nation just now.

FOR ME THE TRAGEDY of the TRC is that it was the child of political compromise. In the final days of the writing of the interim constitution, they were blocked on the insistence of the Nationalist Party that amnesty should be given. The opposition capitulated, and it is the last clause in the interim constitution. So the starting point was not the need to heal our nation. The starting point was the need to find a way forward in a very difficult negotiation process. It was only afterward, when people began to ask how it was possible to give amnesty and do nothing for those who are survivors or victims, that we got the compromise that became the TRC. So I think the starting point of the TRC is not a good starting point. Again, I think one of the major defects in the amnesty process is that people do not have to say they are sorry. You cannot force forgiveness, but you can force restitution, and I think we lost an avenue of real progress there. Perpetrators should have been forced within their means to make some form of restitution even if it was only of a symbolic nature.

I would rather say that the TRC was important but it was not balanced. The words we use of healing, reconciliation, and forgiveness are not political words. They are religious words, and the custodians of those words are the churches and other faith groups in the country. The onus is really on those people to take the initiative and not politicians.

THERE IS A NATIONAL DENIAL going on in the white community. I think we must credit the mass media for highlighting the Truth Commission on radio, television, and in the newspapers. The white community was shocked at what really happened. They never really believed this, and when it was brought to their notice they began to isolate people. They said it was those people who did it, those bad people. It was not us. In a sense it was never accepted that we, the white community, went hand-in-hand with what happened. For example, big business has remained very silent throughout the whole process of the TRC as they did during the years of apartheid. They were very happy to work in the old system to their advantage and in the new system in the same way.

So the process isolated the wrongdoers, and white society exonerated itself by denial. I was not expecting anything else. What was good is that it showed people what actually happened and how bad it was. People say that they never knew it was that bad because they did not want to accept it. Now they know!

For me one of the keys to a reconciled society is that people can talk to each other. So when we begin in our education system to integrate people and when one person learns the language of another, say English or Afrikaans and say Zulu or Sotho, so people can really talk to one another, that, for me, is a key to the future. An integrated education system can play an important role in the future of our nation.

ONE OF THE MAJOR TRAGEDIES of the Truth Commission is the unwillingness or inability of the government to pay restitution. So for the twenty-one thousand people who came forward and got nothing, they feel victimized a second time. That is serious. The vast majority of the allocation for urgent interim emergency relief has not been used yet because there is no infrastructure in the department of justice to deal with it. The government has point blank refused to implement the long-term relief policy, and that is going to leave a very bad taste about the TRC. When you think the amount suggested is three billion rand over six years, which is half a billion per year on the national budget, it is nothing in that budget. Even if they were to put on a "shame tax" or "sin tax" as they call it, you would soon have that money. The political will to finish the Truth Commission is not there and the victims got victimized a second time. This is not acceptable and will have to be challenged by civil society. The TRC ends in tragedy.

This is probably the most comprehensive Truth Commission in humankind, and, therefore, not to finish it and bring it to a satisfactory close is really sad. You know, only twelve percent of the people got to the hearings, and the pouring out of their grief to a competent and listening body did help to bring some healing. It would be nice now, however, to think that the policy that was suggested by the reparations subcommittee could and should be implemented and then bring it to a close and build on that for your future generations.

IT WAS GOOD that we had the participation of religious people. It depends on how you see the process. Was it a secular process or a religious? I think the process itself has to be acknowledged as a religious process, and therefore to have a number of people from the religious fraternity was a good thing. The choice of the Chairperson was excellent and he did a really good job. I understand that it was not for everybody, but the majority of people saw it as a religious process and that is fair enough. The churches and other faith groups play an important role in our society. Reconciliation is their domain and so it was good to have the religious representatives there.

I have spoken to a number of people who have different persuasions on this issue, but to me to see it as a purely secular process in the midst of our religious society would have been lopsided. The people on the Commission reflected our society, and we are a religious society. We may not practice it but we are a religious society!

THE RELIGIOUS GROUPS have really fallen down in taking this reconciliation process seriously. And yet they have so many opportunities to do so, and I think they *must* take the initiative to organize events, healing events, to bring the people together —for example, a walk for peace and reconciliation, using stadiums for people to gather to hear each other's stories, events that stretch out hands across the divides. That is the role of the church, but they are not fulfilling that role. It is their role and not the role of government to do this. But they have retreated into a laager since the late eighties.

We have to challenge the church leadership to accept their role. It might just be battle fatigue that is causing this malaise, but I believe our leadership has become a lot weaker than it was. In fact we have poor leadership at the level of our churches right now, and maybe that is something we have to go through for ten or fifteen years. People are tired. I find it in my own church. If bishops were allowed to retire I know about ten of them who would retire tomorrow. They are just tired out. But it does mean that if you do not have that leadership at the top it is difficult to inspire it at grassroots levels. So I think it is another golden opportunity being lost by the churches and other faith groups throughout the country.

It may be useful to have our own truth commissions in the different churches. The submissions made were saying how much we did and not talking about our shadow, and the shadows were there but they did not come out. I think we owe it to South Africa to look at the churches. They were always divided, as you know. Each church was a microcosm of the society we were living in then and is a microcosm of the society we are living in now. The actual percentages may change a little, but we mirrored the society then. Today we mirror the society in the sense that you have people in my own church who think the Truth Commission was a waste of time and others who see it as a very important starting point on the road to reconciliation.

Those who think it was a waste of time are those people who are in denial. They are the ones who do not want to believe what happened and who feel that the process was to do with other people and not with themselves.

But they can get away with that because of the lack of challenge in our churches at the present time. I meet the bishops twice a year and am still involved in what we call the Justice and Peace and Human Rights Department, and it really has fizzled out as an issue. They wrote a pastoral letter on reconciliation, but it was so bad—and I wrote it!—because it had to be short enough to be read in three or four minutes. In the end it said nothing. It would have been better to do nothing. There is no one denomination, as far as I can see, who is taking this issue seriously at a national level.

The concern is that if we do not do anything, no one else will, and this golden opportunity in these earlier years of our new democracy is going to be lost.

I THINK IT IS SAD to think we went through this whole process, flawed as it was, and now having gone through the painful process there is talk about giving blanket amnesty. That would be a major insult to the Truth Commission. You cannot give blanket amnesty. It is a sign of encouragement to me that the Amnesty Committee has granted only a small number of the many applications for amnesty. To get amnesty you really have to do something and that is good. Blanket amnesty—No!

I think the real question there is the following: Are we going to see civil claims in the civil courts relating to events in the past? For example, would the South African Council of Churches take the government to court over the bombing of Khotso House? That might be very interesting. But it could turn the Truth Commission into an ongoing fun fare and that would be terrible. We cannot go on a witch-hunt through the legal system. But it is possible that someone who has lost a loved one, and the person responsible has not received amnesty, can resort to the law. Possibly the Legal Resource Centre or Lawyers for Human Rights could pick that up as a test case. We need a test case.

I DO FEEL THAT MANY OTHER COUNTRIES are looking at South Africa, and I think that people in the churches should be ready to answer requests from places such as Rwanda, Burundi, and Northern Ireland. We have a story to tell not just about the TRC. The story began in February 1990, and it is still going on. It is important in that we need success stories in the world when we look at the tragedies that are taking place, especially on this continent. We need to be able to share our story of hope. We should not be afraid to say that we have something to share with you and simply tell our story. We should be more organized in that regard, proactive in telling the story. We have something to say that can help the world.

I think they made a bold effort in the Truth Commission. They did not fail, and they did not achieve, but they were not put there to achieve. They laid a foundation on which civil society and religious society can build. That foundation is now there. The report is the unofficial history of the country from 1960 to 1964 and it needs to be popularized; it needs to be put into school curriculum and we need to own it is as our history. It is a sad history, but it is ours.

There was a misconception that the basic premise of the Truth Commission was false: tell us the truth and we will find out what happened and that will lead us to reconciliation. The truth will set us free—and it didn't. In the TRC we found—which is also quite admirable—that there is a call for justice. People do not want revenge. They do want justice. And I think that is a fair position to take by a people who have suffered so much. It illustrates the maturity of a nation. No talk of revenge, just justice. Somehow we need to win back the concept of justice within the country. However it comes, we have to admit that what happened was wrong, and we have to put in as many mechanisms as possible to make sure it does not happen again.

AFRICAN INDIGENOUS CHURCHES

The African indigenous churches arose from a native African aversion to a missionary emphasis on western culture. It is an expression of Christianity through African customs. The first group was in 1884 when a black Methodist broke from the white-dominated church of that time and formed the Thembu National Church. They are a major force in African religious life. The following is enormous, with the Zion Christian Church claiming up to four million adherents in South Africa alone. Most of these churches, however, are small and local in membership. Soweto, the large black complex near to Johannesburg, has as many as three thousand indigenous churches.

Until recently treated with scorn by the mainline churches, they are now accepted as legitimate members of the Christian community.

ARCHBISHOP T. W. NTONGANE

Wednesday, September 1, 1999

It was a court. And Africans know what is going to happen once you get to court.

ARCHBISHOP NTONGANE is an imposing figure with an imposing voice. He is Archbishop of the Apostolic Methodist Church, Chairman/Administrator of the Khanya African Instituted Churches Training and Research Institute, and President of the African Instituted Churches Association of Southern Africa and of the Council of African Instituted Churches. He is, among others, a leading figure in attempts to bring different indigenous churches into a form of union with one another.

FIRST OF ALL, I remember that God's forgiveness is unconditional. Anything we do for reconciliation is done under that forgiveness of God.

THE PEOPLE in our independent churches like the Old Testament. They are not very comfortable with the New Testament so much. Our idea of reconciliation, therefore, is based on the justice of God shown in the Old Testament.

RECONCILIATION IS NOT A COMPLICATED IDEA. It becomes complicated only when someone or some group wants to dominate and to rule others. I would not like to separate religious reconciliation and secular. It is possible for all people. Reconciliation is needed everywhere in society, in the home and in organizations and in churches.

When reconciliation happens it is between two parties or two people. It needs an initiator who may be the one who is hurt or the one who did the hurting, or even a third party who may see the problem between the two and invite the two to sit together. It needs an objective of reconciliation on the part of both parties. It needs people, all the parties, to come down, to sit down and look at each other and listen to one another. When I say come down I mean sitting down flat on the floor, not on chairs. Everyone needs to be equal and to open up to each other. No one should begin with the idea that they alone are in the right. We must approach reconciliation with an open heart.

Anyone can do it. It can be in the house, whether it is a child or husband or wife. It can be in the church and it can be in a community. The round table idea of the Europeans is a good idea, where everyone is equal. Because we have moved into our own churches does not mean that we do not get some good things from the whites. We appreciate what they did, but the trouble is with the way they did it.

First there were the British. They did not understand us at all. We thought the Afrikaners would understand us and not treat us the way they did. They did do some good things, but their mistake was in not coming to us and talking with us before implementing their ideas. You must not do it *for* the people but do it *with* the people. We Africans want to be in from the beginning. No chief will make a rule without first sitting with the people. It is not our custom for people do something, arrange something, and then ask me to come and take part. If it is done like that it does not belong to me, it belongs to you.

I wish the church had been Africanized long ago and then we would not be having the problems today. That was not a good thing to have white churches there and coloured ones there and black ones over there. If the African tradition of participation had been there at the beginning, that would not have happened.

This is why I went into an independent indigenous church. Some people think the independent churches arose because people hated the white people. No, some of the things they did were good, and we did not hate them. We hated the treatment we were given in not being asked to sit down and take part in making decisions.

THIS SAME THING HAPPENED with the Truth Commission. I think there were some links missing in the forming of the Truth Commission, especially in involving the poor, the people who live in shacks with plastic and cardboard, those who are illiterate. We have to look at the person, not at their status, and we need to look with godly eyes at each person as a person made in the image of God. Those people needed to be represented on the Commission itself. You do not have to have had lots of schooling to be wise, and they could have brought their own wisdom.

The TRC has been helpful in a way. The whole crux of the matter is Mr. Mandela's response to his imprisonment and all that happened to him. If he had responded grudgingly, wanting revenge, I doubt if there would still be a South Africa. That one man did so much, and this nation has not yet really honored him for it. A big gathering, a big feast, is needed to honor him.

IT WAS GOOD that there was the TRC. We are saddened that the selection of the persons working for the TRC was not good, not well balanced. If there were five very high academic people, there should have been five non-academic people who have experienced the system. We can get much from those who read and write, but you can get much from those who can do neither. We are ignoring the illiterate, and do you think that because someone cannot write that they cannot understand? We have lost a lot of wisdom from the ordinary people. Do you think that because they have not been to school they do not know what happened?

One of the big problems was that the Commission became a court. Our people do not feel free in court. You know when you get into a court with all those symbols and clever people you are not free to talk, as in a conversation or at a party. When you get to a courtroom you change automatically. That has been the problem. We did not reach the truth because it was a court where the illiterate felt ill at ease and were not helped to tell their real stories. We thought it was supposed to be more like an Indaba where people can be free to speak and say what they feel and tell their stories—always a case of beer there to help things along—but this was a court.

The leader, the traditional leader, wants to get the truth from the people and nothing else, so he makes it a place where people feel easy and ready to speak from their hearts—not with questions and answers and smart white lawyers. You must feel free, because if once you have become emotional and afraid and not relaxed like you would be at home, you cannot say what is deep in your heart. It was a court. And Africans know what is going to happen once you get to court.

So that what happened sometimes is that people were saying what they think people want them to say. The truth was flavored to make it right for you to benefit and get compensation—whether victimizer or victim. People conditioned the truth for their own good reasons. There are areas where the truth was not spoken out openly. I would have expected that it would not be a court but it would be a conversation, where the people would just sit and talk. There is still much need for recognition of traditional methods and traditional leaders if we are to find real reconciliation.

When I was on the Land Commission they told me that my language was "unprofessional." We need more of that kind of language if we are to hear the truth. Legal people hide the truth rather than find it and expose it.

It is questionable to the ordinary people in the street about who chose the Commissioners. Although we know that the Truth Commission began here in Khotso House as the initiative of the churches, there were too many religious people on the Commission. It was not a good thing to have all those religious people there. It needed to be more balanced, especially with women being there.

THE TRC STILL STANDS ACCUSED by the families of victims that it sided too much with the victimizers. It helped them more than the victims. That is what is said. If I were to advise the Truth Commission I would say that someone from the United Nations should chair the amnesty hearings. We are too proud of ourselves in South Africa. We should ask for help from other people who can give it to us.

GOD INITIATES the whole process of life. This is prophetic. God works through His selected people in the world. There is no turning back from that. God has cycles of operation. How long did it take God to release the people of Israel? And He did it with a forced removal! He removed other people to make room for the people of Israel. And God used the people of the churches to release the people of South Africa, this time to stop forced removals and to bring Mandela to be our President. We are where we are because of the churches.

We shouted at Regina Mundi and other places, like the walk in Cape Town. The church was howling to the international community to hear our cry and help us release Mandela.

We need to continue shouting. The church cannot be complacent. The task of the church leaders is to show godliness. We must remind the government that we voted for them and they are accountable to us. They would not be the government if the church had not brought the apartheid system to its knees. And now we should be picking up this government. We must remain prophetic and not be co-opted and absorbed.

The church has been co-opted, if not adopted, by the present government. Never make the mistake of trying to silence me when I oppose you by offering me a position in your company. For governments and companies will change in five years, but the word of God continues and we need to speak the prophetic word of God and not be absorbed by the government today.

We need an interdenominational—not interfaith—revival. We need a new liberation gospel in Soweto and other townships. We need to revitalize the church especially among the young black people. Once they looked to the church for leadership and help. Now they wonder what we are doing. We cannot fold our arms and say we are waiting for the coming of the kingdom of God. We need churches to reach out to those who live in shacks and not just those who live in big houses.

ORTHODOX

The Coptic Church in Southern Africa is one of the oldest of all Christian churches. It was not able to practice its faith during the years of apartheid when there were many strict regulations about foreign church leadership. Although small in number, the church adds a rich experience of faith to the kaleidoscope of Christian practice.

BISHOP MARCOS

Saturday, October 23, 1999

Reconciliation, according to the biblical principle, is when we acknowledge the rights and the duties of everybody, and we recognize the value of each other. No woman is less than the man in the world or no man is less than the woman in the world. And it is the same thing between whites and blacks and any other color.

BISHOP MARCOS is the head of the Coptic Church in Southern Africa. Quietly spoken and overtly gentle by nature, Bishop Marcos welcomed me to his office and home in what was once a northern Johannesburg suburb school building and now is transformed into a cathedral and monastery of the Coptic Church. The elaborate decoration and symbolism of the cathedral itself stands in stark contrast to the small and simply furnished office and monastery.

I BELIEVE THAT THE PRINCIPLE of the TRC was biblical. The Lord says that if somebody confesses his sins and asks for forgiveness he should be forgiven. This means that he truly confesses. He puts down his mistakes of the past and understands what grievances he has caused for himself and for others by his doing so. I look at it more from the biblical point of view than the political point of view. I don't like to interfere in politics at all. But our responsibility as religious leaders is to declare what is right according to the word of God and then let the politicians do their job.

I believe that the TRC has helped to remove from the minds and hearts of the people the grudge that was accumulating over the years because some people came along and said, "I am wrong. I have been wrong. At that time I was under a certain mood but now I know that what I have done is wrong. So I ask for forgiveness."

Those who did not acknowledge their mistakes—truly something should be put on them to make them say, "I am sorry I have done wrong." So if the TRC did not accomplish all of what it should have done for reconciliation, it did at least do a great deal of hushing down the feeling of the grudge that was in the hearts of many people. There were many people who have been really harassed and treated in a very savage way, and definitely that accumulated anger and, let me say, grief and pain. Definitely this has been hushed to a great extent. The main thing that I was really happy about was that it was all based on a biblical principle. I think it has done a great deal of good.

I T WAS A GOOD THING that many of the people on the Commission were from the religious community. They were able to stress the biblical principle that when a sin is committed a person should confess and acknowledge that he has done wrong. He is sad about it. He commits himself that he will not do it again and he asks for forgiveness.

And that forgiveness includes correcting, as much as he can, the wrong he has done to others. The Lord praised Zacchaeus, the short man, when he said that he will give half of his money to the poor and if he has wronged anybody he will pay him fourfold. This caused the Lord to say, "Salvation has come to this house." This means that the offender has not only to say "sorry" but also to pay back what he has taken from others. This is a biblical principle, and I felt this Commission, when I heard about it, to be a very intelligent idea.

ANY HUMAN BEING, white or black, who says "I am sorry" and "I have done wrong" is not belittled in the eyes of the society, but on the contrary he will be very much glorified and respected and honored. People who do not want to say "I'm wrong" are dishonored because they are belittling themselves. We are human beings with weaknesses and limitations. No matter how intelligent and bright we are, we have our weaknesses. And we, if we acknowledge our weaknesses and confess them, should be honored. So I think the TRC has helped everybody, whites or blacks. The whites needed it more because they were the governing class. But every white who came forward and acknowledged his mistake and asked forgiveness, I think, should be honored very much. And I believe that the atmosphere, according to my own understanding, is quite favorable for the reconciliation process.

THE VICTIMS WERE ALSO HELPED. One of the things that can make man to feel the grief more and more is when nobody listens to him. This is human character. I myself was faced with somebody in Kenya many years ago who locked me in a room and put a sword over my neck for twenty-five minutes, threatening to kill me and cut me into pieces. The Lord saved me from this ordeal, but one of the worse things after I was released from this experience was that I could not find anybody to listen to my story. It was very difficult. I had to keep it inside. I was talking to the Lord Jesus Christ only, and it was very, very, very hard on me.

Once you air it out and when you see sympathetic ears listening to you it makes a lot of difference. So I think the blacks who came to express their experience as victims of that ordeal have been helped by finding a sympathetic ear. They found a Commission which is assigned by the government to listen to them and tell them that their pains may have happened twenty, thirty, fifty years ago but they are not dumped or buried. Somebody is listening to them. We hear what you have gone through, we acknowledge your pains and sufferings and the beloved ones whom you lost and the dead people who are aggrieved. And definitely it must have helped some of them. It may be that at the moment it has provoked their grief and suffering and a lot of tears, but I believe that later it must give them a soothing effect in their lives.

RECONCILIATION, according to the biblical principle, is when we acknowledge the rights and the duties of everybody, and we recognize the value of each other. No woman is less than the man in the world or no man is less than the woman in the world. And it is the same thing between whites and blacks and any other color. Every human being has his value in the eyes of God, in the eyes of man, and in the eyes of society. What happened here in South Africa was a real injustice toward some by others.

Let me say that the world of today is full of injustice as one human being, whoever he is, tries to find supremacy over another due to color, religion, tribe, or language. There are many, many, many reasons where man can try to dominate others. Reconciliation is a spirit in which I should acknowledge the freedom of everybody and the value of everybody and their beliefs without belittling them. I go to India and I see somebody who is worshiping a cow. I should not belittle him. This is his way. I may try to persuade him to do something else but not to persecute him.

And reconciliation is truly to say, "If I have wronged you in the past I am very sorry and I will not do it again." And then we sit together in very quiet diplomacy and through listening to one another we try to iron out the differences and remove what has been in the past. We open a new page and we start with a new spirit of humanity and love for one another.

We have an amazing prayer of reconciliation in our liturgy. We reiterate the story of how man fell into sin and how man disobeyed God and how God made the move as a very gracious God to come forward and say, "You have wronged but I am coming to take your hand, to come and reconcile with men."

So reconciliation needs both sides to make an effort to let the past go and start anew. It can start from either side. And it should be also in the hearts of both sides, and both sides should take an active part in it.

IN THE SECULAR WORLD people would speak about material things. But in the secular world, I believe, reconciliation can happen through diplomacy, listening to each other, giving each other a chance to talk and to express feelings. It calls for tolerance and acceptance of each other.

I have had some experiences in secular committees in which these same spiritual principles play a role, even if it is hidden when you are working on secular reconciliation. We can speak on the level of dignity and honor and material things and work for reconciliation in the secular world. If two partners in a business fight with each other, there are so many ways to reconcile them by looking at documents or papers or contracts or agreements. They have to be careful not to trespass on one another or cheat one another. The

Lord shows us a difference between greed and need. This applies in the secular world.

I DON'T THINK THE TRC is needed anymore. What should happen in South Africa now is trying to uplift those who have been underprivileged, and also trying to let everybody have equal opportunities according to his abilities. Some people who have been underprivileged think of their rights, but they don't think of their duties. This can cause a big problem. Everyone who wants to take a position in the society and wants to be a valuable citizen and equal to others should understand that he has duties in the same way as he has rights.

Equal rights for all can come through hard work, study, and all sorts of efforts to make us both productive citizens and people able to push forward to improve our country and live peacefully together. We need to provide the means for this to happen.

We need also to fight the causes of crime. Reconciliation, in my terms, would be effective when we see the rate of crime going down in this country. What are the causes and the places of breeding of criminals? We have to look not only to fight crime but also to fight the breeding places of criminals. In America you do not see flies because they destroy the breeding places of flies. We need to look to the breeding places of crime in our society.

For the church this means we have to lift the spiritual understanding of the people. The church should really have a message for the people that does not flatter them but helps them to examine themselves through the light of the word of God. We all need to change. This includes those people who are very good citizens and who are faithful and hard working. All of us need to change.

First of all I need a change every day. Change my mind to start positive thinking and to start forgiving those who have wronged me. The Bible is not written in vain—but are we really living the Bible and then teaching it? Or do we only have words, words, and more words? I believe that many churches have only words, and to change the people it takes time, it takes effort, it takes a lot of energy, and it needs a lot of patience.

I think the churches should start to work hard on the depth of their own sermons. Their sermons should have a deep life and real commitment illustrating selfless sacrifice for the sake of the congregation to try to change others and not let things go on as they are.

We need ecumenical meetings on this level so that we can influence each other. Many church leaders are very busy with their own affairs. So we need simple retreats and quiet times together, praying together and exchanging views about each other. We do not come to say how good we are, but we come to say how needful we are of help from one another. We all need pastors who will hear us and help us to change.

And let me say that at these retreats or quiet times we need not to sit on chairs or high thrones. No! We need to sit on the floor, to sit at zero level and humble ourselves. With contrite hearts we sit there in the dust and say that without the grace of God, without the guidance of God in my life, I am dust and ashes.

And as we sit on the ground there every one of us should throw out his ego; that is one of the greatest enemies of Christ. The greatest enemy of whole goodness in the world today is ego. Suppose that I'm a very successful church leader with thousands of followers: the ego should still not play a part in my life because any goodness in me is not of me, it is from Christ. So we sit on the floor together without ego and say, "Come, let us sit together." We can discuss the many things that challenge Christianity today. Many of them are very strong financially, economically, and influentially. They are spreading in the world and we are living in our differences as Christians. Catholic, Protestant, Presbyterian, Orthodox, and Methodist are spending energy defending their egos and keeping structures going. And the institution becomes the temple I worship. I worship the institution itself and not Christ anymore.

Can we sit on the floor and say how weak we are, how needy we are? Let it be a starting point. And I have no doubt that the Lord Jesus Christ who humbled himself to that extent, and even lower by washing the feet of his disciples, would enable us to find ourselves there. Believe me, reconciliation starts there, and if we don't do it voluntary today the challenges that are increasing and mounting in the world will push us into the dust themselves.

The Lord Jesus spoke about our oneness. It was a commandment. It was a prayer. And he gave us a commandment also that we love one another. But we take the Bible, the word of Christ who died on the cross, and it becomes the business we are selling in competition with one another.

The nature of the Christ we propagate is peace and love. How much peace and love do we have among ourselves? I believe that this is not the Christianity that the Lord Jesus meant to bring to the world.

Groups of this sort will come about if people have the mind and heart to listen to one another. An initiative of this kind begins with a few people. We don't plant a tree; we plant a seed and let it grow. We start as a group of two or three people at first, then it becomes four or more, enjoying sitting together and really concentrating on this issue, and then it will propagate itself. But to invite people and tell them, "Come and let us sit in the dust and talk together," they will say, "Agh, these people are crazy."

Let me tell a story. Queen Helena, the mother of Constantine the Great, the first Christian emperor, was known for her faith. She longed very much to look for the true cross of Christ. So her son gave her all the facilities to go to Jerusalem, and there she found the true cross. She knew that this was the true cross through a miracle where this cross brought a dead man back to life. Anyhow, Constantine was baptized and became a Christian. So he came to Jerusalem to place the cross of Christ in a big cathedral there to be called by the name of the Holy Cross. The bishop of Jerusalem at that time was a very holy man. There were great preparations, and it was decided that the emperor of Rome was to carry the cross of Christ on his shoulder and enter the cathedral. So Constantine came dressed in a very, very expensive dress bedecked with many jewels. There was a crown on his head and his shoes were made of gold. He carried the cross of Christ and tried to enter the church, but he could not even take one step with the cross on his shoulders, not even move one step. He fell down and then he tried again and could not move. The people came and supported him as he tried once more, but again he fell down. Then the bishop came next to him and whispered in his ear and said, "Your majesty, the one who carried this cross was naked, was poor, was hungry and thirsty, and he was crushed under pain and sorrow. You can never carry the cross as you are. It will not be possible."

Constantine understood the bishop, and he went and he removed all these rich things. And when he came with a simple dress he could carry the cross!

JEWISH

⌘ ⌘ ⌘

MR. FRANZ AUERBACH

Thursday, September 2, 1999

Another problem is that, on the whole, victims remember what happened to them better than bystanders do, let alone perpetrators. Perpetrators want to say: "Forget it, we did it, it does not matter anymore." Bystanders say: "Yes, we know it was there but don't keep reminding us." But victims don't have that luxury.

⌘

Franz Auerbach is a well-respected expert in education and a champion of interfaith activity. Of the Jewish faith, he is a Vice-President of the South African Chapter of the World Conference on Religion and Peace and the Chairperson of the working group of the National Religious Leaders' Forum.

I DID AN EXERCISE for the World Conference on Religion and Peace about three years ago where we sent our letters to Christian, Hindu, Muslim, and Jewish groups. We asked them: "How does your religion see reconciliation?" We got replies from all of them. I compiled those into a single document, and what is quite clear is that all of them mentioned similar elements in the process of reconciliation. Here is the compilation:

What is reconciliation?

- Acknowledgment;
- Confession (which has different forms of expression);
- Remorse;
- Seeking forgiveness;
- Making restitution by those who have wronged others.

They also stress the religious duty of the victim of wrongdoing or injustice to forgive the perpetrator, so that:

- "The victim may then obtain forgiveness for his or her own sins" (Judaism);
- "Since pardon is rewarded by God" (Islam);
- "Forgive our trespasses as we forgive them that trespass against us" and "Confession brings forgiveness by Christ" (Christian);
- "Pray that I will not commit the same wrong again, and ask God to bless me with divine qualities" (Hinduism).

All religions teach that human beings do have a conscience, knowledge of good and evil. Therefore:

- We should acknowledge our wrongdoing and redress injuries and grievances.
- We must seek to restore harmonious relationships with our fellow humans and with God. We must offer restitution and ask for forgiveness.
- There must be a sincere desire not to commit such wrongs in the future.

All the religions stress that as far as possible wrongs and injuries inflicted must be redressed—with this, repentance is inadequate:

- Islam speaks of the need "to develop a community sharing commonly accepted moral and social elements of justice."
- Judaism reminds us that "harming a fellow human being is a sin against that person and against God."
- Christianity asserts that we should "forgive first to initiate reconciliation as that is the example which Christ set."
- Hinduism warns us that our deeds will be punished or rewarded on merit—if not in this life then in the next one—but that through forgiveness and repentance we will exert a positive force that will neutralize the negative one caused by our wrongdoing.

Those are the key elements across the board for all the religions. That does not necessarily mean that the adherents of the religions would agree that all that applies to them personally, although from one perspective that is what it should mean.

I THINK THAT THE ELEMENTS involved in all reconciliation practices, whether religious or secular, are very much the same. Acknowledgment, confession, remorse, forgiveness, and restitution have to apply to reconciliation if you want it to mean anything.

IN SOUTH AFRICA we are in a situation where many whites are inclined to say, "I did not touch anybody and I paid fair wages. I didn't put up signs saying 'Whites only' even if I obeyed them. So I don't have anything to be remorseful about." Black people, on the other hand will say, "You benefited from the system. You got a good education and I got a bad education. You had the privileges and I had nothing." And that creates a problem. But really, I don't think that the secular concept of reconciliation can be very different. And you have the problem of the state saying that it is not able to make restitution because there is not enough money.

I am quite comfortable with the statement that apartheid was a crime against humanity. But that means that it is not only the people who suffered gross violations and who appeared before the Truth Commission who suffered. Millions of other people suffered also. Forced removal is a violation of human rights, but all the people who were subject to forceful removal did not appear before the Truth Commission. We should acknowledge them.

It is also true that many white people are inclined to say, "Look, I was not an activist but I voted for the opposition political party." In reality, taking the world as a whole, can you really expect ordinary human beings, of whatever color, to do more than that? If people were fired by moral commitment of a high order, the world wouldn't be the way it is. That is acknowledged by the Jewish faith in the fact that we have a Day of Atonement every year. If we really got better we, presumably, would not need it anymore!

I think what is needed in South Africa to achieve reconciliation is not specifically aimed at reconciliation but reconciliation cannot really happen without it. Our society has been structured so that relatively few people in different communities know each other at all. So, they don't really know what things were like for others, how they perceived things.

I have experienced this for myself when making some attempt to have dialogue with fellow South Africans who are Muslims, because of the Jewish-Muslim stand-off. One of the things you learn is that Jews tell you that they were persecuted, even before the Holocaust. We know that is true. But Muslims have a similar view of Christian Europe having oppressed Muslim society. I didn't know this before, and it has been very helpful. You are not going to understand Muslims if you do not learn that.

I had slightly more contact with black South Africans because I worked in a night school, not that that is a very deep contact. There were elderly people coming three or four times a week to learn to read and write. Now that is a heavy thing to have gone through. Because I worked on the Committee for the Repatriation of Exiles I heard some stories about the pain of exile and the difficulty of adapting to it. Then there were people I knew who could not study what they wanted to because the doors were closed to them. I think it is necessary to hear people's stories across the same table before you really have the feeling of why we must feel remorse, why we must make restitution.

Given also the numerical imbalances, even if you organize that type of contact, a lot of black people would still not be able to tell their stories. But maybe what is most important is that those in the privileged groups become aware. If all of them were aware, that would already be a great step forward. The Truth Commission report is a powerful thing. It is true that if you read it you will learn a great deal about the past. But how many people bother to do that? What can we do to make people read it to promote reconciliation in the end? You are only going to do it if you have enough interest, enough contact, and enough conscience. There needs to be a lot of promotion of contact and understanding. This is something the religious communities can do. But it is a difficult process.

I THINK THE TRC has helped greatly within the framework that was set for it. There was a wish on the part of those who represented the disadvantaged sections of South African society to let people tell their stories. Obviously that was a good thing. The problem is with amnesty. It arose from political compromise. The then-government would not have signed the interim constitution unless it contained the phrase "There shall be amnesty." They didn't define it at that time, but that was the condition for getting the democratic election and a majority government. It is a condition which many people, particularly those who are genuinely interested in justice, feel very uncomfortable about. It is the compromise we made.

But we did at least get the truth through the TRC. And it seems to me that we have to accept that truth itself is the form of justice. It is not a perfect form of justice, but it is a form of justice because at least you say the truth. Another value was to confirm what people already knew: namely, that the state applied torture and the state, occasionally, murdered to get rid of its opponents. One can possibly understand that the state went that route because of the situation they faced.

In the absence of a negotiated settlement such as the Eminent Persons Group tried in 1986, they were faced with a population which, no matter what they put forward, was not satisfied. The carrots of homelands and tricameral parliaments did not work. They could not make much of an impact on the majority, so all they could think of was greater repression. The idea was that if only you kill or neutralize or liquidate (whatever horrible word you use) the leaders, then the rest would be all right. But, it didn't work like that, and anybody who knows anything about previous revolutions or major political changes knows it does not work that way. You don't need a leader to be told that you are angry, that your intelligent grandmother is a kitchen maid because of the color of the skin. You do not need an agitator to tell you that, even though it is true that sometimes very downtrodden people have learned to accept their fate.

WHITE SOUTH AFRICANS have come to accept responsibility for apartheid to a limited extent. It is easier to get them to accept a social responsibility than a personal one. It is true, for example, that because of better education we are better functioning, more knowledgeable, and, therefore, better earning human beings because of the way the system ran. But you cannot really say from that, you shouldn't do that for me if you didn't do for others. What one should say is that it should be done for others as well. In other words, everybody should have had a good educational system.

With regard to personal responsibility, one of the things one could do is to make a personal contribution to something like the President's Fund. I have made the suggestion publicly that we give one month's income to the President's Fund, even if we do it in a number of installments. If that caught on it would release an enormous amount of money. But it has not caught on and I have to accept that. That may be arrogant of me, and maybe some people did and I just do not know about it. I am reminded that the Truth Commission had a register where people could sign. What percentage of the white population availed themselves of that opportunity? It seems as if there were very few.

So I think white acknowledgment of responsibility is only to a limited extent. The continuing question is, what can we do to increase the number? I have to admit that I don't really know. Those of us who feel it must be acknowledged must say it more. But one tends to be restricted to one's own circle of acquaintances, and they are your acquaintances usually because they think like you do anyway.

One thing that worries me arises from part of the work I am doing for the Jewish Board of Deputies. I have for the last six months or so regularly read the journals of the Afrikaaner right-wing. The hatred that spews out of every issue of that is quite unbelievable. Not only is it against blacks but also against Muslims and against Jews. It is terrible poison. I mention it because it seems they actually believe it, and how you touch people like that I do not know.

They tend to argue that the apartheid scheme was a better scheme of running the society than we have now. They will say that letters are sometimes delivered less fast than previously. The fact that many people had no mail delivery at all at that time is ignored. It got worse for the whites, therefore it is a worse system. And that brings us right back to the matter of not knowing what life is like for other members of our society. When you confront people about the suffering of the black population, they will say that they did not know. I think that is a cop-out because we did have newspapers like the *Rand Daily Mail*. It did not tell us everything, but the amount it did tell us was very substantial. We could get information if we wanted it and, although we did not have an entirely free press, we did have a relatively free press. The opportunity to know was there.

If you have any imagination at all you should be realizing some of the things that happened. I heard three or four TRC hearings, and I will never forget the first one, where I heard a lady saying that she had been kept in solitary confinement for thirteen months. Why she did not go mad I do not know. Thirteen months in solitary is enough to drive anybody insane. Even one thing like that makes one realize the evil of the system. But, of course, there are those who will say she saw her warders and so it was not solitary confinement really, or those who would say it was not thirteen months, it was twelve and a half and she must be lying.

B Y ALL I HAVE READ about the Commission, it seems that victims and survivors benefited enormously, especially those who were able to tell their stories. The Commissioners went out of their way to show respect for the dignity of the people who appeared before the Truth Commission, irrespective of whether they were old or young, articulate or not. It must have been a profoundly affirming experience to realize that they actually are interested in what you want to say.

It is sad to say that apartheid, and other systems too, I expect, taught whites to disrespect those with color. I always remember that I once wrote a letter to a newspaper expressing indignation that in many white households children were not taught to respect the age of domestic servants. That elicited a heart-rending letter from a domestic servant saying that I was so right and that it particularly hurt to be treated that way. Kids, aged eight, order a woman who is a grandmother around in quite inhuman fashion. Now, they are not born with that, they are taught it. Not necessarily in so many words, but they merely copy what they see each day.

In many cases, finding out what actually happened to your loved ones was helpful. I think that made a great contribution. Yes, I think the TRC was a great help. Obviously, it didn't go as far as reparations, it didn't bring back the dead, and it didn't heal everyone who came before it. But it was a lot better than if it hadn't happened at all. The fact that it was spread over a long time also helps in that it was not just a three-week wonder.

I THINK THE FACT that there were a number of people with a religious background on the TRC was the right thing. In the end, if reconciliation doesn't have a spiritual element, then what is it all about? Presumably, people with a spiritual or religious background have a deeper understanding of the spiritual side of human nature. That can only be helpful. You want people with understanding and compassion on such a Commission.

In South Africa, it is true that the majority of those who supported the government genuinely believed that the separation system was the best way of running the society. They thought it better than mixing people of different racial groups. It is quite true that when you mix people, they sometimes fight. But what it is also true, which they didn't fully accept, is that if you separate people to that extent, you make enemies one of the other, and that is much worse than a bit of infighting.

The theory of the apartheid system was that there should be separation with equality. But as the judgment of the American Supreme Court in 1954 showed, you can't run separate and equal systems in matters such as education. One of the ways in which, at the end, the apartheid government justified some of those things was to say that blacks don't need elaborate schools because the parents don't have elaborate homes. If you applied that to the poor among the white community there would be a revolution!

I NEED TO ASK if there is such a thing as a religious community. There are congregations. I get the feeling that the pronouncements of religious leaders do not always percolate very far down into congregations. We also know that not all nominal Christians, Jews, Muslims, and Hindus actually belong to congregations, and even some of those who do don't attend regularly. I am one of them.

I am not sure that very much is done about fostering reconciliation, except some preaching. It is obviously better that it is preached about than it is not, but how far that actually softens the hearts of people I do not know. On the other hand, we have had some very nice demonstrations of compassion for the victims of the tornado that destroyed so much in the Cape and after a fire destroyed shacks in Alexandra. So maybe that shows some measure of compassion in our society that may work toward reconciliation.

One of the things that is very sad is that, collectively, black South Africans seem to believe that all whites are rich and most whites are racist. Now, people working in interfaith communities do not really believe that, but one has to face that it is a minority. It is also true that a lot of younger people in all communities know little about what things were like thirty years ago. They have never seen or experienced the "Net Blankes" signs. They do not really know what it was like. They did not go through such experiences as being kicked out of your neighborhood and having it renamed Triomph. It is difficult for many to understand what all the fuss is about.

Another problem is that, on the whole, victims remember what happened to them better than bystanders do, let alone perpetrators. Perpetrators want to say, "Forget it, we did it, it does not matter anymore." Bystanders say, "Yes, we know it was there but don't keep reminding us." But victims don't have that luxury. The Jewish attitude to the Holocaust fifty years later shows that very well. Armenians remember the Turkish massacre of 1912 or 1915. That was a long time ago. People do not forget. And the Anglo-Boer war concentration camps were better remembered by the next generation than by those who were in them, it seems. They have a collective anger, whereas those who went through it may remember a kindness here or there, an Emily Hobhouse kind of event. Collectively, ethnic groups tend to nurse anger and that makes the whole reconciliation process quite difficult. People get accused of digging the past out when one needs to understand that the remembrance of past hurt is a natural human quality. So, if you want to be sympathetic or empathetic, you need to say, "I would like to find out, tell me what happened to you."

Collective anger can be very difficult to deal with. I think reconciliation in the end needs to be translated into a personal element if it is going to have any meaning. We need to see and know the person who has been hurt. Numbers and figures do not mean anything without that personal touch and contact.

Incidentally, maybe one thing that white people could repent and do something about is the names of people. In a huge number of cases they do not know the surnames of the people they employ. They know the surnames of all the white people they employ. That is natural. But black people remain with Christian names only. Maybe that is a road for appreciating other people. Another way, of course, is to learn a black language. That is an acknowledgment of the humanness of a person.

A few individual religious leaders seem to put energy into reconciliation. They try to make sure that people meet across the race line. They try and break down the stereotypes white people have of blacks by inviting such people as the President to special events. I think many religious leaders make the effort but, by and large, we still socialize within our own groups. So we do not meet many people. Whites do generalize about blacks. It comes back to the need to actually meet and put a face and person to the issue. We need to work at contacts.

THE MATTER OF BLANKET AMNESTY weighs two huge problems that are virtually irreconcilable. The one is that if the whole amnesty process has any meaning at all, then those who didn't apply must be treated differently than those who did. I don't think that there can be any question about that. The other is that if we spend the next twenty years having apartheid trials, then that is not going to be helpful for reconciliation.

WE MUST NOT BE CYNICAL about reconciliation. We need to work hard at it and have the debate out in the open, not with accusations but in an attempt to build bridges, listening to people. Maybe we should find a mechanism where we identify white people willing to listen and black people willing to talk. We need to teach that hurts are not forgotten, and they are even less likely to be forgotten if you say, "Forget about it."

Bystanders and perpetrators do not seem to have thought this through. It would be nice if all the nasty things that happened in our history could be forgotten, but humans do not work like that. At the same time, we must not get into a revenge mode either. We must work at it to get the balance right.

Religious constituencies are the right groups to help us work at it as a nation.

CHIEF RABBI CYRIL HARRIS

Monday, August 30, 1999

The task of true reconciliation, critical to the kind of future this country will have, still awaits us. Although a degree of understanding has been achieved and there was a marked absence of retaliation and vengeance, the long process to bring us all together in a workable way has hardly begun.

Head of the Union of Orthodox Synagogues, Rabbi Harris is originally from Scotland. He queries everything with a traditional rabbinical sharpness softened by a gentle sense of humor. In typical fashion he asked me to join him for this interview immediately before lunch so that I could then enjoy his congenial hospitality.

RECONCILIATION means that you achieve, hopefully, a state where individuals, communities, or groups are able to relate to each other without carrying the baggage of the past with them because there has been either expiation or reparation or they have come to some kind of mutual understanding, which allows them to go forward. That's how we would see reconciliation, and it is very applicable to the present South Africa.

There is slight difference in the religious side, especially in Judaism, because you are not allowed to reconcile unless there has been full restitution. If, for example A steals R5000 from B and then says he is sorry for stealing it but he has spent the money and cannot pay it back, there is no chance of reconciliation. Not only has A got to do repentance for having stolen the money, but he actually has to pay it back. You are not going to get parity unless, at the very least, there is an honest attempt to pay restitution. The victim has to accept the genuineness of the perpetrator. It is subjective because you are dealing with people. How this can be worked out in the South African context I am not sure.

But reconciliation, in Judaism, must contain true repentance. This is a crucial element. If, for instance, you have wronged somebody publicly, it's no use asking God for forgiveness. You have got to go to the wronged person three times. Even if they spurn you on the first two occasions, you've got to go three times. You have got to be genuinely sorry. If the person doesn't accept it after three times, it becomes that person's sin for not accepting the reconciliation.

You have to understand first of all where the error is. This is important, and in that sense the telling of the truth was very important in the Truth and Reconciliation Commission. And then we go on to being sorry. That has to be genuine regret. There has to be some kind of confession with the result not to do it again. And, finally, there has to be putting the thing right with one's neighbor.

So these are five crucial steps, which are together in a package called repentance. How you extrapolate from that to the situation here I am not sure. There has been the first stage, which is knowledge of the sin, and we can call that the truth. The TRC has exposed knowledge of the sin and this is very crucial. It's a matter of whether some of the people are genuinely sorry. One wonders with some of the amnesty applications. There has to be a confession of the sin, and we can say that has happened more or less. The resolve not to do the thing again I suppose has happened, but not necessarily for the right reasons. What there hasn't been is an honest attempt at reconciliation in the sense of trying to help the victims in some way.

M OST REGRETTABLY I do not believe the TRC has contributed to national reconciliation. Let me read what I have written for my own book on the matter:

My problem was with the juxtaposition of finding out the truth on the one hand and the desired aim of promoting reconciliation on the other. These seemed to me to be antithetical companions. At a conference of politicians, lawyers and clergymen to discuss the whole ethos of the TRC before the Commission itself was set up, I expressed the view that "the more truth we discover, the less likely we will be able to reconcile. Exposure may well prove divisive." I was promptly attacked as a "conservative" who failed to understand the pain of the victims, a pain that had somehow to be overcome prior to the building of our Rainbow Nation. Archbishop Hurley, just retired from Durban, agreed with me that if a proper job were done in uncovering the horrors of the apartheid era, it might well prejudice the chance of good relationship in the future.

Dr. Alex Boraine, the TRC's Deputy Chairman, subsequently told me that he was convinced that as the aim was for restorative, not retributive, justice we could indeed, once the bitter truth had been established, move onwards and upwards to a genuine process of reconciliation. Archbishop Tutu kept emphasising that reconciliation based on falsehood, on avoiding the reality of all that had happened, could never be a true form of reconciliation and would not last.

Reconciliation means that you achieve a point at which individuals, communities and groups are able to relate to each other without the baggage of the past interfering—this is because there has been either expiation or reparation or they have come to some kind of mutual understanding. However, in South Africa, now that the Commission has finished its work, I feel that while justice has more or less been regarding "the truth," reconciliation is still some way off.

Reconciliation between individual perpetrators and individual victims was partially achieved at some of the hearings, but the much wider area of relationships between the white beneficiaries of apartheid and the huge black population which suffered, and the other population groups in between, has hardly begun. So deep are the divisions along both racial and economic lines that South Africans cannot be considered to be much closer in any significant way as a result of the Commission's work.

The task of true reconciliation, critical to the kind of future this country will have, still awaits us. Although a degree of understanding has been achieved and there was a marked absence of retaliation and vengeance, the long process to bring us all together in a workable way has hardly begun.[1]

Sorry that sounds so critical. It is a factual assessment. I want the TRC to succeed as much as anyone else. Reconciliation has not happened as a result of the truth. It has happened significantly with some very noble individuals. Good Christians, I may say, who are able to forgive and then forget. But it hasn't happened within the cliques and the groups, and one gets the impression that some elements in the Afrikaner world, who did not want it in the first place, have become more distant. And that makes it all very difficult.

It was widely expressed when the report came out last year that it displayed the chasm between the people. Amnesty has proved difficult also. I find that very hard. It makes nonsense out of justice. There was Khotso House, and then the most horrendous attack against a religious institution, the St. James' massacre, when you just go in firing rifles at Sunday worshipers and because you have got a political reason to get you off, which they did, you walk free. And the Amy Beale killing could be considered a racist murder. Her parents have had the courage to forgive. I find it amazing that they have that level of ability and faith.

My problem is that we desperately need reconciliation, but I was right at the beginning, if you follow my line of thought, that the more stones we were going to upturn—and we had to upturn the stones—the more we find out what the enemy had done. You cannot then simply be "lovey dovey." It takes time. It certainly takes time.

Desmond Tutu has asked me constantly why the survivors can't forgive the Nazis for the Holocaust. I tell Desmond, "That is their problem, not yours or mine." We cannot express the forgiveness. You have got to have gone through it to want to forgive and in a sense, with respect, it is an impertinence to hoist it on to people.

I THINK HALF THE WHITE POPULATION are too busy looking after themselves, but I think there's another half, hopefully the more influential half, who recognize that whatever they have got today is a benefit of the apartheid era so that, in logic, they owe something. And morally they recognize that because there is so much deprivation in the country, they have a moral obligation to help. I am hoping that half wins.

Certainly the other half will probably disappear. They are going to leave either because they do not want a black government anyway or because of fear. It is significant that we just had the results of a survey of the Jewish community. It was a thousand-house survey. The figure was forty-two percent who said that they are prepared to help, not just that they thought about it. There was a much higher proportion who felt obliged to help, but forty-two percent said they felt a personal obligation to actually *do* something about the situation. I find that quite an encouragement. Forty-two percent is a highly significant minority.

Also there is a matter of utilization of the skills and resources. When a person is in law they should be helping with a legal clinic; somebody in building should help in building cheap houses; and somebody in welfare, with knowledge of social welfare problems, should make that expertise available. And this should be in general and not just among one's own community.

It is said that a lot of Jewish people have left the country. That has happened over a long period, and this same survey has shown a re-migration of thirteen percent: one in every eight who leave do return. This survey asked the leading question "Where will you be in five years' time?" and all but twelve percent, that is eighty-eight percent, said definitely they would be in South Africa. Our problem is not the number—it tends to be high in the immediate postgraduates' group, which is a skills thing, what the sociologists call a dependency ratio.

I THINK THE TRC helped the victims in the sense that the whole world had an opportunity to understand better what happened to them. I think that has ameliorated their sense of frustration. I recall listening on the radio to the very first hearings. I was in Cape Town. The people were speaking in Xhosa, and I was listening to the English translation, which was very bland and matter of fact. I found I was crying. I couldn't believe that human beings would do this to other human beings.

I think in the sense that now that everybody knows what "he did to me" this has helped. I do think that the truth can be some kind of consolation. Whether it has been fully assuaged is, of course, another matter, in that we have not got round yet to reparations. I get the impression that they are only partially satisfied with what has happened. Again, the truth has helped, but we are still searching for reconciliation.

I LIKE TO THINK that religious people have a finely honed sensitivity to malpractice and inhumanity and torture. And I certainly think that Archbishop Tutu himself played a major role in plumbing the depths. He didn't let anybody let anyone off the hook. I think what helped the survivors more than anything was the understanding. I think they felt they had a group of people who were capable of feeling the extent to which they have been damaged psychologically as well as physically. And I think that has helped tremendously.

THE MAIN THING WE DO, although there are a hundred and one little examples, is Tikkun, which is a major upliftment program. It operates across the board, and we really want to use the Jewish resources, Jewish skills, and Jewish know-how to help. It is done by individuals, by small groups, and through community projects. It covers literacy, agriculture, and small business development. There is help in regard to sport with the organization of a soccer league in Soweto. Culturally we have got a choir and there are choir exchanges. So it is a matter of building bridges as well as helping.

We have government recognition now, thankfully, and it's beginning to take off—just one example of how deeply we are committed. We got hold of an anonymous Jewish manufacturer of winter coats. He gave us six hundred-odd coats, which he could have put for sale or whatever. We used our Hillbrow Centre, and we had tickets for the people who formed a queue. One of the black women who lives on the streets helped by giving out these tickets and getting it all in order. Many of the people told us that this was the first new garment they had ever owned in their life. Some of them were six-year-old children and some of them were eighty-year-old men and women. The first new garment they had ever owned in their lives—very rewarding work.

We are determined to do more and more. At last week's Jewish Board of Deputies Congress a resolution was passed calling on the Jewish community to put their collective shoulder to the wheel in more and better ways. President Mbeki spoke at the opening of that congress, and he asked for a national consensus. The pledge was given to him that the Jewish community would help. So we are committed to outreach programs and upliftment in every possible way.

We employ a black woman at one of the projects. We never try to do this work at a distance or try to impose it from outside. For example, my wife's literary class, they come every night and they are learning how to read and write Sotho. That is one to one. It is not done at a distance; it's done increasingly with grassroots, to cope with grassroots demand.

That kind of thing is the most important thing our religious groups can do, but I would say that some of the religious groups are among the most deprived. There are religions in South Africa who are well placed to set up the infrastructure to help each other. I did ask at the National Youth Leaders Forum that we should have a twinning arrangement between congregations. Let us say a Jewish group in Sandton should adopt a Christian church in Soweto. They should be twinned. That has not happened yet but I see that as a development. I mentioned the giving out of coats. We also at that time had a party for the kids. And on a different occasion we asked the Jewish youth groups to come to serve at a party. Parents were worried about their children going into Hillbrow, but they turned up en masse. More girls than boys: maybe they are braver! It is very fascinating and it is a very rewarding work. It is certainly only a drop in the ocean, but those drops add up and are important.

NOTE

1. See Cyril Harris, *For Heaven's Sake: The Chief Rabbi's Diary* (Constantia, South Africa: Lionheart Publishing, 2000), 216.

MUSLIM

In numbers the Muslim faith is very much a minority among the varied faiths of South Africa. It is a vociferous faith group. Under the National Christian government of apartheid days it was ignored and marginalized. It is now making the most of its new-found acceptance and freedom to speak openly in the new democracy.

DR. FARID ESACK

Tuesday, August 15, 2000

So true reconciliation must first have mutual responsibility. It must be proportionate, and it must carry in it an element of willing forgiveness. But above all it must carry within it tangible manifestations of the commitment to make amends.

DR. FARID ESACK, a Commissioner of the Gender Equality Commission, describes himself as a Muslim progressive theologian. His viewpoint is strong, and there is little or no compromise. The position he held so fervently during the struggle against apartheid remains exactly what it was, and he is often pitted against the movements and shifts of expediency and gain of our fledgling democracy.

W E HAVE AN ARABIC EXPRESSION called the *tasamuh*, which means a mutual letting go of the hurts and the pains of the past, and that comes the closest in our tradition to the expression "reconciliation." It carries with it an element of mutuality, and so does the expression "reconciliation," and the problem is that so often that mutuality is obscured.

One doesn't quite know whether mutuality implies similarity. Does it imply "I forgive, you forgive"? Is there a moral equivicacy inherent in it all? Are the people who threw stones, burned tires, chanted slogans while a policeman's home, perhaps with him inside it, was being burned as culpable as people who threw other people out of helicopters over the Atlantic Ocean and tortured people while they held them in prison? The whole reconciliation idea lends itself to some very wishy-washy, unclear, western liberal, Christian-loving Lord, un-thought-out notions, and so it is a problematic expression for me because it carries with it all of these possibilities.

What is reconciliation for me ideally? It is a proportionate acknowledgment of all the crimes of the past, meaning there must be acknowledgment from all sides of culpability. There is an acknowledgment, for instance, on my part of how I used the tools of eloquence to whip up the emotions of people. We need to acknowledge that there was an element of using people. You can say that you used the people for the greater good, and you can say the end justifies the means, but people are not like taps that you turn on and off so that all of a sudden after liberation you become a good guy and will not use people any longer. There is culpability, but proportionate culpability. My using that skill is not the same as that person on the South African Broadcasting Corporation who lied to people consistently every day.

So true reconciliation must first have mutual responsibility. It must be proportionate, and it must carry in it an element of willing forgiveness. But above all it must carry within it tangible manifestations of the commitment to make amends. For me that means that a minister in the apartheid regime will say, "I will sacrifice my pension and will give up all of the money that I have earned, for it is ill-begotten money. I will give it up. I will go and rent a comfortable small flat in a nice suburb, and all the other I will give to a reparations fund." There must be tangible and proportionate evidence of your willingness to share what you earned at the expense of others.

If that is not part of the deal then what has happened happens: "Finders keepers, losers weepers." All those who lost so much and then came to the TRC to weep are still weeping. And the ones who are the finders came and they said they were sorry but they were the finders and they kept it and those who came to weep are still the weepers. These are some of the inherent elements in the kind of reconciliation that has transpired here. Our need is the clear thinking and analysis that underpins this kind of love and forgiveness from, say, Albert Nolan or Charles Villa Vicencio or Frank Chikane's kind of thinking.

FIRST OF ALL, I am not sure about this neat distinction between religious and secular. I think there are spiritual elements in all human activity. We can approach things from different angles. When, for example, you asked me about reconciliation, my mind immediately went to an Arabic expression which is part of my theological and spiritual heritage; and so I do not only think linguistically, I think spiritually. I am sure that for many people it depends where they come from and their experience of life.

When Muslims go to Mecca one of the unwritten conditions of the pilgrimage is that before you make the pilgrimage you go to all the people you have interacted with and you ask them for forgiveness. You are going to Mecca to meet your Lord, and you cannot go and reconcile with God until you have reconciled with those whom you have dealt with. So you ask for forgiveness for all the wrongs known and unknown. I forgive you for all that you may have done toward me knowingly or unknowingly.

What it means for me at a personal level may have its origins in my faith, but how it expresses itself are in the same ways. I do not know how an African traditionalist or a Methodist person's reconciliation can necessarily differ in tangible terms from any non-religious person's. Eugene de Kock[1] may be a Christian or a neo-Nazi and his move for reconciliation may come out of that, but I do not care what that is. It is the tangible expressions that matter. Those concrete results, they have to be there.

I THINK THAT THE QUESTION OF RESTITUTION, the question of giving up your ill-begotten wealth, the question of serving your time out, paying your debt to society is important. You see, the whole thing about forgiveness now is that it is synonymous with letting people off the hook. I do not think it has to be like that.

The problem is that reconciliation is the product of a negotiated settlement. It does not arise from the demands of those who have been aggrieved. So throughout that process their demands were listened to, but they were listened to within a framework where nothing could be done about it. They could not even demand that the oppressor says sorry. Saying sorry was not part of the deal. Political settlements do not take cognizance of saying sorry.

For me reconciliation can only take place when there is a massive redistribution of wealth. There is culpability in the silence of so many people who are white, who benefited from apartheid. And they were not only white. I remember in Lenasia in those years there was one house that had six garages. Who can need six garages? Frankly I do not believe it is possible for people to be so wealthy except it is purchased on the backs of poverty.

I delivered the keynote address on the subject of poverty and the constitution to a group of magistrates and lawyers, and I said the problem is not poverty, the problem is wealth. It is like saying you are sitting with a problem of child abuse. Child abuse is a manifestation of a problem but those abused children are not the problem. The problem is the problem of wealth. We say that domestic abuse is a problem. The problem is patriarchy, the religious legitimization of violence against women. There is a social commodification of women. The point is that the redistribution of all the ill-gotten gains of the social and economic system that underpinned apartheid is a precondition for reconciliation.

A second thing is that there is need for a whole movement among white people toward black people. I am not talking about the sucking up to black people: that is a sickness. The sort that says, "I must not criticize a black person or I will be called a racist." That is another form of racism. I am talking about an active form of participation in the days and the issues that are of importance to black people. They are not sharing the days that are set aside for the nation. These are for everyone, but we still have whites who want to hold on to their own days and ignore the others. So they are not coming on board this whole new South Africa that we have. They are swallowing the change as if it is a bitter medicine that they have to swallow, and the sooner they can get done with this damn thing the better with it. And so I think that a whole movement among white people is required.

There was a marked absence of whites at the TRC hearings, for instance. The only white people at the TRC were people who were involved in the struggle. These are the people that knew the stories. You had no need to be at any of those hearings. You knew what had happened, you knew those stories with your years with the SACC, and all the whites who were there were people like you who knew the stories. Where were the whites who did not know the stories?

I DO NOT THINK the Truth and Reconciliation Commission has contributed to national reconciliation. I think the TRC has succeeded in making some whites feel good in the same way that Mandela had that "feel good" factor about him and in some ways made them less hesitant to enter the new South Africa. The TRC was a time to "let that stuff come out and get it done with. Not that we shall stare at it or do anything about it, but let it come out and let's get all the winging and whining and blaming it all on apartheid over and done with." So to the extent that it made whites feel better in moving toward the new South Africa, in the same way that Mandela played a significant role in the "feel good" factor for white people, it was useful, but as far as reconciling blacks and whites in any meaningful way I do not think the TRC did anything.

THE TRC let white people off the hook. It did not assist whites to acknowledge any responsibility or culpability.

THE SURVIVORS FEEL CHEATED. They came to the TRC to tell their stories and that was all that happened. There are some attempts to deal with the pain by Michael Lapsley and the Kulumani groups and groups like that, but they came, they told their stories, perhaps had their moments of glory on TV and that is all. There is anger.

I THINK IT WAS A SHREWD MOVE to have a number of religious people on the TRC—shrewd with all the pejorative connotations that shrewdness carries with it, because you invest this body with an aura of beyond-ness and all the kinds of unquestioning that goes with beyond-ness. You do not take God on. You do not swear at God. So the TRC assumed an aura of beyond-ness so it was not helpful at all. We needed a far more clinical approach with social scientists, political activists, and not just from the left but people with a far deeper sense of what is really required to bring this nation together in a more sociological and political sense—what is required from the perpetrators, rather than this religiousness.

The problem with religious people so often is that we represent God and we speak in the name of God, and because we are leadership figures in our communities we also speak for the people. The local parish priest can offer redemption for your sins or Desmond Tutu can sit and say, "Let's pray together" at the TRC. But there is an element of infantilism in all of this. I am reduced to a child, and I put the responsibility for my life in the hands of these elder religious figures. So I think that was not helpful.

It was helpful in the sense that it achieved what it set out to do. It put a political bandage over the apartheid era so that we can limp into the new South Africa. From that perspective it was helpful. But it did not get people to engage critically in questions about what the hell we are letting ourselves in for and what route we should go. We needed far more clinical thinkers on the panel rather than the passionate manifestations of our nation's pain that was manifested so brilliantly by people like Desmond Tutu. Problematic as I think it was, that was useful, but it certainly did not make for a good combination in the end.

THERE IS A RELIGIOUS TASK IN RECONCILIATION. All of us, all human beings, have degrees of culpability—and I am not talking in the sense of that rabbi who said that those people who were gassed were responsible themselves for what happened to them. No, I am not talking that kind of rubbish. But there is a level that all of us share from a religious perspective: that all of us are weak. In the words of the Quran, "And we have created humankind weak," or the Christian term, not that I agree with it, that we are born in sin.

None of us are without blemish. If we take this religious element into reconciliation it deprives the situation of arrogance, the arrogance that says, "I am somebody because I am black whereas you are nobody because you are white and you are not entitled to open your mouth any more." The problem is that being a victim becomes a label for all sorts of things, including a license for oppression, the scenario of Israel and Palestine, for example, so it can easily become a scenario in South Africa also. When the label of victim is carried too long there is danger.

So the point I am trying to make is that, yes, there is a religious responsibility to inject certain elements into notions of reconciliation.

I do not think that minority religious communities are really doing anything about reconciliation. This in part is because the TRC was seen as a very Christian process, so in the Muslim community nobody speaks about it. It is not an issue. People still live in their own ghettos, and we carry on as we did before as if nothing had happened. Not that we do not have anything to offer. We do have something to offer, but unfortunately we were not asked at the time whether we also had anything to offer. There was one

Muslim on the Commission. It seemed as if they said, fine, there is someone with a Muslim name so they are covered, but no one in the Christian community suggested that if so and so has a Christian name let him represent the Christians. No, you had to have an authentic religious article.

IF YOU WERE TO ASK ME what are the responsibilities of the religious community at this time in South Africa I would say that one of the responsibilities is to critically engage with notions of reconciliation, to foster reconciliation that is based on justice. It is essentially a prophetic role. It is a prophetic role to the diverse South African communities.

I do not buy into this two-nation theory that says there is a nation of black and a nation of white. Neither do I buy into the theory that there is a nation of just rich and poor. I think that many black people are showing themselves every bit as greedy and as ferocious in climbing social and economic ladders as the worst examples of any of the whites. When it comes to the darker skinned blacks of the rest of Africa, we show ourselves every bit as xenophobic and racist as the most rabid white racists.

It is the responsibility of religious leaders and religious communities to keep on pointing that out and being a prophetic voice. We have to go beyond the margins of party politics that says that if you are black you have to identify with the ANC and if you are white you have to identify with the Democratic Party. We have to remind the nation that political power always has the potential to corrupt, and no human beings, because of the state of weakness that we are born into, are beyond this. We therefore have to remain vigilant. There is nothing in human history that shows that once you have been hurt you will not hurt others.

And this must be done in partnership with the rest of society. You can't have the religious element sitting on the side to be the prophets and the overlords and ready to call the nation to order in the so-called moral crisis that always seems to have to do with sex. A far more comprehensive kind of thing is needed.

I think many Christian communities and the South African Council of Churches, or what is left of it, and groups like the Institute for Contextual Theology and the Catholic Department of Justice and Peace are examples of what can be done by religious communities.

The regrettable thing is that these often have the blessing of the mainstream communities but it is by proxy. It is similar to the way in which the churches used people such as Allan Boesak and Desmond Tutu in the struggle. The Anglican Church, for example, owned Desmond Tutu, but this meant he was their escape hatch and fall guy. Desmond is there so the church is there. Allan is there so the church is there. But the churches were not there. So what is happening now is that the church sets up these divisions so that the whole church doesn't engage with the issues. The Catholic Church can remain as patriarchal and loyal to the Pope as ever and at the same time have a justice and peace division. The church has this remarkable ability to surface in every hole. The Muslims and other groups play the same game by the way. It is not just the churches.

The issue is power. How do we give the image of opposing power and at the same time not see that we are part of the powerful and be ready to give up our own power? That is our struggle.

NOTE

1. Eugene de Kock was a leader in the apartheid-supporting police groups trained to kill anti-apartheid opponents. He is currently serving a life sentence.

MR. BASHIR VANIA

Tuesday, May 16, 2000

Too many books are being written, too many conferences are being held and this is the problem. Nobody is doing anything. Everyone is just talking and writing about it. Nothing is being done, especially by the former perpetrators, to really assure the victims that they do have their interests at heart.

THE ISLAMIC INFORMATION CENTRE is hidden away in a suite of offices over a fast-food outlet deep in the apartheid-created Indian township of Lenasia. I cannot help but feel that it needs to be in the heart of a white, mainly Christian suburb. Mr. Vania is its Director and also the Administrative Assistant of the Islamic Relief Agency in Lenasia. He is a quiet-spoken man, as unobtrusive as the Information Centre itself.

I WOULD SAY RECONCILIATION is the coming together of people on the basis of forgiveness and positive change. Obviously I assume that people want to reconcile because of positive self-interest. When I say positive, as opposed to negative, self-interest, I mean to imply that people would want to get together on the basis of peace, presuming that by getting together in the long run it would be better for everybody. In the case of negative self-interest the conflict would continue out of self-interest, and in the long run everyone would lose, as violence is bad for everybody and everybody loses.

Coming together on the basis of forgiveness, positive self-interest, and positive change would be my idea of reconciliation. That to my mind is a general human view, not just Islamic.

The Islamic view is that any person who is just and fair should be the first to initiate the move, whether you are the victim or the perpetrator. It does not really matter who initiates it. If the victim initiates it he would be doing it from a position of weakness, and that might make the perpetrator, if the perpetrator is an unjust person, take advantage of that. But if there were to be genuine reconciliation, then I think that both the victim and the perpetrator will want to get together on the basis of self-interest, and that would be a fairer type of reconciliation. From an Islamic perspective anyone who is fair and just should be the initiator.

I EXPECT THAT MOST RELIGIOUS PEOPLE think that a secular approach to reconciliation tends to be amoral. Obviously the advantage of that is that it could be more flexible. A lot of religious people would be concerned about it though, as it would be based on interests rather than morals. One gets this quite often in terms of foreign policy. For example, when America talks in terms of their foreign policy they talk quite blatantly of self-interest and not morals. Strict morals do not feature prominently in the secular approach, and religious people would not be happy with that. The secular approach is based almost exclusively on self-interest, and it is, therefore, unencumbered by strict moral codes.

I N SOUTH AFRICA we need a freedom from fear and mistrust. We do need to free ourselves from this. Secondly, when we talk of reconciliation we should not talk only of forgiveness on the part of the victim but some sort of reparation on the part of the perpetrator. I do not think enough of that has been done on the part of the perpetrators, so obviously more needs to be done at that level. Former victims of apartheid, for example, do not feel that enough is being done. They still feel marginalized; they still feel that much more can be done.

There needs to be a stronger return to moral ethical codes as well. I do not think that that is being done either. Perhaps people are more interested in writing theses on human rights rather than really getting down to doing constructive work. Not enough is being done at ground level. Too many books are being written, too many conferences are being held and this is the problem. Nobody is doing anything. Everyone is just talking and writing about it. Nothing is being done, especially by the former perpetrators, to really assure the victims that they do have their interests at heart. True reconciliation needs both parties to come together for their mutual self-interest. What has happened is that the perpetrators have come to reconciliation for their own self-interest rather than the self-interest of the victim as well. More needs to be done on that front, definitely!

THE TRC EXPOSED EVIL and reported on it. I am amazed that many of the people who tacitly supported the apartheid regime did not know what was being done in their name, whether due to deliberate blindness or simply because they were quite comfortable in the status quo. The fact is that many people did not know or pretended not to know and the TRC has exposed this; therefore people find it extremely difficult to deny what has been done in their name and also, hopefully, recognize their part in the evil. Anyone who turns a blind eye to evil is part and parcel of that kind of conduct. I think that from that perspective the TRC has done an enormous amount of good by allowing the victims to speak out, allowing their stories to be told.

PRIOR TO THE TRC many white South Africans tended to rationalize or justify what was happening. After the TRC some tended to admit some sort of responsibility, but between the theory of accepting and the reality of accepting there is a huge gap. They may have accepted that they were part and parcel of the problem but do not want to be involved in the solution. They have not done enough to show that they accept responsibility.

As I have said, forgiveness is one thing and reparations is quite another. White South Africans are not doing enough currently to try and rectify some of the wrongs that were done. I think they just depend on the government to see to that. In this country where the situation is so unique, the private sector and the religious sector should get more involved at ground level to set things right. The government and human rights activists are too busy trying to ensure a liberal constitution in order to impose first world American social values in regard to matters such as the death penalty, pornography, and abortion. Too much emphasis is put onto that. I think the average person is not bothered about that just now. We want more jobs, less crime, more hospitals, and things at that level. There is not enough being done on the reparations front.

The TRC exposed the evils of apartheid, but nothing has been done to put that right. An enormous amount of work remains. The farm problem in Zimbabwe has recently shown, for instance, that the land issue needs attention.

We do something when it is in our own self-interest, but when it is in the interest of the victim, the other person, we do not try as hard as we should. That is a dangerous thing because ultimately your interest is really tied up with that of the victim. For instance, we are asked to be charitable to the poor, but really when we are charitable to the poor we are not doing the poor any favors: we are doing ourselves some favors, even if only stopping uprising and theft. So if you are charitable and do things to uplift the under-privileged it is for your own good. We tend not to project that far and look only to our own immediate needs at this time. We need to convince the rich and the powerful that it is in their own self-interest to do more for the poor.

Obviously in this country the rich and the powerful are primarily of European origin. This is not so in all countries. In Pakistan, for instance, it would not be white people, but the principle remains the same. If the rich and the powerful do not do anything for the helpless and the downtrodden, then ultimately they are asking for trouble. Inevitably in this country at the moment it is the whites who need to be convinced. Twenty, thirty, or more years down the line it might be different. Perhaps then we can talk of the haves and have-nots irrespective of color.

THE VICTIMS have been given an opportunity to share their pain. That is important from a psychological perspective. They have set the record straight. From that perspective they have benefited, but I think from the perspective of reparation I do not think enough has been done for the victims. A sympathetic ear is about it! More needs to be done.

OBVIOUSLY IT WAS HELPFUL to have religious persons on the Truth and Reconciliation Commission, but then I am prejudiced! I am religiously inclined. Religion is always an important factor in anybody's life. Even an atheist has a system of beliefs, a code of conduct—and, in one way, even atheism is a religion. Yes, it was important to have religious people there, and the government would be foolish to discount the importance of religious people.

I think in this instance I was happy that religious people were involved. As to whether Islam had a fair representation, I suppose it is debatable; but if not, I do not have a big problem with that so long as religious people with a strict moral code were there. That is the most important. The most important thing is that the victims get a fair representation. Muslim or non-Muslim was not an issue. Yes, it would have been fairer to have a greater Muslim representation, but the victim is the important person to think about. Did they get a fair hearing and do they feel satisfied that justice has been done?

If one looks at the Quran, chapter six verse fifty-four, for example, it says that God tells that you should ask for forgiveness and amend your conduct. That is important. If I do something wrong and ask for forgiveness I hope and presume that God will forgive me, but there is the other part that says you have to amend your conduct. It is the amending of your conduct that shows your sincerity. Now I think possibly that that is what many Muslims felt upset about. The first part was implemented, the forgiveness, but the amending of conduct was not implemented. Simply turning the other cheek is noble, it might be good, but is it fair or is it just in every respect? And this would be the problem for the Muslim, that not enough justice was done; ultimately in the long run that will lead to many, many problems. I think it has done so already to a certain extent.

I THINK THE RELIGIOUS COMMUNITY has to create an awareness of what was done, and I think they need to ensure that similar things do not happen again. That can only be done by propagation, by talking about things. And the religious community needs to persuade its followers that forgiveness is good but is rarely enough. Things need to be done to repair the damage. I am speaking on all religious fronts now. The emphasis needs to be put on that aspect. There is an emphasis on forgiveness and coming together but not enough on reparations.

Islam puts a lot of emphasis on justice. It is very difficult to obtain peace without justice, and from that perspective Muslims can do an awful lot. Firstly, we do need to get back to our moral principles to create awareness of injustices and then try and right the wrongs as far as we are able. That is extremely important in Islam.

The principle of jihad is important for a Muslim. Jihad does not mean holy war. Obviously all wars are unholy, and holy war is a contradiction in terms. If you are holy you do not need war. Jihad really means struggle, struggling to right wrongs, and it can take many forms. Teaching people to write is a struggle. It is a form of jihad. Fighting just wars to protect the innocent and helpless is a form of jihad. Educating people is a form of Jihad. From that perspective Islam is very strong on justice. Muslims do try. We are only two and a half percent of the population, but you find that for that number we do tend to get around quite a bit! I think it is our strong sense of justice.

Our small organization, for instance, tries to be involved in community work. I think that is a way of helping the people of this country. Education is another aspect of it. I think as Muslims we do have a task to try and inculcate a sense of fairness, of justice, in every person in this country. We may not be doing enough but we are trying.

In education, Islam does not really differentiate between religious education and secular education. The truth is neither religious nor non-religious. We have tended to emphasize the so-called religious education to teach about Islam without realizing that we should not differentiate between the two. This has been a mistake. Obviously morals are very important for Islam, and from that perspective there is much that needs to be done in this country with issues such as the death penalty and abortion, together with human rights. Obviously morals come into those issues, and it is the duty of Muslims to educate the public from an Islamic perspective. But, as I have said, we do not differentiate between religious knowledge and all knowledge. Knowledge is knowledge. We do now have some Muslim schools, for example, to rectify the oversight in acknowledgment that we do need to do more on every front.

Fortunately most religions do have common moral principles. "Thou shalt not kill." "Thou shalt not steal." Firstly, we need to establish that people are aware of moral problems in our society. Once they are aware then we have some sort of common basis to examine ethics, say Christian ethics as against Islamic ethics. But first we need to establish the fact that we have some moral standards that are similar and then we can debate the differences. In this country at this present time we have to establish that these codes exist.

But the important thing is that all debates are a means to an end. It is to clarify matters and then to work together on those things we have in common. Religious people do not talk enough to each other. We need to do that so we can work together and not against one another. The politicians are debating human rights but the religious people are not doing enough of that. Ultimately the purpose of the debates must be to get down to work. If we simply talk to one another we shall run into problems in the long term.

We like to think that the Islamic Information Centre is contributing toward reconciliation. I am called upon to give a lot of talks to make people aware, both within the Islamic community and without. Sometimes I am asked to chat about Islam at churches. We also do relief work all over the country. So in our own little way we do what we can and, as I say, one person or one small organization can make a difference. So yes, there is a lot of goodwill and there are Islamic organizations that are doing something.

B LANKET AMNESTY IS A PROBLEM. Secular approaches to reconciliation tend to be perhaps overflexible and unencumbered by strict moral codes, and in the long run that is not justice. Do we give everyone blanket amnesty? If you do, you are allowing great injustices to be committed. On the other hand, if there is no blanket amnesty you are going to have to choose whom you are going to forgive and whom you are not. On what basis? What kind of moral codes? What message are you sending? If you are powerful enough you can get away with anything? It is a problem.

In Islam the principles of polity, equity, equality, liberty, law and order are interwoven and intertwined—the one is not discrete from the other. Islam does not advocate the rendering unto Caesar what is Caesar's and to God what is God's. In the Islamic methodology all physical, social, economic, educational, and religious praxes belong to God and revolve around Him—and Him alone.[1]

NOTE

1. This quotation is taken from *Political Principles in Islam,* published by the Islamic Information Centre.

OTHER RELIGIOUS
TRADITIONS

Baha'i Faith

There are only a small number of Baha'i in South Africa. They are very active in all interfaith activities.

MRS. SHOHREH RAWHANI, MR. KRISHNA NAIDOO, MR. GAVIN RAMOROESI, MR. JERRY JACOBS, AND MRS. JUDITH RAMOROESI

Saturday, June 18, 2000

It is the will of God that humanity reconciles and unites, and so this very proactive step that South Africa took will draw the blessings and the bounties of God upon it. This is one country that, either knowingly or unknowingly, is working toward the will of God.

This was a group meeting held at the National Spiritual Centre of the Baha'is in South Africa in Johannesburg. The views expressed were said to be the official standpoint of the Baha'i faith together with individual interpretations and expressions given in response to my questioning. The difference can be noted by the use of "we" as against "I."

T HE BAHA'I FAITH essentially tries to tie spiritual principles to life. Essentially the Baha'i faith says that all the errors of the world are symptoms of the spiritual ills within mankind and the result of man being estranged from his Creator. So if we talk of reconciliation we are talking of the heart and soul of man being reconciled with his Creator. In that sense then if you look at the estrangement that men feel toward each other it is actually the result of man's estrangement with his Creator, which is at present, we believe, the concept of the organic oneness of mankind.

We say that a manifestation of God, a Divine Teacher, has come in the name of Baha'u'llah. He has come with principles and teachings the whole purpose of which is to bring man closer to God. The understanding is that if you reconcile with the will of your Creator all the virtues that are needed for man to rise to where he should be will manifest themselves. This will include relationships with one another over race, religion, class, or creed. So the teachings of the Baha'i faith are essentially geared toward bringing man closer to his Creator, and if you concentrate on that, the behavior and the practice of man will change, will transform in the way he relates to his fellow human beings. We do focus on building love for our fellow man, but this is also a direct by-product of man connecting with the will of his Creator. That is our starting point.

The fundamental principle of the Baha'i faith is the oneness of mankind, so everything else that the Baha'is do is around that one pivotal principle which is to bring about the unity of mankind.

F ROM A BAHA'I POINT OF VIEW, forgiveness is linked to the individual. I can forgive you for doing something wrong to me, but in terms of justice—and Baha'is firmly believe in the building of a just society—justice is the domain of society and is manifested through its laws and constitution. For example, Judy has hurt me and I forgive her, but it is the task of society to deal with Judy for causing that hurt. So the difference between forgiveness and justice for Baha'is is that the individual does not take vengeance; he forgives because that is of the heart, but in terms of applying justice in society that is a legal/constitutional matter.

Baha'u'llah asks that every individual Baha'i bring him/herself to account each day. We all take responsibility for our own actions. When we follow that law it means that I acknowledge the wrong that I have done to any other person. Whether I go and ask that person for forgiveness is a matter of character, but I have the obligation to bring myself to account each day before God. From that it may be that I will be the one who makes the move, but what we do as individuals before God is the essence. Although we do not have a priesthood or religious leaders, there is an administrative order made up of elected groups of individuals at local, national, and international levels to whom all individuals are ultimately accountable in cases of noncompliance to the laws of the Baha'i faith.

What about the days of apartheid? That was an unjust system. You could not rely upon it for justice.

If you look at the principles, they were in direct contrast to the laws of the land. For instance, right from the start it was a multiracial grouping. We continued during the time of apartheid to build the multiracial community. We never said the white Baha'i are there and the black are here. We continued to operate according to the basic principle of the oneness of mankind. We suffered police visits and some persecution for our beliefs. We do not make a judgment on the law itself because we have a mission of creating a new world based on the principles of Baha'u'llah. The fact that there are rules of government is transitory; they come and go, but the teachings of God are consistent and eternal. The social principles may change according to the times we live in. This was our dilemma, trying to live according to principles in a country that was totally contradictory to those principles. We survived, together with our principles.

(To Gavin Ramoroesi:) What was your own experience of those days of apartheid?

I am a second-generation Baha'i living among people who have been through the dreadful things brought about by apartheid. I was a teacher in 1986 in Soweto when there was a lot of violence not only between the government and the blacks but, and this was even more horrific, between blacks and blacks. It was a difficult time. It was really tough on us especially as Baha'is, because you were either with the movement or with the government, and if you were not in the movement you were portrayed to be with the system. When you have to stand with the principles behind you and the consequences of what is happening in the society about you as well, you have to make clear judgments. You look at yourself and you ask, "If I take this action will I be infringing on my beliefs? And this way, will I be infringing on my community?" Finding a bridge between what you are as a black youth and what you are as an individual Baha'i, plus your social responsibility as a member of the community, was difficult. As a Baha'i I could not divorce myself from the community I was living in, but neither could I divorce myself from the beliefs I was brought up with. That is the difficulty I am talking about.

FROM A BAHA'I PERSPECTIVE the religious deals with the development of the soul. You begin with the assumption that there is God, and our purpose in life is to develop the soul so that you pass on to the next life. You seek the development of the faculties and the tools for the next life. But the secular concept of reconciliation seems to be on the material side. We see the day when the two become one. Secular will be based on spiritual principles. At present there is a distinction between them which sometimes causes contradictions.

I THINK BASICALLY AS A BAHA'I that what is needed is for the people of South Africa to look at the principles the Baha'i faith has brought to see where they have worked and where they have brought peace to that community. The principles of Baha'i faith, we believe, are the answer to the problems of South Africa because everything in it is working toward the unity of the human race, this one family concept. One hundred sixty years ago when Baha'u'llah came he said that the future of humanity will be unity in diversity, and that is interesting because that phrase has become the one for our new coat of arms. It is in the Baha'i writings of one hundred sixty years ago.

So we believe that if the people would turn to and apply the principles that have been brought by this latest Divine Teacher from God, then we will have unity in diversity because this is what God has willed for humanity. Therefore, the only way that humanity will achieve it is through God and not through politics and social endeavors but turning to the principles of God, which include social development. That is what will bring peace and reconciliation to our country. We need to achieve the unity of our races in this country, in their diversity.

CERTAINLY THE TRC has contributed to reconciliation at a certain level but not in totality. There is still a lot of doubt among people about the process. I am not saying there is anything material that would be able to compensate those who suffered for what they have gone through. The knowledge of who did what and where your relatives are, as was the case, and the reburials that have taken place has helped. A lot of things were settled but nothing material will ever heal that feeling, only the spiritual side will compensate this.

I would say that the TRC has taken South Africa forward, especially for those people who went. It has helped them tremendously even if the experience was traumatic.

IF I AM HURT by someone else and I have to reconcile, it is going to take me time. I am going to watch him, the person who hurt me, very carefully. I can only reconcile with him when I see he is opening up, when he is changing. During the process of the TRC on television there was no opening up. Yes, there were tears from some of the perpetrators, but the victims were not quite sure whether reconciliation works.

Sometimes when I watched the TRC on television and saw that the perpetrator did not show any sign of remorse at all, that hurt me. I feel that this person was not there for the purpose of reconciliation but to get amnesty and go scot-free, and that hurts. That is when the TRC fails, when individuals do not even show remorse for what they have done. I also know that not regretting what they have done is even more detrimental to their souls. When I see one soul going down without realizing it, there is yet another hurt and a big challenge as well.

MEMBERS OF THE Azanian People's Liberation Army took the responsibility for the killing of three Baha'is in East London. We spoke to the next of kin of the victims, and they decided they would never oppose the amnesty if that was what government felt would help to develop the country. They said that in their hearts they had already forgiven the individuals for their actions because of the extraordinary situation in this country that made such things happen. They wanted to know why they had done this, and once that had come out their hearts were settled.

THE AMNESTY PROCESS within the TRC raises many questions. We said that as individuals we forgive and that justice is left to society to determine and apply the rule. It was perhaps a necessary political decision to allow amnesty through the TRC as we went from one extreme form of society, to try and normalize it. Politically it may have been correct, whereas viewed from the point of justice it did not serve the purpose of justice, but it was an expedient decision to make to move forward.

WHEN WE DIE I believe we stand before God and you are answerable to God, so whatever we do on this material plane may be good to keep society stable, but does it clear the human soul from whatever wrong is committed? God is the one who judges, so on this plane you make a decision of society, but at the end of the day you stand before God as an individual answerable for what you have done.

IN A WAY it was good that there were many Christian representatives on the Truth Commission. The majority of South Africans are Christians. Even though there are a lot of people of other religions who were hurt by the government, they could all wholeheartedly go to the TRC. They did not look upon those Commissioners as Christian pastors but as community leaders given this great responsibility.

I never looked upon them as people coming from Christianity. I know Bishop Tutu, but I did not take him as a Christian only and did not see any portrayal of any particular Christian church. Maybe I was being too broad-minded, but I did not see that and I would not classify them as Christian leaders. They were there for a purpose, and they were there as South Africans, not as representatives of a particular religious group, and I think they did a fairly good job.

There could not have been any other way. You could not have a Commission made up of party politicians. You needed a different input. If you look for fairness for justice for healing there is no other way than to bring in the religious. Whether it was fairly balanced is another thing, but you do need that religious input.

THE FOCUS that the Baha'is have always had is the moral imperative. That is the value that the religious communities bring which needs to drive the development of mankind. What we see around is a lack of it. Morality is lacking and we would ascribe that to the fact that the spiritual principles are absent. It is an apartheid world. Throughout the whole world it is an unwritten pattern of behavior, and we talk from our separated compartments. If the religious communities have a role to play it is to bring these fundamental principles of morality through Christianity, Judaism, Islam, Hinduism, and Baha'i faith, etc., to bring these to the fore. It has to influence and inform the decision makers of our world and exemplify this, live it out.

We try in the Baha'i community to be a model, and there are great expectations and responsibilities upon Baha'i to live out the principles. We are not perfect and we are growing, but we measure ourselves in relation to the extent to which our lives exemplify our teachings. The way we relate to each other, how we conduct ourselves in our daily life—that is the way we measure ourselves.

ONE OF THE THINGS that South Africa has achieved with this proactive step to bring about unity through the TRC and the whole emphasis on reconciliation, not just at the top where the leaders of the ANC and other parties shake hands but at the grassroots, is to draw the blessing of God. It is the will of God that humanity reconciles and unites, and so this very proactive step that South Africa took will draw the blessings and the bounties of God upon it. This is one country that, either knowingly or unknowingly, is working toward the will of God.

Hindu

The Hindu faith is much larger in membership than either the Jewish or Muslim groups in South Africa. It is, however, heard of little because of its traditionally quiet manner of operation. It is strongest in the warm Indian Ocean coast areas centered on Durban, where the original Indian labor was brought in by the colonial powers to work in the sugar cane farms of that area.

MR. N. RATHINASAMY

June 7, 2000

More and more I begin to feel the Indian community, Hindus in particular maybe, are beginning to shift away from the mainstream of life. They just carry on to live their own lives because they find themselves isolated in many respects. They find that work opportunities are being lessened by the day and affirmative action is there. Everyone talks about the days when you were not white enough and now you are not black enough, which is true.

༄

I was fated in Lenasia—the apartheid-created Indian township south of Johannesburg—to have to find people in offices hidden through side doors and narrow staircases! Mr. Rathinasamy is a businessman operating from a small office above a garage. He was the first Chairperson of the Hindu Co-ordinating Council of Gauteng and is the Chairperson of the Human Services Trust. During our conversation I discovered that he is also the rather proud father of Truth and Reconciliation Commissioner Ms. Jasmine Sooka.

THERE IS DIVISION among the Hindu community. The Hindu Co-ordinating Council is aimed at bringing people of different organizations and movements together to cooperate. It has a small success especially at the time of Hindu festivals.

The Human Service Trust was founded by Swami Krishna, who came from India originally and established a service-orientated group in Mauritius. He tried to do the same here, getting people together to devote themselves to service based on their religious background to provide services to the community that are not provided by any other group. It is a welfare agency. I have been involved with that since 1976.

RECONCILIATION IS, I think, an attempt made to overcome differences to get rid of misunderstandings and to meet one another again in a harmonious manner. It obviously requires acknowledgment of wrong. If you are the person who committed the wrong and you are not prepared to admit that, then I cannot see how there can be any kind of reconciliation. Tied up with that is that the person against whom the offense was committed has to truly and really forgive. It is not like the Afrikaans saying that you forgive but you do not forget. I think that if you think of genuine reconciliation the forgiveness has to go with a willingness to forget. You must forget the past. If it is not obliterated from your conscious mind then again and again in the future it will be recalled, and eventually the act of reconciliation will be destroyed completely.

The first move for the act of reconciliation must come from the perpetrator. I would think that in the first instance the victim would not even be prepared to face the perpetrator or meet them on any ground. I think this is one of the good things about the Truth and Reconciliation Commission, that it compelled the perpetrators to face the victims. And the fact that the victims were willing to come also and give evidence indicated that they were prepared ultimately to meet. From the reports one has read, with many of them it was an act of relief for them being face-to-face with those who had committed dreadful acts against them or their families. They were relieved ultimately to know what the truth was and who was responsible.

Mind you, the perpetrators here in many cases made contrition but I do not believe it. I listen to the statements made by Eugene de Kock[1] and wonder about them. Then recently there was Craig Williamson.[2] I cannot see that there is any real contrition on his part, and I think, therefore, that I do agree with the relatives that it seems to be a travesty of justice that such people are getting off scot-free.

THERE MUST BE DIFFERENCES between religious and secular approaches to reconciliation. The religious is supported by the teachings of your faith while the ordinary one is involved in the cut and thrust of ordinary life, and I do not think forgiveness would come into that necessarily. A Hindu approach would obviously be a religious approach with emphasis on forgiveness, both asking for forgiveness and giving forgiveness. Hindus may not make a great deal of noise like some other religions, but those who have imbibed the teachings of their priests and their parents will act accordingly.

There has been a spirit of forgiveness and overlooking hurts that crop up in marriage, for instance, which was not necessarily so in other religions, where you could easily divorce or get rid of one partner and marry another one. But we must be honest and say that our children are not being brought up truly as Hindus in the present age. There is a small group maybe. The other thing is that even if they have had this upbringing they move out of places like Lenasia, and they live in the plush suburbs of the town and lose contact with their community. The only time they come back may be for a special occasion, such as that of a man who now lives in Sandton[3] and came back here to Lenasia only to organize his daughter's wedding. But this is a frightening aspect of life, especially with the Hindu. Wherever the Muslims go they build their mosques and they continue to establish their classes and their teachings. But wherever the Hindus go there are problems developing. The vernacular disappeared from the Tamil group a long time ago. If you talk to any Gujurati-speaking people nowadays you find they have the utmost problem getting their children to keep up the tradition. They want to leave as soon as they can and the parents no longer really use it at home anyway. There is this encroachment of the secular world.

I THINK IN MANY RESPECTS the TRC has done a tremendous job because the mere process of getting people to come forward to confess to whatever crimes they have committed in pursuance of the apartheid state meant that first of all the world at large became fully aware of the kind of society we lived in here from the 1950s onward. And I think for the community that was so involved in it, sections of the white community and sections of the black community who were the active perpetrators of the offenses, there must have been a sense of catharsis for their communities just by the fact that they are now speaking out and revealing these things that they have kept hidden all these years. I think even to Eugene de Kock, the one they called Prime Evil, it must be a relief to be able to say, I have done all these things but now I have said it all out and perhaps someone has forgiven me for it. So I think the perpetrators must have a sense of relief on the one hand and, on a more material level, there is the fact that they escape prosecution and they will not be hounded in the future.

For the victims, I think with many of them they had not known what happened to their children, to their fathers and daughters. People just disappeared from the face of the earth, and we are only learning now even about what happened to SWAPO [the South West Africa People's Organization] insurgents so many years ago and how they were thrown into the sea. You haven't the foggiest idea about what happened. You had a grown-up son and he suddenly disappeared, and now to know what happened to him must bring about some sense of relief.

But I do think that even in spite of the fact that some have got to know what happened and some have openly forgiven the people who perpetrated these crimes against them, for many there is still a lingering sense of doubt about the whole procedure, a feeling that they have done such dastardly crimes that they should be punished. You cannot expect an attitude that you forgive completely. And when I read about some of the people who get amnesty, one begins to think that one can share in the feeling of those who refuse to forgive.

I would think that because of the fact that a large section of the community has not participated in the TRC, Afrikaners particularly, and in the black community there are so many who have suffered so much, there must be a feeling of injustice here. There is a sense of justice not being carried out properly and, by and large, they are not prepared to forgive everybody about it. But at least the fact that it has been brought out into the open could be a lesson, to the future citizens of this country that they cannot allow a situation like that to develop again. I had assumed the Germans had learned that lesson, but now you hear about neo-Nazis and begin to think it takes fifty years and you go back to where you were on square one and the same thing develops again. I think the TRC record will help this nation not to be involved in that.

Many Natalian Hindus suffered as victims. There were many Indian activists, many of whom were Hindus. Some of these are now in leadership positions in Gauteng. The Hindu teaching on forgiveness would encourage them to forgive because you are not supposed to bear rancor, and it will blemish your presence. And when you think of the fact of reincarnation, things like this, where you are unable to forgive, harm your soul and therefore will prevent you from ascending to a higher level. We have a great element of forgiveness in Hindu philosophy where you are called upon to have a generosity of spirit.

I WOULD SAY A SECTION of the white population has accepted some responsibility for the gross violations of apartheid, but it is still a fact that unfortunately the security forces have not come forward and the army is more or less silent. How many generals have come forward? And now we are learning about the crimes that they ordered but nobody has said a word, not even General Constant Viljoen,[4] who admits to a few paltry things and that is all. But as the head he was surely aware of what was happening. The same applies to our former President: he just defies everybody, and obviously he was part of the terrorist apparatus of this country. He says he is not guilty and knows nothing and will ask forgiveness for nothing. I think that it is very unfortunate, but he is an old man now and we can just leave him.

It is difficult to give any general picture of the white population. We live in an isolated community, so I meet very few whites now when I am, what shall we say, township-bound.

I WOULD THINK THE TRC helped the survivors in getting them knowledge about whatever happened to the members of their families that were harmed, as well as by exposing the people who perpetrated these things. Some of them indicated that they were sorry for what they did, and I suppose if you accept that it was offered in a genuine sort of contrition it does give you some kind of psychological relief. But I still think that at the back of their minds they cannot be completely reconciled to the fact that the perpetrators go free. I still think that many of them are not happy with that particular process. You see again and again people complaining about the fact that justice was not done here. You see people hiding behind the fact that because everything is politically motivated it can be forgiven. There was this amazing character recently who tried to say that he killed his wife because it was politically motivated. What a farce! He did not get amnesty, fortunately, because he does not deserve it.

I would think that there is a good case for reparations when you think of the fact that many wives have lost husbands who would have been the breadwinners. There are father and mothers who lost sons who would have grown up to be their life support as well. And, of course, the fact that their lives have been so completely devastated would demand that there should be some form of compensation. Some relief is needed monetarily, and it can surely do something to alleviate the sense of loss. I cannot understand how, after six years to grapple with the situation, this government has not made a real attempt at making any real kind of reparation. What they have paid out is measly.

It is like Robert Mugabe and the land. It has taken him twenty years. Small amounts have been paid. That is all. What about the old people? Some relief could make their lives a little easier but they have done nothing of the kind. You have to have question marks about this action of the government. Is it because so many of them were exiles? Many of those who stayed in the country and went through all the process of oppression are not in government anymore. These are people who were part of the resistance movement

in the country and who were imprisoned for their beliefs. The people spent
their exile years studying to get degrees, and perhaps they do not appreciate
the sufferings of the people here in South Africa in the seventies and eighties. Those were the most severe years of oppression and by that time most of
them were out of the country anyway.

I WOULD THINK it was helpful to have a considerable number of religious people on the TRC because I think with all religions they teach
forgiveness, and they expect humility and believe in confession as well. Yes, I
think that having so many religious persons present on the TRC was a very
good thing. In spite of the way that the *Citizen*[5] would make fun of Desmond Tutu, I think that he was the best possible Chairman for the job, under the circumstances. He brought a touch of humanity into what could
easily have been a legal exercise.

IT IS DIFFICULT to answer about the religious bodies and what they
should be doing. Religious bodies could play a great part in providing
counseling services to the victims more than to anybody else. Unfortunately
Hinduism does not go in for counseling and confessions. It is more ritual-
based, and unless you have someone who is determined to deal with this on
a weekly basis in the sermons that he makes I cannot see how they can really influence the attitudes and thinking along those lines. People may go to a
Hindu priest now and then for advice, but by and large not. Hindu families
tend to keep everything within themselves and expect guidance from the
elders within the family.

More and more I begin to feel the Indian community, Hindus in particular maybe, are beginning to shift away from the mainstream of life. They
just carry on to live their own lives because they find themselves isolated in
many respects. They find that work opportunities are being lessened by the
day and affirmative action is there. Everyone talks about the days when you
were not white enough and now you are not black enough, which is true.
When they use the term "black" in affirmative action they mean Indian,
coloured, and African men and women, but when it comes to practice it
does not work that way at all. So by and large Indian people seem to withdraw into themselves and that is not very good.

Our Hindu welfare agencies cater for everybody. Long before the new
dispensation came into being an organization like Johannesburg Indian Social Services (JISS) catered for everybody in the areas in which they worked.

For example, they have a school for the mentally handicapped here in Lenasia Extension 8. It started off dealing mainly with youngsters from the Indian community. Today that school is eighty percent black because they have gone out with an outreach program. The Indian Blind Association renders their services to all groups as well. We also have clinics in various places where we serve the entire population groups. More and more of the services are devoted to African people. Muslims can have organizations to serve only Muslims because they have people in Soweto and congregations there. Hindus do not because we do not evangelize. The Hare Krishna movement has some people of different racial groups but the people come along voluntarily. Nobody goes out to look for people.

M Y FINAL WORD would be to say that the TRC was a bold experiment. It was an attempt made to ensure that the hurts of the past are uncovered for one thing and some kind of treatment given to it so that people can say, we know this happened to us, we know who was responsible, and let us put it behind and get on with our lives.

NOTES

1. Nicknamed "Prime Evil," Eugene de Kock was a leader in the apartheid-supporting police groups trained to kill anti-apartheid opponents. He is currently serving a life sentence.

2. Craig Williamson is a confessed agent of the apartheid regime.

3. Sandton is an affluent, mainly white, suburb to the north of Johannesburg.

4. Constant Viljoen was the army head in apartheid days. He is currently in Parliament as a leader of the Freedom Front political party.

5. The *Citizen* is an English-language daily newspaper.

ESSAYS AND PERSPECTIVES

❧ ❧ ❧

THE ROLE OF THE CHURCH IN PROMOTING RECONCILIATION IN POST-TRC SOUTH AFRICA

ᔥ ᔥ ᔥ

Hugo van der Merwe

Centre for the Study of Violence and Reconciliation

The church fought for liberation and after that we were confused. We did not know what to do. The enemy was gone. We could not pinpoint the enemy.[1]

FIGHTING INJUSTICE WAS, it seems, a much simpler task than rebuilding social relations. The struggle within the various churches to develop a new vision for their role in society is, it seems, the beginning of a long process. While this crisis of vision is not unique to the church, it is something that goes to the heart of many religious beliefs.[2]

Social divisions are what necessitate reconciliation. The apartheid era presented the church with the challenge of fighting the fundamental source of this division—apartheid. In many respects, this battle for justice was one that built the legitimacy of the church as a political actor with real power to promote social change. It is therefore not surprising that the task of overcoming social divisions and (re)building relationships in a democratic

South Africa is something that is now seen by society and by church leaders as a key part of the church's role.

This paper uses the interviews conducted by Bernard Spong (alongside previous research by the author) to examine the way the church interacted with the TRC and how this has affected the approach of the church in addressing the challenge of reconciliation after the closure of the TRC.

Reconciliation as a Religious Calling

As reflected in the interviews of the church leaders, they generally see reconciliation as a task for which the church is uniquely qualified.[3] They claim to understand it better (or at least more deeply) than other actors in society, and feel that they are well situated to address this concern.

I also believe that the term reconciliation is a very Christian or a biblical term. I do not think it belongs to the secular world. At the same time, I am not advocating a position that this is to be clearly monopolized by the churches but I think that the depth of it could be missed if it is not looked at from its roots.[4]

What specifically the churches can contribute is, however, still not spelled out in the interviews. What new understanding they bring to the subject (beyond what is found in social sciences) is not clear, and the practical strategies for engaging society are clearly still in their infancy.[5] The church is, it would seem, still at a very early stage of converting their potential into reality. It would appear that the churches' sense of self-righteousness as inherent gatekeeper of true reconciliation is one serious obstacle to pursuing this task, as there is much in secular society to draw from in developing new strategies. Some respondents, however, took a more integrated approach to religious-secular divisions.

I am convinced legal processes can only go so far. They are very important because they provide a framework in which interaction can happen in society. So much of our work, religious work, is attitudinal. It is about values and it is about committing yourself to something that is not often easily definable.[6]

The distinction drawn by most interviewees between religious and secular approaches to reconciliation (and their pejorative view of the latter) would reduce their ability to learn from other civil society initiatives to build reconciliation.[7] This distinction is generally simplistically understood as between idealistic and pragmatic approaches, or as between social-psychological and political-legal conceptions of behavioral change. In practice these are different sides of the same coin rather than contending approaches to social change. They also interact in complex ways that need to be further explored rather than contrasted and rejected.

Non-religious civil society initiatives in South Africa see their linkages with religion, spirituality, and church structures as an additional resource from which to draw. This conversation and cross-fertilization between religious, political, social, and psychological approaches is clearly needed to strengthen the churches' role in promoting reconciliation. A more positive approach is conveyed by Dr. Farid Esack, a Muslim theologian: "I am not sure about this neat distinction between religious and secular. I think there are spiritual elements in all human activity." This view is also reflected by a number of other respondents who draw a strong link between their religious understanding of reconciliation and their African cultural roots. The Rev. Wesley Mabuza, Director of the Institute for Contextual Theology, explains:

But I need to say that this idea that there is secular on one side and religious on the other is a western approach. For us it is an *ubuntu* situation. Whether you are religious or not, what is the human thing to do in this situation? From the African mind I would have problems with this demarcation. I would say reconciliation is reconciliation.

Their views about differences between religious and secular approaches did not, thankfully, prevent the churches from playing a strong role in establishing and assisting the TRC (in partnership with various secular structures). The TRC itself, in fact, presents a very interesting combination of religious and secular approaches. This mix was probably responsible for many of the TRC successes as well as some of its failures.

The Church's Impact on the TRC

Without the input of religious figures, the TRC would have been quite a different phenomenon. While the conceptualization of the TRC legislation and the drafting of the act were essentially political processes driven by pragmatic political concerns, the lobbying activities of churches and other NGOs did bring about some key adaptations in the final legislation. While not affecting the fundamental shape of the TRC, these inputs pushed the TRC toward a more victim-centered approach.[8] The Religious Response to the TRC[9] was launched in October 1994. This structure provided a network function for a number of NGOs (not only religious ones) to engage with the policy issues raised by the TRC. It was, however, only in 1995, when the draft legislation was released, that religious bodies and other civil society structures started engaging more seriously with the process. Structures such as the Religious Response to the TRC made submissions to Parliament regarding the legislation and made inputs into the process of selecting Commissioners.

Once the TRC was established, the churches became even more actively involved, particularly within local communities. Many churches provided direct assistance in facilitating the implementation of effective gross human rights violation hearings. The TRC made extensive use of church networks when setting up human rights violation hearings in local communities. Through the South African Council of Churches and other religious networks, local ministers were drawn into the process of coordinating meetings, arranging publicity, taking statements, and other crucial functions to ensure effective community engagement in the hearings.[10] In some cases, churches also assisted in creating a (limited) support structure for victims seeking counseling.

In collaboration with the TRC, church structures also made key inputs into two TRC events: the religious sector hearing and a children's hearing. A wide range of churches participated in the religious sector hearing in East London in November 1997. At these hearings, churches made submissions about their role during apartheid. Some used the opportunity to look at their own history of human rights abuses, and apologized for their role in apartheid. Others used the opportunity to recount their experiences of struggle against apartheid abuses.[11]

The Religious Response to the TRC was invited by the TRC to formulate a program for children who were too young to testify at a public hearing. The children were instead involved in drawing, storytelling, and sharing experiences with one another.

The most profound impact of religion was, however, through the shaping of the TRC's approach to the implementation of its mandate by particular religious leaders. The strong religious influence of numerous Commissioners and key staff directed the TRC's activities in a particular way. While the TRC's activities were clearly circumscribed by the legislation, the interpretation of the mandate was given a very particular form, and the tone of its proceedings was fundamentally altered.

In various ways this gave the Commission certain strengths. The ability of the Commission to engage victims and perpetrators in an empathetic manner, to promote a message of repentance and forgiveness, and to gain credibility in a range of communities was probably considerably enhanced through this participation. Interviewees particularly credit the TRC for providing a more humane and approachable face.

I do think it was helpful to have religious figures on the Commission. Otherwise it would have been very dry and analytical. Religious people brought spirituality and compassion and understanding. They brought the spiritual attributes that we actually need. If it had just been a secular thing it may very well have just deteriorated into a legal process.[12]

The participation of religious leaders also came at a cost. Firstly, the TRC was not very effective as a mechanism to establish "historical truth." Its use of public hearings to promote healing and build public empathy undermined or sidelined its ability to gather information and analyze the dynamics of human rights abuses.[13] Its focus on personal experiences and morality diverted attention away from processes of social reconstruction such as conflict resolution and community development. It could also be argued that a more legal approach could have resulted in more criminal investigations and thus more amnesty cases or prosecutions. What would have happened without the religious leaders depends ultimately on whether they were replaced by psychologists, sociologists, historians, politicians, or lawyers.

Confusing Law and Morality

The input of religious leaders into a process such as the TRC did, however, give rise to particular problems. The amorphous twinning of religion and law created serious moral dilemmas in the way the TRC approached certain issues. A key example of this was the way in which Commissioners conflated the legal process of amnesty with the religious concept of forgiveness. Repeatedly in their public pronouncements, Commissioners referred to the amnesty process as one that implied forgiveness of perpetrators. The gross human rights violation hearings have many examples of this:

Commissioner: I want to ask you one question concerning this matter. If the perpetrators, the police are forgiven, are given amnesty, do you see any danger concerning people's lives in Adelaide?[14]

While some respondents in this study recognize this problem, others reflect this same conflation of religious and legal concepts. Bishop Marcos, head of the Coptic Church of Southern Africa, for example, argues, "I believe that the principle of the TRC was biblical. The Lord says that if somebody confesses his sins and asks for forgiveness he should be forgiven."

For victims, this created tremendous confusion and moral doubts. The TRC is presented as a body that supports the granting of amnesty within the framework and conditions provided by the Act.[15] For most victims, the amnesty provision is a fundamental rejection of their right to (criminal and civil) legal recourse. The implication that the Commission would grant forgiveness simply on the basis of disclosure of the truth (without repentance or compensation for the victim) is deeply undermining of their right to refuse forgiveness.

Rather than seeing the process as one of law (forged by political compromise), victims are now faced with a morally and religiously sanctioned process of absolution. For victims who are ready to forgive, this may be an additional social aid in their healing process, but for those who oppose amnesty (or resent it being granted), it could well be seen as a rejection of their moral sense of injustice. The more complex perspectives of the religious leaders interviewed here, however, provide some solace. The complexity of the process of forgiveness is given much more recognition than was their experience through the TRC.

The Internal and External Role of the Churches

The problem of reconciliation in South Africa is incredibly complex. There are many levels of social division that need to be overcome. The churches' ability to reach a large portion of the population combined with its moral influence provide them with a potentially powerful role in many arenas of society. For this potential to be translated into concrete action, it appears that the churches need a strong principled commitment, a clear understanding of the dimensions of the problem and of the dynamics of reconciliation (rather than simply the ideal), and a clear organizational strategy.

While the respondents show a very detailed understanding of the challenge of reconciliation, they seem to despair at the size of the task and often question the extent of their church's commitment to this new responsibility. Fr. Sean O'Leary, Acting Director of LUMKO, reflects the views of most interviewees when he states:

The religious groups have really fallen down in taking this reconciliation process se-riously. And yet they have so many opportunities to do so, and I think they *must* take the initiative to organize events, healing events, to bring the people together—for ex-ample, a walk for peace and reconciliation, using stadiums for people to gather to hear each other's stories, events that stretch out hands across the divides. That is the role of the church, but they are not fulfilling that role. It is their role and not the role of government to do this. But they have retreated into a laager since the late eighties.

Respondents also express a general concern about the lack of coordina-tion and organizational coherence of reconciliation work, both within and among churches. Wolfram Kistner, a Lutheran theologian, sees this as an important obstacle in the development of such work:

We sometimes feel that the church is doing nothing, but there are many church peo-ple involved in many ventures—but they are isolated. We need to link them up so that they can strengthen one another, to feel that they are not alone, and share not only their failures but also their successes. And give hope to one another.

The various interviews demonstrate very clearly that there are individ-uals with a strong yearning for reconciliation. There are also numerous ex-amples of concrete actions to promote reconciliation in addition to a strong core of support for developing reconciliation into a key pillar of the church's mission in society. There are, however, also many obstacles to the development of a concerted campaign and the implementation of reconcil-iation programs in the broader society.

The biggest challenge perhaps, and the biggest space for change, is the fact that churches largely reflect the social divisions of society. This is very clearly recognized by respondents who talk about their churches' efforts to deal with the problem, but also reflect on the difficulty of dealing adequate-ly with the challenge.

Most obviously the problem is reflected in the racial composition, divi-sions, and mistrust that still exist in the churches. Churches are often divid-ed internally along racial lines—divisions between different congregations, branches, and so on. These internal divisions make the churches excellent laboratories for reconciliation. For a church to seriously consider itself as an agent of reconciliation, it would have to first look at how these internal divi-sions can be dealt with. Some respondents see this internal process as a basis from which they can learn and develop their ability to tackle problems in society. Bishop Phaswana, of the Central Diocese of the Evangelical Luther-an Church of Southern Africa, argues:

Once the churches started to operate in their own isolation we began to miss the boat. We must work and operate within our denominations for the sake of growing strength and vision to go out into the community. . . . Denominations must meet on their own not for their own sake but for the sake of gaining strength and sharpening the vision to go out and share with others.

What is reflected in the interviews is that this process has been fairly ad hoc. While there are exciting examples of successes and inspiring attempts at promoting change, they do not give the impression of a coordinated program to address the history of the church and the relationships among members of the church, and to change the way that the church reflects society.

Reflections on the transformation of the church hierarchy have not, it appears, progressed as far as many would like. This aspect of church transformation would seem to be quite crucial in assessing the future role of the church. While one component of this process is obviously broadening the racial composition of church leadership, another is the manner in which the ethos of church leadership and authority relate to a social message of empowerment and valuing differences. Only a few of the interviewees addressed this issue, most particularly the comments of the Rev. Wesley Mabuza:

We still have ministers who want to teach their people what is right and what is wrong instead of empowering the people to discover for themselves. I detest the continuous patronizing in ministry that our churches seem to dish out to congregations. The religious community has a lot to do on its own. Never mind what it can give to the country. If it can get right it will automatically get the country right. I am not so naïve as to believe that the hierarchy of the churches will give away power to empower the people so easily. The pretense that churches are places where there is justice and we know what justice is about is a pipe dream and the sooner we acknowledge it the better.

Numerous people working with the TRC found it to be extremely authoritarian in its internal operations, and thus questioned its ability to effectively contribute to the promotion of open participation and empowerment and facilitate a break from a history of authoritarian rule. Similar questions need to be asked of the church: What internal values does it still cling to that may limit its ability to promote external change?

Churches are also generally institutions with their own legacies of racial discrimination and insensitivity in relation to their own black members and clergy, or in relation to black communities. These histories were not wiped out by their good deeds in opposing apartheid. They constitute a legacy that will undermine trust and respect unless they are dealt with openly. As many interviewees reflect, the churches could well make use of internal TRCs. While some efforts have been made by the churches to acknowledge their role in supporting (or not sufficiently opposing) apartheid, and admit their own discriminatory practices, a more transparent participative process of engaging with the past could provide a more solid foundation for building a new vision.

The churches' role in addressing reconciliation more broadly in society should obviously be informed, limited, and complemented by its internal reconciliation process. While the church can only play a limited role externally without having its internal house in order, the internal process will never be completely finalized. The external role is thus one that needs to continue, but will only reach its full potential through being energized by the fruition of its internal processes.

Reconciliation Strategies

There are various strategies of reconciliation identified by interviewees that fall broadly under the umbrella of reconciliation. While some initiatives seem to predate the TRC, others appear to be attempts at building on the momentum of the TRC process and providing more people to participate in processes of storytelling and dialogue.[16] While some essentially duplicate certain activities of the TRC, most also attempted to extend them to new types of divisions and deepen them to provide a more serious engagement with issues. These strategies have been used for internal reconciliation processes and/or for promoting broader national and community reconciliation.

Reconciliation sermons: The most obvious role for the church (and the most commonly mentioned by interviewees) was to provide guidance regarding the values and journey of reconciliation through sermons. While some felt that not enough attention was given in developing this message and addressing it consistently, it seems to have been a very common phenomenon for the churches to take on this role in their regular services.

Symbolic events: Symbolic events, such as mass gatherings, memorial services, marches, and public celebrations, are commonly cited as things the churches should be doing, but are not. Interviewees express some regret that such events have been the province of political parties, when religious bodies could have used these opportunities. The Day of Reconciliation, an annual public holiday, is cited as one example of an opportunity that is generally squandered by the church.

Counseling: The role of counselor was mentioned by a number of interviewees as a particular strength of church leaders which was utilized effectively within the TRC, and which could be extended to those who did not have access to counseling services through the TRC. There is, however, a recognition that more training needs to be provided to equip church staff with appropriate skills. Another component to the role of counseling is to provide space for confession. Some interviewees felt that perpetrators of human rights abuses were not sufficiently given a space where they could confront their sins and make a sincere confession.

Storytelling: The experience of the TRC seems to have imbued respondents with immense appreciation for the significance of storytelling. They recognize that the TRC only gave a very small number of people this opportunity and see churches as having an important role in expanding the space for such processes.

Cross-racial dialogue and community building: The church recognizes that whites and blacks in South Africa still live in very separate worlds and see a need for opportunities where people can share their experiences of society—both of the past and the present. The Rev. Dr. Desmond van der Water explains:

Perhaps where it will count is where you bring people together in small ways to encounter one another, working together, breaking down the stereotypes and cultural barriers. The church is very well placed to facilitate that kind of coming together as it is a safe environment to do it. We have a big and exciting task at that level to foster reconciliation between alienated race groups.

Advocacy on behalf of victims: A number of respondents mention their frustration and anger with the lack of reparations from the government for victims. While not reflected in the interviews, churches have been active in lobbying the government for more appropriate reparations.

Victim-perpetrator mediation: A few respondents stressed the importance of facilitating dialogue between perpetrators and victims (or victimized communities) directly so as to promote individual and collective healing.

Social justice and poverty alleviation: Many respondents stressed the importance of poverty and economic inequality as fundamental obstacles to reconciliation. While these interviews do not clarify the churches' role in this regard, the importance of development initiatives and advocacy regarding economic justice is generally supported. The need to confront white church members with the need for social upliftment, and their responsibility for this, arises from whites having benefited from apartheid.

These strategies are very similar to those used by non-religious NGOs in South Africa. The fact that they are conducted under church auspices adds a new dimension to the intervention and provides access to different types of groups and communities.

Impact of the TRC on the Reconciliation Work of the Churches

For many churches, the TRC largely served to reemphasize the huge amount of work that still needs to be addressed in terms of reconciliation. It has made it clear that reconciliation has not yet been achieved and does require extensive further work. This has, in the opinion of many, been useful and opened the door for further reconciliation work. As noted by one NGO staff member: "The work of the TRC has created waves. They have created greater awareness among churches of the need to look at reconciliation. Churches are now confronted with how they engage their congregations in reconciliation processes."[17]

This impetus only seems to have materialized in the wake of the TRC. During the life of the TRC, direct church action was largely absent. It could be asked whether the religious participation in the TRC actually served to demobilize the churches' role in facilitating reconciliation (at least in the short term). In effect, for the period during which the TRC operated, it became the reconciliation body that fused state and church power in a very charismatic manner. The TRC drew into its ranks various people who had been working for the church on reconciliation issues. The church initially saw the TRC as a body that would take on more of a reconciliation role, rather than simply acting as a *truth* commission. Many in the churches saw their role in assisting the TRC as their contribution to reconciliation.

It was only in the second year or so of its operation that the TRC became clearly aware of its own limitations and started portraying itself as simply "laying a foundation" for reconciliation through providing truth and a space for dialogue.[18] It realized that reconciliation is something that would take decades and generations. It then started talking about handing over the task of reconciliation to the churches and civil society upon its completion. This two-stage approach to reconciliation was, however, not clearly strategized. The coordination between the TRC and the churches was mainly to ensure the effective functioning of the TRC's work. Very little was done to develop a clearer long-term strategy to take the work of the TRC beyond its lifespan.

The fact that the churches face a crisis of vision after the closure of the TRC is perhaps because of the expectations that they laid at its door and, to some extent, the responsibility which they appeared to have transferred onto this para-religious structure. The TRC has provided the churches with many insights and channels to pursue, but the blurring of the line between politics and religion involved in the process has left churches with little clarity about their responsibilities in the new society.

NOTES

1. From the interview with the Rev. Dr. Maake Masango of the Presbyterian Church of South Africa.

2. This crisis of vision is one that appears to affect mainly the progressive groupings within the respective churches. Because the churches as a whole did not directly engage in fighting apartheid, the struggle for a new vision is probably only seen as a challenge for a section of the church.

3. In a statement titled "The Challenge of Reconciliation," published by the Gauteng Council of Churches, it is, for example, claimed that "the state cannot bring about repentance and true reconciliation. Only we the religious bodies in our land can do this."

4. From the interview with the Rev. Charity Majiza, General Secretary of the SACC.

5. In "The Challenge of Reconciliation" cited above the churches proclaim that "models are needed for the practical implementation of reconciliation." However, while the need and basis for reconciliation are clearly articulated, a process for intervention is left to the readers to develop for themselves: "We need to search for and become involved in any action or programme that focuses on reconciliation." It is a process that is still to be defined.

6. From the interview with Ashley Green-Thompson, Director of the Peace and Justice Department, SACBC.

7. See, for example, Hugo van der Merwe and Undine Kayser, "Community Reconciliation in South Africa—A Review of NGO Initiatives in the Post-TRC Era," forthcoming from the Centre for the Study of Violence and Reconciliation.

8. While church structures were central actors in the lobbying process, the key drafters of the legislation were politicians, legal academics, and human rights lawyers. See Hugo van der Merwe, Polly Dewhirst, and Brandon Hamber, "Non-Governmental Organisations and the Truth and Reconciliation Commission: An Impact Assessment," *Politikon* 26 (May 1999): 55–79 for a more detailed analysis of civil society influence on the TRC.

9. See Undine Kayser, "What Do We Tell Our Children?: The Work of the Centre for Ubuntu in Cape Town (formerly the Religious Response to the Truth and Reconciliation Commission)" (Jo-

hannesburg: Centre for the Study of Violence and Reconciliation, 2001) for a detailed review of the work of the Religious Response to the TRC.

10. Sometimes this relationship was, however, quite frustrating for local church leaders who felt that, while they were providing essential assistance to the TRC, they were not given much space to influence the way the TRC engaged with their communities. On this point see Hugo van der Merwe, *Community Reconciliation and the Truth and Reconciliation Commission: An Analysis of Competing Strategies and Conceptualisations,* unpub. Ph.D. dissertation, Institute for Conflict Analysis and Resolution, George Mason University, Virginia, 1999.

11. This hearing was one of several TRC sectoral hearings that were convened to develop an understanding of the role of institutions in promoting (and failing to protect) human rights.

12. From the interview with Lesley Morgan, Coordinator of the Justice and Social Responsibility Division of the Uniting Presbyterian Church of South Africa.

13. For a more detailed analysis of this problem, see Audrey R. Chapman and Patrick Ball, "The Truth of Truth Commissions," *Human Rights Quarterly* 23 (February 2001): 1–43.

14. From TRC Human Rights Violations Hearing held in Grahamstown, 7 April 1997.

15. This was further conflated by the Commission's support for the extension of the amnesty date to May 10, 1994.

16. Less than ten percent of victims who made statements to the TRC were given the chance to tell their stories at a human rights violation hearing.

17. From an interview with Athol Jennings (Vuleka Trust, on January 16, 1998), cited in Hugo van der Merwe, Polly Dewhirst, and Brandon Hamber, "The Relationship between Peace/Conflict Resolution Organisations and the TRC: An Impact Assessment" (Johannesburg: Centre for the Study of Violence and Reconciliation, October 1998).

18. For a more detailed analysis of the TRC's various conceptualizations of reconciliation, see van der Merwe, *Community Reconciliation and the Truth and Reconciliation Commission.* While much discussion occurred within the TRC about the meaning of reconciliation, little consensus emerged from their debates.

PERSPECTIVES ON RECONCILIATION WITHIN THE RELIGIOUS COMMUNITY

Audrey R. Chapman

American Association for the Advancement of Science

There is a difference between a secular and religious concept of reconciliation. I really agree with the person who said that the Commission was a civil commission that hijacked Christian terms.[1]

I think that, in one way, the Commission could not have functioned without religious people, not only Christian but also committed religious people from other religions. It would not have worked out without the person of Archbishop Tutu. To me, this raises the question of whether a model of this sort can be transferred to another country. South Africans in general are a religious people, and I am not sure whether you could do something similar in a rather secularized country.[2]

ONE OF THE MOST NOTABLE FEATURES of South Africa's Truth and Reconciliation Commission was its emphasis on forgiveness and reconciliation. The TRC was also unusual because religious thinkers and clergy played major roles (Chairman, Deputy Chairman, four other Commissioners, and the Director of the Research Department). The powerful presence of one of South Africa's most senior clerics as Chair, the liturgical character of many public hearings, and the use of religious terminology infused the TRC with a decidedly Christian atmosphere. Even more significantly, key members of the Commission had a religious conception of its mandate. In his interview in this volume, Piet Meiring, a former member of the TRC's Human Rights Violations Committee, recounts Archbishop Tutu's view that the term "reconciliation" is so loaded religiously that it is necessary to fill it with religious content. And so it was by many Commissioners: victims were encouraged to forgive perpetrators and perpetrators, albeit far less frequently, to confess wrongdoing and reconcile with victims.

South Africa's post-apartheid context and the experience of the Truth and Reconciliation Commission offer an opportunity to explore the process of reconciliation in a transitional society and the efficacy of various strategies for promoting reconciliation. The TRC model also raises many issues about how to conceptualize reconciliation and its requirements, particularly the differences between political and religious approaches. One recurrent question relates to the appropriateness and impact of the religious contribution to the TRC.

These issues were explored in the interviews with the religious leaders. The interviews also provided an opportunity to elicit their evaluations of the TRC and its contributions to promoting reconciliation. This essay analyzes the views of those interviewed on these topics and discusses their implications.

Religious Foundations of Reconciliation

As might be expected, given the backgrounds of the subjects, the interviews stressed the religious foundations of reconciliation. Most, perhaps all, of the interviewees would agree with the statement made by several sources that ultimately reconciliation between people depends on reconciliation with God. Others made the even stronger claim that there can be no reconciliation outside of faith. A few—Lesley Morgan, the facilitator of programs on reconciliation for the Uniting Presbyterian Church, for example—did not believe that a secular form of reconciliation is even possible.

Characteristically, the Christians interviewed categorized reconciliation as a Christian or a biblical term and interpreted the meaning of reconciliation through a New Testament prism. Frequently, they claimed that the term "reconciliation" refers first and foremost to God's supreme act of rec-

onciling humankind and the creation to God's self. The passage in 2
Corinthians 5:18–19 (NRSV) was paradigmatic for several:

All this is from God, who reconciled us to himself through Christ, and has given us
the ministry of reconciliation; that is, in Christ God was reconciling the world to
himself, not counting their trespasses against them, and entrusting the message of
reconciliation to us.

Those who noted that God became reconciled to humanity through the
death of Jesus often added that reconciliation is a very costly thing. One ex-
ception was Archbishop T.W. Ntongane of the Apostolic Methodist Church,
who explained that people in the (African) independent churches prefer the
Old Testament and therefore based their idea of reconciliation on the justice
of God expressed in that text.

Members of the other religious communities who were interviewed—
Jewish, Muslim, Hindu, and Baha'i—also identified reconciliation as important within their faith traditions. Franz Auerbach, Vice President of the
South African Chapter of the World Conference on Religion and Chairperson of the Working Group of the National Religious Leaders' Forum, reported that his survey of religious understandings of reconciliation did not
find significant differences in perspectives among persons of Christian,
Hindu, Muslim, and Jewish backgrounds. All of these faiths identified reconciliation as requiring the same elements: acknowledgment, confession
(which had different forms of expression), remorse, forgiveness, and restitution by those who have wronged others. According to Auerbach, the conceptions of forgiveness that were conveyed stressed not only the need of
wrongdoers to seek forgiveness, but also the religious duty of the victim of
the wrongdoing/injustice to forgive the perpetrator(s).

Approaches to Reconciliation

None of those interviewed for this volume disputed the need for reconciliation in South Africa. Respondents noted multiple sources of division—race,
class, social status, economic status, and even religious affiliation. Many of
them described the task of promoting reconciliation as an important religious vocation. Few contested the appropriateness of the government taking
initiatives to foster greater national unity. Nevertheless, almost none of the
sources seemed to have a clear conception of the nature of or requirements
for promoting reconciliation.

Many of the interviewees conceptualized reconciliation as a process during which people get rid of the burdens of the past and make a new beginning. The Rev. Dr. Desmond van der Water, General Secretary of the United Congregational Church of Southern Africa, stated, for example, that reconciliation has two major dimensions: an acknowledgment that there has been a fracture or a break in a relationship and a desire to be reconciled. Dr. Farid Esack, a Muslim theologian and a Commissioner for Gender Equality, spoke of the Arabic concept of *tasamuh*, which means a mutual letting go of the hurts and the pains of the past.

In reflecting on the requirements for reconciliation, the interviewees frequently emphasized the need for a genuine transformation of relations. Several spoke about reconciliation as requiring internal as well as external changes. Yet there were few, if any, concrete suggestions or proposals as to how to initiate or promote such a transformation. Some spoke of the need for openness, mutual respect, and an ability to listen so as to discern the truth of each other's experience. Others emphasized acknowledgment, confession, remorse, forgiveness, justice, and/or restitution. It was unclear, however, whether these were perceived as requirements for or dimensions of reconciliation.

Few of the respondents made the TRC's mistake of reducing reconciliation primarily or exclusively to effecting an improved relationship between former victims and perpetrators. While many respondents believed that reconciliation had an interpersonal dimension, they also affirmed that it was a broader communal concept as well. Bishop Dandala, the Presiding Bishop of the Methodist Church of South Africa, stated, for example, "it needs to be said with equal vigor that when we talk about reconciliation, particularly in a context like ours, it cannot only be an individual thing because of the way we dealt with one another as communities." He went on to note, "there has to be a fair amount of collective acknowledgment of collective sin, collective shortcomings, and the ability for people to deal with those things that still divide us as communities."

Nevertheless, much as in the TRC report, far more of the interviewees spoke about the relationship between individuals than the collective dimensions of reconciliation. This predilection may reflect their personal experience. Traditionally, clergy and religious communities have had far more involvement with pastoral relationships between individuals than initiatives to promote national reconciliation. And it is also considerably more difficult to attempt healing communal divisions.

Secular (Political) and Religious Approaches
to Reconciliation

The interview subjects who addressed the relationship between religious and secular or political approaches to reconciliation generally stressed their differences. The Rev. Selaotswe Tsingtsing, the minister at St. Mungo's Uniting Church, for example, explained that as a religious person he views reconciliation in the context of his relationship with God and his understanding of God as love. In contrast, he believed that reconciliation at a secular level involved members of a community coming together for purposes of creating social relationships for the benefit of all. For the Rev. James Buys, the Moderator of the United Reformed Church, the primary difference is the premise from which reconciliation proceeds; that is, whether reconciliation is motivated by religious values or political goals. According to Buys, for Christians the redemptive act of Christ in reconciling the human community with God is paramount. In contrast, legal requirements were paramount within the broader political context. Buys identified the legal framework related to amnesty as framing the TRC process.

Some equated differences in the scale of the relationships as informing the distinction between religious and political approaches to reconciliation. Like the TRC, some of the interviewees understood reconciliation as applying only or primarily to interpersonal relationships. A few were explicit about this, and for many others it was implicit in their comments.

Notably and unfortunately, many of those who distinguished between political and religious approaches to reconciliation had fairly minimalist, often pejorative, conceptions of the nature of political reconciliation. Several of the interviewees equated secular approaches to reconciliation with the mere end of hostilities or the beginning of a process of negotiations. Fr. Sean O'Leary, the Acting Director of the Pastoral Institute of the Catholic Bishops Conference, reflected that secular society employs the rule of law as the way of dealing with deviation and therefore did not require forgiveness or reconciliation. Bashir Vania, the Director of the Islamic Information Centre, went so far as to characterize secular approaches as amoral and motivated by self-interest.

A smaller number of the interview subjects denied that the distinction between religious and secular approaches was valid. Bishop Phaswana of the Lutheran Church claimed that the dichotomy between the religious and the secular did not enter into African thinking. Dr. Farid Esack argued that it is not possible to make a neat distinction between the religious and the secular because there were spiritual elements in all human activities. The Rev. Wesley Mabuza, Director of the Institute of Contextual Theology, attributed the demarcation between secular and religious approaches to reconciliation to a western mind set, and like Bishop Phaswana, he observed that this approach was inconsistent with the African heritage. For him the critical issue was not whether someone was religious or not, but whether the proposed reconciliation initiative would restore the dignity of the person who is hurt and the one who is asking for forgiveness. He cited the traditional African concept of *ubuntu* as central. He also observed that the requirements of Christianity gel with African culture, which explained the readiness of the majority of Africans to become Christians.

I think it is significant that regardless of their perspective, few of those interviewed believed that a religious interpretation of reconciliation applied directly to social and political relationships on a national level. This observation was often paired with criticisms of the manner in which the TRC confused religious and political approaches to reconciliation. Dr. Wolfram Kistner, a Lutheran theologian, was among those critical of the TRC's conflation of religious and secular approaches to reconciliation. For him reconciliation in the religious sense required repentance, forgiveness, restitution, and making a new beginning, but, like many others, he considered this to be the task of the churches, and not of a truth commission. Similarly, Bishop Patrick Matalengoe of the Anglican Church characterized the TRC as a "civil commission that hijacked Christian terms."

Like the report of the TRC, there are significant points of inconsistency in the interviews regarding the issue of the relevance of religious approaches to societal issues of reconciliation. On the one hand, as noted above, many of the interviewees distinguish between secular and religious approaches, and some of the religious leaders are critical of the TRC's tendency to apply religious conceptions of reconciliation. Yet most of the respondents, even those who are critical of the TRC, continue to utilize religious terminology to discuss reconciliation. Moreover, most of the interviewees, regardless of their perspectives on the TRC's approach to reconciliation, considered it to be appropriate for so many Commissioners to be drawn from the religious community. There is even something of a self-congratulatory note about the contributions of the religious community to the TRC process. Thus it is unclear whether the fundamental critique is that the TRC did its secular work badly or that it did not do its religious work properly. [3]

Forgiveness and Reconciliation

Analysts have linked the TRC's unprecedented emphasis on forgiveness and restorative justice to the influence of the religious community. Yet the interviews in this volume manifest a far more complex assessment of the relationship between forgiveness and reconciliation in the TRC process. Even those who understood reconciliation as requiring forgiveness do not equate the two. The Rev. Basil Manning, Chairperson of the Centre for Anti-Racism and Anti-Sexism, for example, conceptualized reconciliation as tied to the acknowledgment of wrong on the one hand and forgiveness on the other, but he also stressed that reconciliation is much broader than that. He commented that reconciliation "is not about revenge; it is about the doing of I am sorry."

Significantly, many of the respondents were uncomfortable with or critical of the TRC's conflating reconciliation with interpersonal forgiveness. For example, Mr. N. Rathinasamy, the first Chairperson of the Hindu Coordinating Council of Gauteng and Chairperson of its Human Services, described an emphasis on forgiveness as characteristic of religious approaches to reconciliation, but not transferable to the secular arena. Similarly, the group of Baha'i faith representatives distinguished between forgiveness as an option for an individual and justice as the appropriate domain of the society.

There was particular unease with the unreciprocated form of forgiveness the TRC frequently promoted. Unlike the TRC report, few, if any, of the respondents advocated that all former victims had an obligation to forgive their perpetrators. Generally, the views in the interviews were closer to the perspective of the 1985 *Kairos Document* and its critique of "church theology" than the unconditional forgiveness of the TRC. The *Kairos Document* argued against making reconciliation into an absolute principle that must be applied in all cases of conflict or dissension. It emphasized that there can be no reconciliation and no forgiveness without repentance and without the promise of justice. [4] The view of Dr. Kistner that it is highly questionable, even in a religious sense, for people just to be forgiven and not to be asked to do something in return, very likely would be broadly supported among the interviewees. Many of them believed that at the very least the perpetrator should be required to make a sincere admission of wrongdoing, but such confessions, let alone statements of contrition, were not a requirement for amnesty by the TRC. Moreover, even when perpetrators, such as Eugene de Kock, acknowledged their crimes in the TRC Amnesty Hearings, the respondents did not believe that they were sincere. Others, like Rev. Manning, tied forgiveness to concrete efforts to compensate for the legacy of the past. Mr. Rathinasamy went so far as to claim that under the circumstances it was a travesty of justice for the perpetrators to get off scot-free.

Like some of the secular critics, some viewed the TRC's pressure on former victims as unfair, one-sided, and unbalanced. Victim advocates have been critical of the TRC for its efforts to delegitimate and suppress the anger of former victims. Several of those interviewed appeared to be sympathetic with these concerns. The Rev. Frank Mabuza, for example, was angry with Tutu and others on the TRC who criticized blacks for an unwillingness to forgive and/or let go of their anger. Notably, Dr. Willie Botha, a leading Dutch Reformed theologian and Afrikaner, expressed the view that the oppressor is in a better situation to start the reconciliation process by asking for forgiveness than the victim. Yet like many of the others he acknowledged the difficulty of getting perpetrators to do so.

The Role of Confession and Repentance in Reconciliation

While the TRC Commissioners presiding over the victim hearings often coaxed or pressured former victims to state that they forgave perpetrators, the judges who presided over the amnesty hearings did not make similar efforts to actively solicit acknowledgments of wrongdoing and contrition from perpetrators. Nor did the official requirements for amnesty include repentance for political crimes. This imbalance has been an ongoing source of criticism, particularly from organizations representing former victims.

Significantly, much like the *Kairos Document,* there is almost complete accord in the interviews about the importance of confessions of culpability from perpetrators and the far broader group of persons who benefited from the apartheid system, as well as the need for repentance. The Rev. Charity Majiza, General Secretary of the South African Council of Churches, emphasized that repentance and forgiveness are both essential elements in the reconciling act. This means that one has to take responsibility rather than shifting the blame elsewhere. The Rev. Frank Makoro and the Rev. Ramakatsa Mathibedi of the Baptist Convention of South Africa began their interview by observing, "When we talk of reconciliation, the first thing we must address is the question of acceptance of the wrongdoing. That means taking responsibility rather than shifting blame somewhere else." Several of the interviewees associated the requirements of confession and repentance with African culture as well as religious faith. The Rev. Dr. Maake Masango, minister of the St. Giles Presbyterian Church, commented, for example, that in the African community someone who has done something wrong is ostracized, even isolated, until that person confesses.

Acknowledgment

Has the TRC process been conducive to prompting the majority of white South Africans to come to terms with their own complicity in overtly or tacitly supporting the apartheid system and benefiting from its structural inequalities? There was agreement in the interviews that the TRC process, particularly the public hearings, had certainly managed to communicate the sufferings imposed on the black population. Thus many of the whites, even those who had preferred not to know about the abuses inflicted by apartheid, could no longer deny the horrors of the apartheid system. Franz Auerbach compared the situation of such white South Africans to the post-World War II period when many Germans claimed that they had not known what had taken place under the National Socialism of Hitler. He also commented that South Africa's relatively free press meant that there was a far greater opportunity to know about these abuses during the apartheid years than in Germany during the war years.

Yet knowing about the abuses of the past does not necessarily translate into an acknowledgment of responsibility. Like many other commentaries on South Africa, there was a near consensus in the interviews that the beneficiaries of apartheid had yet to come to terms with their moral complicity and culpability. Several of those interviewed suggested that many members of the white community are still in a state of disbelief or denial. Piet Meiring, himself an Afrikaner, believed that many of his friends, his own people, and even the Dutch Reformed Church are now in a state of deep despair and suffering from an identity crisis. He compared the current situation of the white community to the stages that someone experiences during an existential crisis related to terminal illness or the death of a close family member: disbelief or denial, followed by anger, then rationalization or bargaining, deep despair, and eventually, only after having worked through the process, acceptance. Meiring commented that all white South Africans, English as well as Afrikaners, were also having problems sorting through their role in the new South Africa.

Several of the interviewees were distressed that most members of the white community still denied that they had benefited from the apartheid system. Several noted that many persons in the white community sought refuge by still stressing their own lack of involvement and/or responsibility for the abuses of the apartheid system. At best, some of the respondents believed that a minority of white South Africans had accepted responsibility for the past. Rev. Mabuza estimated that on a scale of ten the white community scored at three. Bishop Matalengoe was less generous. He put the percentage of white people ready to acknowledge the wrongs of apartheid at 5 percent. Others expressed the view that things are changing, but very slowly.

Several, Wesley Mabuza, for example, were critical of the TRC's inability to bring whites to a place of asking for the forgiveness that Africans were willing to offer. He attributed this failure in part to the absence of a collective voice pleading for the white community to ask for forgiveness. The failure of the Dutch Reformed Church, which served during the apartheid period as the virtual equivalent of an established church, to take a more meaningful initiative was particularly problematic for some. Yet, given the historical role of the Dutch Reformed Church in providing the theological justification for the apartheid system and the criticism this evoked in the anti-apartheid movement, it was striking how few of the interviews dealt with this issue.

Dr. Botha attributed the negative view of the TRC within the Afrikaner community to two factors: negative reporting by the Afrikaans media and the failure of the churches to help the Afrikaners accept the TRC process. He reported that the national executive of the Dutch Reformed Church was advised by some of the National Party leaders to keep away from the TRC, and therefore the churches did not encourage the people to attend the hearings or become involved in any way. According to Dr. Botha, this distance was then compounded by cultural factors. The Afrikaner people do not easily concede their need for forgiveness because of their tradition about being strong and tough and not showing their feelings in public. Crying, especially in public by a national leader like Archbishop Tutu, therefore seemed quite inappropriate. For many Afrikaners the emotionalism encouraged by the TRC seemed staged, and this was irritating and off-putting. He cautioned, however, that growing individualism also made it difficult to speak about the Afrikaners as a community in the same way as in the past.

Several respondents were disturbed that many whites are now comparing unfavorably the quality of life and the services provided by the democratic government with the situation under the apartheid administration.

Some attributed this view to the failure to take into account that the resources that formerly benefited a small minority now had to be stretched to cover the entire population. A few of the interviewees also reported that despite the revelations of the TRC some whites still argue that the apartheid scheme was a better way of doing things.

Restitution as a Requirement for Reconciliation

The TRC was based on a restorative approach to justice rather than a punitive model based on determining guilt and then imposing penalties on those responsible for the abuses. The TRC sought to repair past injustices through providing truth about the past, affirming the dignity of former victims, and providing symbolic and financial reparations. One of the several innovations of the TRC process was to link the verification of victim status to the receipt of financial reparations and stipends for medical and therapeutic treatment from the state. The TRC also made recommendations about symbolic reparations, primarily in the form of monuments for victims.

The importance of economic and social reparations to effecting true reconciliation was a theme repeated many times in the interviews. Many of the interviewees underscored that true reconciliation must carry within it tangible manifestations of the commitment to make restitution. Piet Meiring relayed a story that Archbishop Tutu had told of a man who stole a beautiful pen from somebody and then after many years requested forgiveness for doing so. According to the story, the victim embraced the former thief, telling him that he was forgiven, but then asked for his pen back. Prof. Meiring suggested that the many South Africans who had profited from the past, especially members of the white community, should now be ready to give the "pen" back. Moreover, for many of the respondents appropriate restitution should be on two levels, individual and structural.

Interestingly, many of the respondents did not believe that the burden of restitution should fall primarily or solely on the government. Several recommended that both the perpetrators and the broader community of beneficiaries of the apartheid system should contribute to reparations. Bishop Matalengoe defined perpetrators very broadly as all those who readily accepted the franchise under the apartheid system, and stated that they should now be required to pay reparations, presumably through some mechanism to redistribute income or property. To accomplish this goal, some interviewees suggested imposing an extra tax on those who were oppressors. In the absence of a government-imposed reparation tax, several respondents recommended that the beneficiaries of apartheid make voluntary donations into a reparations fund. Dr. Esack commented, for example:

For me that means that a minister in the apartheid regime will say, "I will sacrifice my pension and will give up all of the money that I have earned, for it is ill-begotten money. I will give it up. I will go and rent a comfortable small flat in a nice suburb, and all the other I will give to a reparations fund." There must be tangible and proportionate evidence of your willingness to share what you earned at the expense of others.

Several of the interviews were critical of the TRC and perhaps the political system for the failure to require some form of restitution from perpetrators to victims of apartheid. As Fr. Sean O'Leary commented, "You cannot force forgiveness, but you can force restitution." He went on to say that the TRC should have forced perpetrators to make some form of restitution, even if it were to be of a symbolic nature.

Unfortunately, it now seems unlikely that the government will implement even the TRC's modest recommendations regarding financial reparations for victims. Many, likely most of those interviewed, were very disturbed about this development. Generally the interviewees sympathized with the plight of the victims, who came forward to tell their stories to the public and then gained nothing except further pain and at times a sense of shame. Bishop Phaswana may have spoken for many other respondents in his statement that "the victims feel that they have been doubly taken for a ride—victimized by the apartheid system and now by the government they have elected because the government through the TRC raised expectations of restitution. These expectations have not been fulfilled." A few also made critical comments about the priorities of a government investing scarce funds in buying weapons and appeasing multinational companies while neglecting to provide compensation to victims.

The Role and Requirements for Economic Justice in Reconciliation

Beyond the provision of providing limited reparations to victims, many of those interviewed, both black and white, spoke about the need for greater economic justice in the form of a redistribution of resources as a requirement for reconciliation. Many respondents emphasized the need to acknowledge that there are financial costs to achieving a meaningful form of reconciliation. The view of Bishop Kevin Dowling, the Chair of the Justice and Peace Department of the Southern African Catholic Bishops' Conference, that "reconciliation really has to do with justice" was likely shared by many of the others interviewed. According to Bishop Dowling, "In the end real reconciliation, I believe, in our country is only going to happen when people experience economic transformation, economic justice."

Fr. Dale White commented that while the TRC addressed personal aspects of forgiveness, it is the economic dimensions of forgiveness that are blocking true reconciliation. He spoke of the affluent people, both white and black, wearing a kind of blanket that protects them from seeing what is happening to the poor and from becoming aware of the systems that are grinding the people into poverty. White, who equated forgiveness with reconciliation, went on, "Forgiveness, as I understood it, is the forgiveness of the unjust steward, the forgiveness that reaches the poverty that they were imposing on others and has it removed."

Some conceptualized the call for economic justice as the unfinished business of the TRC. Fr. O'Leary commented:

In the TRC we found—which is also quite admirable—that there is a call for justice. People do not want revenge. They do want justice. And I think that is a fair position to take by a people who have suffered so much. It illustrates the maturity of a nation. No talk of revenge, just justice. Somehow we need to win back the concept of justice within the country.

Many of the interviewees mourned the failure of the white community to respond to the challenge of promoting greater economic justice in the country. Lesley Morgan commented that most white people supported equality between the races, but an equality that would not require any personal cost. While they would like black people to be uplifted and have access to the benefits the white community has received, they were not willing to make any personal sacrifices to bring it about.

The Role of the Religious Community in the TRC

Like the TRC report, the interviews seemed to speak with two voices about the appropriateness of the religious role and religious influence in the TRC. Despite some of the concerns expressed about conflating religious and political conceptions of reconciliation, most of the respondents were quite comfortable with the strong religious representation on the TRC. Many considered it an appropriate expression of the religiosity of South Africa and the leadership role of the faith communities in the opposition to the apartheid system. One person even characterized the TRC as itself a religious experience. Some respondents commented that religious people brought special attributes—spirituality, compassion, and understanding—that added depth to the TRC process and prevented it from deteriorating into a dry legal proceeding. Still others expressed appreciation for the opportunity for people in the Christian community to come to know better about the commitments of other faiths. One interview, perhaps representing the views of others as well, stated that the Commission could not have functioned without religious people and therefore raised the question as to whether the South African model could be exported to other countries.

What accounts for this "double vision" of criticism and support for the religious character of the TRC, sometimes even by the same person? It may reflect the realization that the religious involvement brought both benefits and liabilities. For example, Dr. Kistner, who was one of the strongest advocates for the religious contribution to the TRC, also acknowledged that it sometimes confused people, such as when the Commission made a transition from a pastoral style to a more legal procedure. Similarly, some of the interviewees may have a great deal of admiration for the personal role played by Archbishop Tutu but also realized that the religious character he sought to impose on the TRC was not appropriate. Beyond this inconsistency, the interviews often reflect a more fundamental inability to come to terms with the broader issues of the character of national reconciliation and the relevance of religion in a truth commission process. Perhaps it may also be difficult for persons of faith to view a civil political process through a secular perspective.

Some interviews were consistently critical of the religious role. Dr. Esack characterized the incorporation of religious figures into the TRC as a "shrewd move" because it invested the Commission with "an aura of beyond-ness." But it also had negative consequences. According to Dr. Esack, the involvement of religious leaders discouraged people from engaging critically. He believed that South Africa would have been better served with a truth commission composed of social scientists, political activists, and people who were experts on effecting reconciliation. His assessment of the religious approach to reconciliation was that "it put a political bandage over the apartheid era so that we can limp into the new South Africa." Rev. Manning suggested that many of the religious representatives were motivated by a "cheap grace" theology: as long as you say you are sorry nothing more is expected. Dr. van der Water believed that having so many religious people on the TRC, especially having an Archbishop as Chairperson, confused the intention of the process. Moreover, he seemed to agree with Dr. Esack that people with a religious background do not have appropriate skills to oversee such a process. Consistent with his criticisms of the TRC composition and processes as being too elitist, Archbishop Ntongane stated that there were too many religious people and too few ordinary people. Alone of all the interviewees, he also noted that women were underrepresented.

Contributions of the TRC

Evaluations of the TRC tended to mention both its contributions and limitations. Few respondents disagreed that there were some or even many good things about the TRC. The assessment of Ashley Green-Thompson that the TRC had at least placed the issues of truth and reconciliation on the national and international agenda was a minimalist view with which few would likely take issue. A few acknowledged that an exercise like the TRC, with limited time and resources, could only be expected to initiate a long-term process. Yet many of the respondents were also disappointed, undoubtedly because of their high expectations, and therefore critical of some aspects of the TRC.

The theme, so central to the work of the TRC, that there can be no reconciliation without a full disclosure of truth was apparently shared by many of those interviewed. Yet several of the respondents also acknowledged the problems in determining the truth about the crimes and abuses that occurred during apartheid. And others were critical of the focus on gross human rights abuses or political crimes to the exclusion of dealing with the structural violations of the apartheid system.

Many, indeed most, of the respondents believed that the TRC had made tangible, albeit limited, contributions to truth-finding. Many stated that the oppression and brutality of the apartheid system were now a matter of public record. The Rev. Dr. Maake Masango commented that the TRC experience helped to seek the truth, "and it is the truth that will set us free." His characterization of the TRC process was that "it brought the truth out of the silent mute world into a communal world." Some, Rev. Makoro, for example, added that having an official body confirm what happened under apartheid is a benefit for the victims. Many of the interviewees commented on the benefit of relatives being able to discover what had happened to loved ones.

Many of the most positive comments pertained to the respect the TRC accorded to victims and their relatives by letting them tell their stories. The TRC's victim-oriented approach was seen as restoring dignity to victims. Several spoke of the TRC as a painful and difficult experience for victims, but also as a cathartic one that was quite helpful.

Nevertheless, few of those interviewed would assess the TRC's truth-finding process as an unqualified success. Several respondents were disturbed by the failure to deal more effectively with the structural dimensions of the apartheid system. Franz Auerbach likely spoke for others as well when he criticized the TRC for focusing so exclusively on gross violations. He pointed out that acknowledging apartheid as a crime against humanity means that millions of people also suffered. He specifically mentioned the TRC's failure to deal with forced removals. [5] Rev. Manning pointed out that apartheid was not just about a government that used excessive force but the way in which it dehumanized people. He asked when and how the damage of the impact of the legal foundations of apartheid, like the Bantu Education, the Job Reservations Act, and the pass laws, would be assessed. Fr. O'Leary was critical of the TRC process because it isolated the wrongdoers and thereby enabled the white society to exonerate itself. By this he apparently meant that by personalizing the blame, the TRC enabled the majority of whites to maintain the myth that the abuses were committed by "a few bad eggs" rather than acknowledging that the suffering was caused by the very nature of the system.

The assessment of the TRC's contributions to reconciliation was generally qualified, even negative. A few questioned whether the TRC should have been called a reconciliation commission at all. In their interview, the Rev. Ron Steele and the Rev. Dick Khoza of the Rhema Bible Church suggested that it was a mistake to assign the mandate of reconciliation to the TRC. Their view was that reconciliation can only come afterward as the fruit of the truth. Now that the TRC had exposed wrongdoing under apartheid, the real job of reconciliation could take place. Chief Rabbi Cyril Harris questioned whether a single body could or should have tried to combine truth and reconciliation. Quoting from his book, he commented: "My problem was with the juxtaposition of finding out the truth on the one hand and the desired aim of promoting reconciliation on the other. These seemed to me to be antithetical companions." He mentioned that even before the Commission was set up he had expressed the view that truth-finding might well prove divisive rather than conducive to reconciliation. Now that the TRC had finished its work he believed that reconciliation between victims and perpetrators was partially achieved in some areas, and he acknowledged that these events were deeply moving. Nevertheless, in the wider area of relationships between the white beneficiaries of apartheid and the black population who had suffered, according to Rabbi Harris, reconciliation has hardly begun. He stated categorically that truth had not brought reconciliation; South Africans cannot be considered to being closer in any significant way as a result of the TRC's work.

Many of those interviewed were also critical of other aspects of the TRC process. The amnesty process was one target, even though many acknowledged that it was the outgrowth of a negotiated settlement that did not accord the TRC much discretion. The imbalance between the treatment of perpetrators and victim was mentioned by several. Another commonly mentioned problem was the failure to provide adequate restitution and compensation. There was also concern that the lack of reparations had engendered anger among the black South Africans.

Continuing Role of the Religious Community

Many, perhaps all, of the respondents, believed that religious communities should be playing an ongoing role in promoting reconciliation efforts. That the church should recognize the need and seize the opportunity was a theme in many of the interviews. As Lesley Morgan asked, "Who does reconciliation if not churches and other religious organizations?"

Several interviewees commented on the need for greater reconciliation efforts within the churches to enable them to come to terms with their own past and to promote more meaningful forms of racial integration in their own bodies. Under the apartheid regime, the religious community was divided into communions that were both supporters of apartheid and opponents and victims of oppression. Some of the major Christian churches, particularly the Dutch Reformed Church, conferred their blessing on the apartheid system, offering religious justification to its practice of racial separation, and others gave the apartheid state tacit support. A few religious communities—churches, mosques, synagogues, and temples—were also sites of transformation, albeit more often through the drafting of official statements and the courageous leadership of a few individuals than through the commitments and activism of members. While faith communities frequently claimed to cut across divisions of race, gender, class, and ethnicity, in most cases they did not. Instead, they were (and continue to be) separated into racially and sometimes economically homogenous groupings both at a denominational and congregational level. Some religious communities were internally divided as well by attitudes toward apartheid policies and the appropriateness of undertaking religious activism. [6] Rev. Mabuza undoubtedly spoke for many others when he reflected, "There is no way the religious community can take part in reconciliation and transformation when it itself is not transformed, when it is not reconciled."

Most of the interviewees, even those who detailed initiatives that were underway, were critical of current efforts to deal with the churches' own apartheid legacy. The relative silence and inactivity of the Dutch Reformed Church was considered to be particularly unfortunate. Nor did they believe that the political transition in South Africa necessarily changed the religious community. Several interviewees, such as Bishop Phaswana, described the continuing racial and ethnic divisions within their own denominations. Some respondents related painful personal experiences in their congregations or denominations. These included the problems of black ministers posted to predominantly white congregations and conversely, the difficulties white staff have in gaining respect and acceptance from black members of their denominations. Dr. Trefor Jenkins and Lindi Myeza, both members of the Central Methodist Church in Johannesburg, painfully described the process of white flight that accompanied the Africanization of worship and attendance in their own Methodist congregation.

Many of the respondents reflected on things the religious community could do to promote reconciliation, both within their congregations and in the wider society. The Rev. Charity Majiza mentioned the importance of incorporating the issue of reconciliation in worship, liturgies, and preaching. Rev. Mabuza and Fr. O'Leary expressed the view that many denominations need a TRC-like body to deal with their own histories of violations and abuses. Similarly, Piet Meiring recommended that local churches should conduct their own mini truth commissions, telling their own stories and sharing with one another so as to try to create bonds between people. Bishop Matalengoe spoke of the need for churches to develop a vision of the reconciled community so that it can be seen as really ministering to the people and offer a reason for living. Dr. Kistner suggested that churches could link with congregations from different backgrounds and experiences so that people could learn from one another. Dr. Esack called the religious community to a prophetic role. By that he meant that one of the responsibilities of the religious community is to critically engage with notions of reconciliation, to foster a conception of reconciliation that is based on justice, and to do so in partnership with the rest of society.

But most respondents who addressed this topic acknowledged that the religious community was not taking the initiative to promote reconciliation. Many even questioned whether the churches had either the will or the resources to do so. Others recognized that significant contributions to reconciliation required far more than making statements and approving resolutions. According to Bishop Matalengoe, most churches are investing their energy at maintaining the status quo, and focusing on their buildings and staff salaries. As a result, workshops on reconciliation are poorly attended and books thrown away into the wastepaper basket. Rev. Manning offered a similar perspective, claiming that the churches are more interested in improving their membership base and finances than in transformation. Fr. O'Leary described the churches as retreating into a laager since the late eighties and attributed this malaise to battle fatigue and the weakening of leadership. Some of the respondents spoke about the disparity between the verbal support for reconciliation activities and the lack of investment of financial and personnel support. Clearly Brigalia Bam, the Chairperson of the Independent Electoral Commission, was correct in her assessment that the churches are not living up to the hopes and expectations of the wider community.

Cumulatively, the interviews suggest that religious communities are having problems reconceptualizing their role in the post-apartheid era. As a consequence, religious communities are inclined to withdraw from the public arena, including from active efforts to promote reconciliation. A few of the respondents characterized the current situation as the loss of a prophetic vocation now that the apartheid system has ended. Yet a closer examination of the role of the religious community under the apartheid system indicates that only a few religious leaders ever carried such a prophetic mantle.[7] Even the religious communities opposing the apartheid system were more likely to do so through drafting statements than by visible acts of civil disobedience. Perhaps the "mythology" of an activist past is itself an impediment to shaping a more effective contemporary role within a democratic political system.

Prospects for Reconciliation

Most of those interviewed would likely agree that South Africa has at last begun the long journey toward reconciliation. However, the respondents would likely assess the progress made and the obstacles remaining somewhat differently. The Rev. Dr. Maake Masango, a black minister in a predominantly white Presbyterian church, for example, cautioned that there was still a need to deal with some of the apartheid legacies in the church, "the skeletons that still haunt us," but he pointed to his denomination's peace and reconciliation ministries as signs of hope and progress. Yet Lesley Morgan, a staff person involved in Presbyterian peace and reconciliation initiatives, generally tended to be critical of these efforts.

Despite the many obstacles identified, most of the interviewees remained hopeful. It is difficult to assess whether the expressions of hope primarily reflect the long sought political transition to a democratic future, the benefits of the TRC experience, the underlying faith of the respondents, or some combination thereof. While many of the religious leaders acknowledged the problems of the present, they anticipated a better future. Acknowledging that it would take time, several even believed that future generations of South Africans would be rid of racism. Lesley Morgan expressed a seeming contradiction, perhaps characteristic of others as well. She began her interview noting that "Reconciliation is impossible!" She then went on "But, I am a Christian so I believe that through God all things are possible."

And if nothing else, some offered prayers. The interview with the Rev. Frank Makoro and the Rev. Ramakatsa Mathibedi closed on the following note:

It is our hope and prayer that as we go along the victims and perpetrators will find each other, and also that the government, civil society, and the religious communities will find a way of helping those who became victims of our past. We must offer something that will help all people face the future with hope.

NOTES

1. From the interview with Bishop Patrick Matalengoe of the Anglican Church, Director of the Truth and Reconciliation Program of the South African Council of Churches, August 23, 1999.

2. From the interview with Dr. Wolfram Kistner, Lutheran theologian, August 18, 1999.

3. This final point comes from Hugo van der Merwe's review of an earlier draft of this paper.

4. *The Kairos Document: Challenge to the Churches* (Braamfontein: The Kairos Theologians, 1985), 8–9.

5. During apartheid, the South African government forcibly relocated millions of Africans and people of mixed racial background to more marginal areas to reallocate their property to whites.

6. See, for example, The Institutional Hearing on the Faith Community, *Truth and Reconciliation Commission of South Africa Report,* vol. 4, chp. 3, pp. 59–92.

7. This was certainly the conclusion of the TRC Report. See chp. 3 of vol. 4, pp. 59–92, which focuses on the role of the faith community.

APPENDIX

THE CHALLENGE OF

RECONCILIATION

THIS DOCUMENT was produced as a result of collective reflection by a group of Christians and church leaders involved in ministries in the East Rand, Johannesburg, Vaal, and Pretoria. The group began in 1997 as an attempt by some local churches to respond to the challenge of the Truth and Reconciliation Commission and then broadened its horizons to the promotion of reconciliation. The text was printed and distributed by the Gauteng Council of Churches and the Justice and Peace division of the Catholic Diocese of Johannesburg.

A Challenge to the Churches

1. We, the Churches, have frequently called for reconciliation in society. This call has been reinforced by the TRC. We recognize the need for the churches to continue the work of reconciliation within local communities. The work of reconciliation is a Christian calling and needs to be willingly undertaken. Why is this not happening sufficiently, and why is it taking so long?

2. One reason is the failure of the Churches to deal adequately with the challenge for reconciliation within our own structures. The time has come for the churches to acknowledge that if we are to be agents of reconciliation then we need to start the process from within.

3. The Church continues to be disempowered by the effects of the colonial past under which it was established. It also suffered under and was co-opted into the policy of apartheid. This makes it difficult for us as we seek to proclaim the gospel and work for the rule of God within our churches and society as a whole.

4. It is only as we ourselves are a challenged church that we can engage in reconciliation with other faiths and sectors of society.

How Apartheid Affected the Churches

5. Many Christians supported apartheid, whether politically, by keeping silent in the face of injustice, or through participating actively in the exploitation of the oppressed.

6. White Christians helped to maintain the economic, military and security apparatus that oppressed black people. Whether they agreed with it or not, all whites benefited from the system simply because of their skin colour. Some white Christians were afraid to speak out against apartheid although they knew that it was wrong. Some supported the cause of justice but were patronizing in their attitude to peoples of other races. On the other hand there were prophetic people within the white Christian community who worked for true justice and reconciliation and sometimes paid heavy prices for their commitment.

7. All black people were oppressed by apartheid. Some allowed themselves to be used to oppress and divide their own communities. Sometimes atrocities were committed by black Christians in the name of liberation, for party political reasons or for personal gain. Some black Christians kept silent in the face of their own oppression. On the other hand, many black church leaders and congregations suffered because of their resistance to apartheid and its injustices.

The Church Must Always Be Reformed

8. The Church must always be reforming herself, and reconciliation is a part of this process. God is calling us through our history to confess, repent and be reconciled. As Churches, we need to hear and respond to this call.

9. If we are to move beyond our pain and guilt into true reconciliation and transformation then we all need to be part of creating transformation. This change needs to happen at the level of the local congregation. It also needs to come from church leaders and to be engaged in by individual Christians in our daily living.

10. We need to change our attitudes towards each other within the Church and also to work on changing those structures of the Church that continue to be oppressive. We need to stop hiding behind excuses and to admit where we did wrong or failed to do what is right. We must face up to the hurt we have inflicted on each other and, in some areas, continue to inflict upon each other.

11. As a direct result of our history, we still live within divided churches carrying the scars of many past injustices and hurts. Our failure to bring about reconciliation has contributed to a situation in which life has frequently been rendered cheap or meaningless. We acknowledge that there are inequalities in the resources available to congregations in townships as opposed to those available in suburbs. The reality of infighting and power struggles needs to be dealt

with. We need to take responsibility for perpetuating denominational rivalry that can and does tear communities apart.

12. In order to take seriously the life and witness of the Church, we must constantly ask questions about the nature of ministry itself. This is because ministry flows directly out of our relationship with God. It we lack a healthy spirituality, we will neither be able to be good stewards of the created order with which we coexist, nor will we live in right relationship with one another. Ministry is all about service. It is about seeking the good of the other and being agents of empowerment. We therefore need to ask ourselves:

Are our leaders inspired by God's spirit and are they prophetic?
Is the Church a place where issues of gender inequality, hierarchy, and racism are taken seriously?
Are we truly seeking to be agents of transformation in society by being transformed ourselves?
Are we still caught in models of ministry that have more to do with control than with being a servant church?

13. We must say we are sorry to God, to one another, and to society for the failure to be good stewards of the responsibility that Jesus entrusted to us. True repentance is achieved by putting in place steps to right what is wrong. It is accompanied by restitution and leads to the transformation of church and society. This is the challenge we must face if we are to be agents of reconciliation.

Some Theological Reflections on Reconciliation

14. We offer the following reflections on reconciliation:

Life is sacred and valuable;
Reconciliation requires confession, restitution, and forgiveness;
The Truth and Reconciliation Commission drew attention to the need for the nation to deal with the past and build reconciliation;
There is no reconciliation without justice.

Life Is Sacred and Valuable

15. We are all created in the image of God and are called to live in a relationship of respect with creation and one another. This has often not been the case in our history as South Africans. The acts of physical, emotional, spiritual and economic violence inflicted on others by dominant groups have caused hurt. Even in the Christian faith community we need to restore respect for each other's dignity and worth.

16. The lack of true reconciliation has helped to create a society where life is viewed as cheap. This is seen in the ways we continue to fear each other, to destroy one another, and to tolerate poverty. It is also seen in the way in which people, particularly the poor, continue to be treated with disrespect. When he spoke with authority and valued the poor, Jesus gave us an example and challenged us to recognize their worth. When we take the poor seriously, we are also able to challenge them to take seriously their own worth and to work for a better quality of life.

Reconciliation Is a Process

17. As Christians we believe that God forgives us, and therefore we are called to forgive one another. God's forgiveness is unconditional; this is why we speak of the mystery of forgiveness. Forgiveness, which leads to reconciliation, is also joyful for it creates the possibility of new life. At the same time God's forgiveness must be accepted in order to be effective, and this acceptance involves confession, repentance and restitution by the offender.

> *The same is true for interpersonal relationships. We may forgive people the wrong they have done to us, and thus make forgiveness accessible to them. But it will only be effective and lead to reconciliation if they are prepared to accept it and show that acceptance by confession, repentance and restitution.*

18. There is no such thing as easy reconciliation. It is a costly process. Confession, restitution, and forgiveness are hard, difficult, and frequently painful processes for all of us. Reconciliation is made possible by forgiveness, but it cannot happen without confession, repentance, reparation and a firm decision by the offender not to repeat the offenses of the past. Without all these factors, reconciliation is not possible, and the past can easily be repeated in the future.

The Challenge of the TRC

19. The TRC drew attention to the need for reconciliation. It did much to help it to happen, but as a state body it could not and did not require repentance. The limited reparations that it recommended are the responsibility of the state. We must hold the state accountable for paying these reparations which unfortunately will be paid for by the taxpayer and not by the offender. This means that the state cannot bring about repentance and true reconciliation. Only we the religious bodies in our land can do this.

20. The lack of repentance and restitution by perpetrators continues to cause great pain to victims and communities who suffered pain and hurt. Un-

like the state, the Church neither believes in, nor is limited by a policy of amnesty without reparation. It is our task to deal with this pain, and also with the issues of guilt, conscience, and repentance, reparation and forgiveness. God calls us to be reconciled. We therefore need to work hard to build up right relationships where once there was separation, rejection and bitterness.

21. The TRC has started the process. It is up to us to build upon this and to bring about wholeness and reconciliation. As we seek to do this, we must work towards new attitudes and patterns of behavior in person to person relationships. We also have to avoid the fault of the elder brother in the story of the Prodigal Son. Unlike his father, he was unwilling to forgive his brother when he repented of his past and sought to start life again. Where people are genuinely sorry and attempt to make reparation there ought to be no holding back of forgiveness. Because life is sacred, we are called to see beyond the sinful actions of people to the basic humanity we all share as children of God.

There Is No Reconciliation Without Justice

22. Because reconciliation is a wholistic process it reaches beyond interpersonal and community relations into the very life of our nation.

23. There need to be changes in the socio-economic and political systems that shape our society. We cannot continue with a status quo where there continues to be a disproportionate distribution of wealth. It is unacceptable for a minority to be economically secure, while nearly half of our population lives below the poverty line. We cannot continue to enjoy the fruits of democracy while we participate in the ongoing militarization of our continent and other parts of the world through our arms trade. We must end the proliferation of small arms.

24. As Christians we are called to offer alternative models to those which do not serve the common good. We must help to set new priorities for our nation. We are challenged to create and to support structures that call for a society that is more just.

Models Are Needed for the Practical Implementation of Reconciliation

25. This challenge which we issue is meaningless unless as Christians we become part of visible actions and experiences that demonstrate a willingness to reconcile and be reconciled.

26. There are many creative ways of being reconciled and we cannot begin to list them all. This document is not meant to be a final word on reconciliation. Groups and individuals should feel free to take from it what is helpful and use-

ful. The document may be amended, changed or added to as is appropriate. We need to search for and become involved in any action or programs that focus on reconciliation. This could be done by sharing our resources, skills, time and energy. In this way we can best demonstrate our willingness to be reconciled by working alongside others who wish to be reconciled.

27. We can and we must address the hurts of the past. The imbalances of resources and skills caused by our past can and must be dealt with. As we eliminate these, a new nation will be born. It will be a nation that not only speaks about reconciliation but becomes a model for how reconciliation may be achieved.

We end by repeating the call for the Church to accept the challenge that the call to engage in reconciliation brings. We commit ourselves to helping this happen and encourage others to do so as well.

RELIGION CENSUS 1996[1]

Religion	Total
Total:	39,806,598
Zion Christian Churches	3,867,798
Other Zionist Churches	2,161,315
Ethiopian-type Churches	965,054
Ibandla LamaNazaretha	454,760
Other African Independent Churches	229,038
Anglican Churches	1,600,001
Apostolic Faith Mission	1,124,066
Other Apostolic Churches	3,517,059
Baptist Churches	439,680
Catholic Churches	3,426,525
Congregational Churches	429,868
Dutch Reformed Church	3,527,075
Other Reformed Churches	386,456
Lutheran Churches	1,051,193
Methodist Churches	2,808,649
Orthodox Churches	33,665
Pentecostal/Charismatic Churches	6,580,587
Presbyterian Churches	726,936
Other Christian Churches	1,360,180
Subtotal Christian Churches	34,689,907
African traditional belief	17,085
Hinduism	537,428
Islam	553,585
Judaism	68,058
New Age	168,783
Other faiths	25,047
No Religion	132,528
Not stated	3,614,178

1. These data are from the 1996 South African national census. Provided by Statistics South Africa.

AN OPEN LETTER TO
PASTORS OF ALL CHURCHES
IN SOUTH AFRICA

This letter was submitted to the TRC in November 1997 with close to 400 signatures of ministers.

TO US, AS PREACHERS OF THE WORD OF GOD, the responsibility is entrusted to proclaim at all times the Gospel of reconciliation with God and our fellow human beings in Christ. This responsibility entails the prophetic denouncement of all forms of injustice, oppression and violence committed against any human being.

As we read and hear what happened in South Africa during the years of Nationalist Party rule, we as preachers of God's Word are confronted with the question: How could it possibly have happened while we as preachers of reconciliation, justice and peace were preaching this message from our pulpits every Sunday?

But the question which disturbs us even more is this: How was it possible that those who intentionally committed murders and sabotage against fellow citizens could have been, as is now becoming evident, members of churches and even regular churchgoers? Was there *nothing* in our preaching, liturgies and sacraments that disturbed the conscience of those who were directly involved in all the evil deeds committed?

Therefore we have indeed more than enough reason to feel deeply guilty for having spiritualized and even gagged the Gospel to such an extent that those in government and those responsible to execute government policy did not feel confronted by our preaching. We are guilty of having allowed the rules to execute the ideology of forced separation for the sake of so-called law and order, without offering united resistance as preachers of justice and peace. We admit and confess that we too were blinded by an ideology which presented itself as justifiable from the Bible. We lacked the gift of discerning the spirits, because we had no real desire to receive this gift.

In the light of the above, we want to confess publicly that we as preachers were co-responsible for what happened in South Africa. In fact, our guilt should be considered as more serious than that of any other person or institution. We, who were supposed to be the conscience of the nation, did not succeed in preventing the most serious forms of abuse of the human conscience. As a result of this, the criminal violation of people's human dignity and even the destruction of human life continued for too long.

But this confession of guilt is not intended to be vague and general. We confess our guilt by mentioning specific examples of our failure to be faithful to the Gospel. We first of all acknowledge and confess that for many of us, especially those in the white community, life was very convenient and comfortable under National Party rule. Many of us therefore could not and would not see the oppression and violation of millions of people in our country, hear their cries for justice and failed to take action.

We furthermore acknowledge and confess that when we sometimes *did* feel uncomfortable about the way the government and other institutions persisted in its abuse of power, we did nothing because of fear. We thereby allowed evil (with the co-operation of Christians) to continue its devastating work against the people of God.

In the same breath, we commit ourselves to call upon Christians to be careful in their support of political leaders and their policies. We furthermore commit ourselves to challenge Christians concerning their political and socio-economic responsibilities.

We also want to make amends for neglecting the needs of the poor and oppressed. Therefore we commit ourselves to the task of guiding God's people towards involvement in actions to eliminate the socio-economic inequalities of our country. We have evaded this responsibility for too long.

We furthermore commit ourselves to the task of encouraging people with the Gospel of hope—especially in these days when many have lost hope and are despairing of the future of our country. This we will do by replacing the longing for the previous so-called better days by dreams of an even better future. The same Gospel therefore also urges us to commit ourselves to engage in the reconstruction of our society.

Although we recognize that some ministers have stood bravely in the struggle for justice, it is our hope that every church minister who reads this document will recognize the challenge facing us all, which we dare not push aside.

We are compelled to make a choice: either we confess our guilt in order to be set free for greater and more faithful service to the Gospel of Jesus Christ, or we ignore this challenge to confess our guilt and thus declare ourselves not guilty of what happened in our country. If you are willing to identify with this document and commit yourself to a process of unified action in a process of healing and rebuilding our nation, send your reply before the end of June, to the following address:

> Ecumenical Advice Bureau
> 7th Floor West Wing, Auckland House
> 185 Smit Street
> 2001 BRAAMFONTEIN
> Fax: 011-403-1485

This document with the signatures will be submitted to the TRC[1] and we express the hope that it would serve as a unified response from ministers. We hereby also wish to extend this invitation to spiritual leaders of other religions to participate in this submission. Thereafter a national conference of all those who have signed this document will be arranged in order to discuss the implications of our confession.

Drafted and signed by:

Beyers Naude, Nico Smith, Cornel du Toit,
Tinyiko Maluleke, Moss Nthla, Nico Botha

NOTE

1. When the letter was submitted to the TRC in November 1997 just under four hundred ministers had became signatories. The majority of South African ministers declined to sign. Nico Smith testified about the letter initiative at the TRC's 1997 faith communities hearing.

INDEX